SALT DESERT TRAILS

LANSFORD WARREN HASTINGS

Author of *The Emigrants' Guide, to Oregon and California.*
Personally guided the first emigrant train across the Great Salt
Desert in 1846.

SALT DESERT TRAILS

A History of
THE HASTINGS CUTOFF

❖

*and other early trails which
crossed the Great Salt Lake Desert
seeking a shorter road to
California*

❖ ❖

By
CHARLES KELLY

❖ ❖ ❖ ❖

Edited and with an Introduction by
PETER H. DeLAFOSSE

❖ ❖ ❖ ❖

WESTERN EPICS, INC.
Salt Lake City, Utah
1996

Royalties from the sale of this book will be donated to the University of Utah Marriott Library, Special Collections

IN MEMORY OF CHARLES AND HARRIETTE KELLY

LIBRARY OF CONGRESS CATALOGING-IN-PUBLICATION DATA

Kelly, Charles, 1889–1971
    Salt Desert trails: a history of the Hastings Cutoff and other early trails which crossed the Great Salt Desert seeking a shorter road to California / by Charles Kelly ; edited and with an introduction by Peter H. DeLafosse.—Hastings Cutoff Sesquicentennial ed.
    p.   cm.
    Originally published : Salt Lake City, Utah : Western Printing Co., 1930.
    Includes index.
    ISBN 0-914740-37-7
    1. Great Salt Lake Desert (Utah)—History. 2. Trails—Utah—History. 3. Trails—Nevada—History. 4. Pioneers—Utah. 5. Frontier and pioneer life—Utah. 6. Hastings, Lansford Warren, 1819–ca. 1870. I. DeLafosse, Peter H., 1947–. II. Title.
F832.G7K45   1996
979.2'4301—dc20   96-26519
                                            CIP

TABLE OF CONTENTS

INTRODUCTION

CHARLES KELLY
TRAILS HISTORIAN

The story of the stranding of the Donner-Reed party in the Sierra Nevada during the winter of 1846-47 has fascinated students of Western history since the rescue of the survivors. In the one hundred fifty years since the tragedy with its gruesome elements of starvation and cannibalism, most of the literature has focused on the events in the Sierra Nevada. The seeds of their troubles, however, had been sown earlier in Utah as travel delays in the Wasatch Mountains and on the Salt Desert put them in jeopardy as they attempted to cross the mountains.

Traveling overland to California, the Donner-Reed party had followed a shortcut through northern Utah that was promoted by Lansford Warren Hastings—the Hastings Cutoff. In the late 1920s, Salt Lake City printer Charles Kelly began researching the history of the Donner-Reed party and other Salt Desert travelers, publishing the results of his research in 1930.[1] A landmark in Donner-Reed party and Utah trails studies, *Salt Desert Trails* focused attention on the role played by Lansford Hastings in the Donner-Reed tragedy and on the difficulties of overland travel through Utah.

From the time he settled in Utah in 1919 until his death in 1971, Charles Kelly—historian, writer, iconoclast, musician, painter, photographer, and first Superintendent of Capitol Reef National Park—passionately pursued researching and preserving stories of the American West. The oldest of the six sons of Alfred Kelly and Flora Lepard Kelly, Charles Kelly was born on February 3, 1889, in the lumber camp of Cedar Springs, Michigan, where his father held the pastorate of a Baptist church. Although Alfred's religious excesses instilled in Charles a hatred of his father and of all

---

[1] Charles Kelly, *Salt Desert Trails; a History of the Hastings Cutoff and other early trails which crossed the Great Salt Lake Desert seeking a shorter route to California* (Salt Lake City: Western Printing Company, 1930).

religions, he learned from his father the craft of printing that gave him a trade with which he could earn a living.

When Charles was a teenager, Alfred moved his family to Dickson County, Tennessee, where he attempted to found a religious colony. The colony failed and, hoping to salvage some of his work by promoting real estate, Alfred contracted the publication of advertising literature with a printer in the nearby town of Burns. The printer offered Charles his first job, giving him an opportunity to earn his own money and a way to escape from his father. Armed with savings of fifty dollars, he announced to his father his intention to attend college.

Kelly enrolled in the Scientific Department at Valparaiso University in the fall of 1907. Located in northwest Indiana, fifty miles from Chicago, the university was founded in 1873 as a non-sectarian, co-educational teaching school where students could take classes year-around. With its location and low cost Valparaiso University attracted a student body from around the world. By 1907 it became the second largest university in the United States with an enrollment of over five thousand students. Charles moved from the insulated world of his father to the cosmopolitan environment of Valparaiso University.

He was an excellent student, earning high marks in chemistry, mathematics, geology, rhetoric, debating, history, and Latin, and he pursued his first avocation—music—by joining the university orchestra as a cornetist. After three twelve-week terms, money ran out and he returned to Tennessee for a year. Kelly returned to Valparaiso in the spring of 1909 for two more terms, but now money was completely gone and his formal education was over.[2]

After leaving Valparaiso, Kelly worked his way west as a printer. In Great Falls, Montana, he met the painter Charles Russell. Russell inspired Kelly to take up his second avocation—painting—which he pursued throughout his life. Kelly finally settled in Salt Lake City in 1919 and married Harriette Greener that same year. Five years later, he became a partner in the Western Printing Company.

---

[2] Valparaiso University, Student Register, 1907-08 and Student Register, 1908-09, Charles Kelly registered for the Fall 1907, Winter 1907, Spring 1908, Spring 1909, and Summer 1909 terms. Valparaiso University was purchased in 1925 by the Lutheran University Association which continues to operate it.

Looking for desert subjects to paint, Kelly discovered the Salt Desert and the Hastings Cutoff. He sought information from Frank Durfee, a resident of Grantsville, and Dan Orr, a rancher in Skull Valley, both of whom were intimately familiar with the Salt Desert. In a series of weekend automobile trips during the spring and summer of 1929, Charles Kelly, his brother Dwight Kelly, Frank Durfee, and Dan Orr located and followed the trace of the Hastings Cutoff from Skull Valley, Utah, to the Ruby Mountains in eastern Nevada. On later trips they were joined by Edgar M. Ledyard, president of the Utah Historical Landmarks Commission.

The Kelly party traveled over Hastings Pass in the Cedar Mountains on the west side of Skull Valley, and over Grayback Ridge at the edge of the Salt Desert. They were able to locate the trail from artifacts scattered along the way. After crossing the sand dunes west of Grayback, they reached the mud flats of the Salt Desert. "The old trail lay before us glittering in the sun. Here were no ruts, to be sure—the surface is perfectly smooth and level—yet the trail stretched away to the west as plainly as though the pioneers had passed only last year."[3] The trail was marked by a discoloration of the surface layer of salt which had been disturbed by the wheels of the emigrant wagons. Following the trail across the mud flats, they came upon the most astonishing site of their trip—the remains of five abandoned wagons.

At the base of Pilot Peak on the Utah-Nevada border, they visited the Cummings Ranch and the McKellar Ranch and interviewed Eugene Munsee who had homesteaded one of the springs at Pilot Peak.[4] They continued across Silver Zone Pass in the Toano Range to Flowery Lake at the base of the Pequop Mountains, and completed their trip at the southern end of the Ruby Mountains. Kelly collected artifacts and photographed scenes along the way.

Unable to find a publisher, Kelly typeset and printed the book in 1930 under the imprint of his Western Printing Company. The book was titled *Salt Desert Trails: A History of the Hastings Cutoff and other early trails which crossed the Great Salt Lake Desert seeking a shorter route to California.* Kelly illustrated the book with his black-and-white photographs. Like nothing else, these im-

---

[3] Charles Kelly, *Salt Desert Trails*, 153.

[4] The McKellar Ranch, the Cummings Ranch, and the Munsee homestead are all part of the present TL Bar Ranch.

ages show the terror and grandeur of the Salt Desert; the scenes of the abandoned wagons are a grim reminder of the hardships experienced by the Donner-Reed party.

Five more books came from Kelly's pen during the decade following *Salt Desert Trails*: *Holy Murder*,[5] *Old Greenwood*,[6] *Miles Goodyear*,[7] *Outlaw Trail*,[8] and the *Journals of John D. Lee*.[9] With the exception of *Holy Murder*, all the titles were privately printed in limited editions by Kelly and bear the Western Printing Company imprint. Kelly's books explored little-known subjects of Utah and Western history. *Salt Desert Trails* put the Donner-Reed story in perspective by focusing on the role of Lansford Hastings and the troubles the party experienced in Utah. *Old Greenwood* and *Miles Goodyear* traced the careers of two minor mountain men, Caleb Greenwood and Miles Goodyear, and the roles they played in the history of the Hastings Cutoff. *Outlaw Trail* told the story of Butch Cassidy, Utah's most famous outlaw, and of Kelly's search for the location of the trail. *Holy Murder* was the first biography of Porter Rockwell, bodyguard of Mormon leaders Joseph Smith and Brigham Young. The *Journals of John D. Lee* contained the first printed journals of Lee, the only person tried and executed for participation in the Mountain Meadows Massacre.

After selling his interest in the Western Printing Company, Charles and Harriette Kelly retired in 1940 to Fruita, Utah, a small hamlet in the heart of the newly created Capitol Reef National Monument. Intending to continue his research and writing, he embarked on his second career with the National Park Service. Al-

---

[5] Charles Kelly and Hoffman Birney, *Holy Murder; the Story of Porter Rockwell* (New York: Minton, Balch & Company, 1934).

[6] Charles Kelly, *Old Greenwood; the Story of Caleb Greenwood; Trapper, Pathfinder and Early Pioneer of the West*; with Photographs by Edgar M. Ledyard and the Author (Salt Lake City: Western Printing Company, 1936).

[7] Charles Kelly and Maurice L. Howe, *Miles Goodyear; First Citizen of Utah, Trapper, Trader and California Pioneer* (Salt Lake City: Western Printing Company, 1937).

[8] Charles Kelly, *Outlaw Trail; a History of Butch Cassidy and his Wild Bunch, Hole-in-the-Wall, Brown's Hole, Robber's Roost*; with decorations by Bill Fleming (Salt Lake City: Western Printing Company, 1938).

[9] Charles Kelly, ed., *Journals of John D. Lee, 1846-47 and 1859* (Salt Lake City: Western Printing Company, 1938)

though the monument had been created in 1937, no custodian had as yet been named. In exchange for housing, Kelly assumed the non-paying job of custodian in 1943. Congress authorized funds in 1950 for a full-time Superintendent at Capitol Reef, and Kelly was appointed Park Ranger in 1950 and Superintendent in 1952. During his tenure with the National Park Service, Kelly continued researching and writing Western history.

Following his retirement from the National Park Service in 1959, Charles and Harriette returned to Salt Lake City, where they spent the remainder of their lives. Kelly was elected an Honorary Life Member of the Utah State Historical Society in 1960, and in 1969 he received the Award of Merit from the American Association of State and Local History. During his retirement, Kelly revised and expanded *Outlaw Trail*[10] and co-authored a revision of *Old Greenwood* with his friend, Dale Morgan.[11]

Salt Lake City bookseller Sam Weller suggested to Kelly a revision of *Salt Desert Trails*, which was printed in 1969 by Weller's recently formed publishing company, Western Epics. It is fitting that *Salt Desert Trails* both opened and closed Kelly's writing career. Following the Hastings Cutoff across the Salt Desert was, as Kelly wrote, "...the greatest and most valuable experience of my life and I am fortunate in having done this research before anything had been disturbed."[12] Charles Kelly died on April 19, 1971, in Salt Lake City.

Writers who knew Kelly have related stories about his volatile personality and his disdain for religion. The quarter century since his death gives us the opportunity to examine Kelly's historical legacy apart from the misanthropic aspects of his character. Kelly was fortunate to have lived and worked during the period between the world wars. The end of World War II brought profound changes to the landscape of the American West, which continue to this day. Kelly documented this regional history while physical remnants still existed and before the post-war changes commenced. In the years since his work it is astonishing how much of the physical history he recorded has disappeared. While others

---

[10] Charles Kelly, *Outlaw Trail* (New York: Devin Adair, 1959).

[11] Charles Kelly and Dale L. Morgan, *Old Greenwood* (Georgetown: Talisman Press, 1965).

[12] Charles Kelly, *Salt Desert Trails*, preface.

pursued the more flamboyant characters of the American West, Kelly's curiosity led him to investigate and preserve the by-ways of Great Basin and Colorado Plateau history.

In the nearly seven decades that have elapsed since Charles Kelly followed the Hastings Cutoff, time and development have taken their toll on the physical remains of the trail. The reader of 1930 could still follow much of the Hastings Cutoff across the Salt Desert. Regrettably, for the reader of 1996, Kelly's explorations are now part of the historical record. Much of what Kelly recorded has vanished forever, and all that remains is his written and photographic record. Today's trail historians owe a great debt to Kelly for "trailing the pioneers" along the Hastings Cutoff.

EDITORIAL GUIDELINES

Salt Desert Trails is a Utah and Western history classic—the granddaddy of Utah trails books—and I have preserved the book as Kelly wrote it. The starting point was the text of the 1969 edition. All quotations were checked against the originals, and Kelly's footnotes were expanded to include complete bibliographic citations—long a desire of Kelly's friend and colleague, Dale L. Morgan. An annotated copy of *Salt Desert Trails*, which is in my possession, has helped clarify some points in the text, particularly information that was added in the 1969 edition. This copy contains corrections and numerous marginalia in Kelly's hand.

Factual errors were corrected by changing a word or two, and, in a few instances, a sentence was rewritten. The most radical surgery occurred in chapter 13, "The Cutoff in 1847." Kelly listed only one Salt Desert crossing for that year; that is, the Miles Goodyear party that returned to Utah from California. In "Gold Seekers on the Hastings Cutoff,"[13] Kelly noted a second Salt Desert crossing for that year, the party under Captain James Brown that was returning from California with pay due the Sick Detachment of the Mormon Battalion. The text in this chapter was replaced with an excerpt from "Gold Seekers" that described both crossings.

The 1969 edition was published with fewer illustrations than the 1930 edition. Kelly had located the only known photograph of

---

[13] Charles Kelly, "Gold Seekers on the Hastings Cutoff," *Utah Historical Quarterly* 20 (1952), 3-30.

Lansford Hastings from Albert Spence, a grandson of Hastings, and it was published in both editions. Kelly may have saved this photograph from oblivion, and this important image has been retained. The remaining illustrations have been selected from the photographs taken by Kelly during his Salt Desert explorations. These photographs are of increasing value to the historian because they document vanished trail features. Kelly was an excellent photographer and his images have an aesthetic appeal far beyond their documentary value. They are among the most haunting images of the Utah landscape ever photographed.

Both the 1930 and 1969 editions of *Salt Desert Trails* included this edition's Salt Desert Trails map, which shows the region's major historic trails. The Hastings Cutoff map, showing the locations of the artifacts the Kelly party found along the trail, is taken from an article Kelly published during the centennial anniversary of the opening of the Hastings Cutoff.[14] Complementing the final chapter of *Salt Desert Trails*, this fascinating article describes the unsuccessful search by Charles E. Davis and the Kelly party for a treasure allegedly buried in the Salt Desert by the Donner-Reed party. Today, Interstate 80 has replaced US 40 shown on this map.

Kelly's interpretations of two controversial points remain. The first concerns the inscriptions at Alcove Spring (see Chapter 7). There is some question today about the authenticity of the inscriptions, but the matter has not been resolved. More controversial are Kelly's conclusions about the abandoned wagons on the Salt Desert. Kelly was convinced that the remains belonged exclusively to the Donner-Reed party (see Chapter 20). Recent research casts doubt on this interpretation.

In the early 1980s, Great Salt Lake began to rise, threatening development around the lake. Responding to this threat, state officials authorized the building of a series of dikes in the Salt Desert to hold the lake water that was pumped at great expense into the desert. Prior to the flooding of the Salt Desert in 1986, the Utah State Historical Society conducted a series of archeological surveys to map the sites of the abandoned wagons, recover remaining arti-

---

[14] Charles Kelly, "Treasure Hunt on the Salt Desert," *Desert Magazine* (December 1946), 11-14.

facts, and analyze them and previously collected artifacts.[15] The survey found very little remaining material at the site. Some of the artifacts that Kelly collected can be found in the Donner-Reed Museum at Grantsville, Utah, but the location of the rest of Kelly's artifacts is unknown. It is impossible to relate these artifacts to any specific emigrant party because of the fragmentary evidence and the corruption of the site.

The recent discovery of a letter from James Pierce, a Park City, Utah, resident who had crossed the Salt Desert as a youth with a party of Forty-Niners, talks about the hardships of crossing the Salt Desert and the abandoning of wagons on the mud flats, experiences similar to the Donner-Reed party.[16] This group followed the Cherokee Trail to Salt Lake City and continued westward along the Hastings Cutoff. The abandoned wagons and artifacts Kelly found probably were a mixture from the Donner-Reed party and later emigrant parties—possibly the Cherokee Forty-Niners—which crossed the Salt Desert, but their origin will forever remain a mystery. The absolute certainty with which Kelly named "Reed's wagon," and its probable error, however, is of little consequence when compared with the sum total of his accomplishment.

SELECTED BIBLIOGRAPHY

Charles and Harriette Kelly donated a large collection of books, pamphlets, magazines, newspaper clippings, photographs, manuscripts, diaries, journals, and correspondence to the Utah State Historical Society in 1960.[17] Included in this collection were two thousand prints and negatives, each identified and labeled. Prior to her death in 1974, Harriette Kelly donated the remainder of their collection to the Marriott Library at the University of

---

[15] Bruce R. Hawkins and David B. Madsen, *Excavation of the Donner-Reed Wagons: Historic Archaeology along the Hastings Cutoff*, With Contributions by Ann Hanniball, Brigham D. Madsen, M. Elizabeth Manion, and Gary Topping (Salt Lake City: University of Utah Press, 1990).

[16] "The Find on the Desert," *Crossroads* 5 (Winter 1994). *Crossroads* is the quarterly newsletter of the Utah Crossroads chapter of the Oregon-California Trails Association.

[17] Charles Kelly Papers, MS B-114, Utah State Historical Society.

Utah.[18] These two collections complement each other and are a treasure trove for today's trail historians. Following the publication of *Salt Desert Trails*, Kelly became acquainted with many writers and historians, including California historian George R. Stewart and poet John G. Neihardt. These acquaintances led to friendships and a lifelong correspondence dealing with a variety of topics in Western history. Kelly's correspondence file related to *Salt Desert Trails* is especially interesting.

While *Salt Desert Trails* is the first work on the subject, the literature of the Hastings Cutoff is extensive. Footnote citations will guide the reader to the major primary and secondary sources. Many manuscript sources used by Kelly in the first edition were later published in books and journals. These citations have been updated in the footnotes. Of particular interest to the modern reader are collections of primary source documents.

Central to *Salt Desert Trails* is the figure of Lansford Warren Hastings and travel along the Hastings Cutoff from 1846 to 1850. Primary source documents for this period were edited, annotated, and published in Dale L. Morgan, ed., J. Roderic Korns, "West From Fort Bridger: The Pioneering of the Immigrant Tails across Utah, 1846–1850," *Utah Historical Quarterly* 19 (1951).[19] Charles Kelly was a close friend of both Korns and Morgan and he contributed much to the content of this volume. Morgan completed the book after Korns' untimely death, and Kelly rounded out the story with his article "Gold Seekers on the Hastings Cutoff," published in the volume following "West From Fort Bridger."[20] Additional source material relevant to the opening of the Hastings Cutoff will be found in Dale L. Morgan, ed., *Overland in 1846: Diaries and Letters of the California-Oregon Trail*, two volumes (Georgetown: Talisman Press, 1963).

---

[18] Charles Kelly Papers, MS 100, Special Collections, Marriott Library, University of Utah.

[19] A new edition of this classic work, revised and updated by Harold Schindler and Will Bagley, was published in 1994 by Utah State University Press.

[20] Charles Kelly, "Gold Seekers on the Hastings Cutoff," *Utah Historical Quarterly* 20 (1952), 3-30. This paper was followed by Charles Kelly, ed., "The Journal of Robert Chalmers April 17–September 1, 1850," *Utah Historical Quarterly* 20 (1952), 31-55.

Brigham D. Madsen, ed., *Exploring the Great Salt Lake: The Stansbury Expedition of 1849-50* (Salt Lake City: University of Utah Press, 1989) contains the original journals of the Stansbury expedition. Doyce B. Nunis, Jr., ed., *The Bidwell-Bartleson Party, 1841 California Emigrant Adventure: Documents and Memoirs of the Overland Pioneers* (Santa Cruz: Western Tanager Press, 1991) contains the primary source documents from the Bidwell-Bartleson expedition, including two little-known journals by James John that fill in details absent from John Bidwell's accounts.

Contemporary trail descriptions will be found in Peter H. De-Lafosse, ed., *Trailing the Pioneers: A Guide to Utah's Emigrant Trails, 1829-1869* (Logan: Utah State University Press and Utah Crossroads, Oregon-California Trails Association, 1994). Separate chapters by Steven Madsen (Spanish Trail), Roy Tea (Bidwell-Bartleson Trail), Jack Tykal (Pioneer Trail from Fort Bridger to Salt Lake City), Rush Spedden (Hastings Cutoff from Salt Lake City to Wendover), and Will Bagley (Hensley's Salt Lake Cutoff) describe the trails in relation to today's roads and identify remnants of the original trails, while a selected bibliography by Harold Schindler describes major books relating to these emigrant trails across Utah.

ACKNOWLEDGMENTS

First, and foremost, I would like thank Sam Weller for bringing *Salt Desert Trails* back into print and for inviting me to prepare this new edition for publication during the 1996 sesquicentennial anniversary of the opening of the Hastings Cutoff. I have also received much advice and support from Dr. Gregory Thompson, Assistant Director for Special Collections, Marriott Library, University of Utah.

Lee Kreutzer, Park Archeologist, Capitol Reef National Park, supplied the photograph of Charles Kelly. Mel Doering, Archivist, Moellering Library, Valparaiso University, Valparaiso, Indiana, helped me to research Charles Kelly's student records. Will Rusho provided prints of Charles Kelly's Salt Desert photos. For my continuing education in Utah trails history I gratefully acknowledge the work of and wish to thank Will Bagley, David Bigler, Robert K. Hoshide, Kristin Johnson, Dr. Floyd A. O'Neil, Dr. Brigham Madsen, Will Rusho, Harold Schindler, Rush Spedden, and Roy Tea for their advice and encouragement.

Peter H. DeLafosse
January 1, 1996
Salt Lake City, Utah

CHARLES KELLY'S SALT DESERT

A Photographic Gallery

Charles Kelly took the photographs in this folio while exploring the Salt Desert in the late 1920s. Time and modern development have obliterated most of the remnants of emigrant travel documented in Kelly's photographs and in the final chapter of *Salt Desert Trails*. Kelly's record remains.

Kelly's photographs are reproduced courtesy of the Photographic Archives, Utah State Historical Society.

FIGURE 1. Skull Valley. Looking south. Lone Rock in the center.
See page 169.

FIGURE 2. Emigrant Trail. Along the approach to Hastings Pass over Cedar Mountain. See page 170.

FIGURE 3. Hastings Pass. Looking east from the summit across Skull Valley. See page 170.

FIGURE 4. Hastings Pass. Looking northwest from the summit toward the Salt Desert. See page 170.

FIGURE 5. Gun Barrel. Found by Kelly party on the west side of Grayback Mountain. See page 172.

FIGURE 6. Dan Orr (left), Charles Kelly (center), and Frank Durfee (right). On the west side of Grayback Mountain. Charles Kelly is holding the gun barrel shown in Figure 5. See page 172.

FIGURE 7. Sand Dunes. On the eastern edge of the Salt Desert, north of Knolls. See pages 172–74.

FIGURE 8. Mirage on the Salt Desert. Looking south toward Knolls and Wildcat Mountain. See page 175.

FIGURE 9. Edgar Ledyard (left) and Dwight Kelly (right) on the Salt Desert, looking south. Note the train passing in the distance.

FIGURE 10. Abandoned Wagons. In the foreground are the bones of an ox. In the middle distance are the remains of two more oxen. The dark spots are the ruins of other wagons. Floating Island to the left, Silver Island in the distance. Note the trail in the lower-right corner running toward Floating Island. See page 177.

FIGURE 11. Wagon ruin named "Reed's Wagon" by Charles Kelly. See pages 181–82.

FIGURE 12. "Having One on Reed." Charles Kelly drinks from a canteen over Reed's Wagon. See pages 181–82.

FIGURE 13. Abandoned Wagon. Part of the running gears of an abandoned wagon. Floating Island to the left, Silver Island in the distance. Note the emigrant trail preserved in the mud flats. See pages 177–78.

FIGURE 14. Emigrant Trail. Trail preserved in the mud flats. Floating Island on the left, Silver Island in the distance. See page 177.

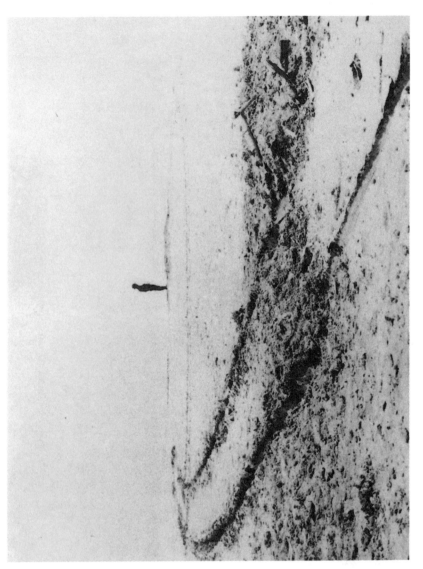

FIGURE 15. The End of the Trail. This is what happened when the Kelly party stopped its car to investigate the low mound in the middle background. Note parts of the century-old emigrant wagon used to block up the wheels of the mired car. It took four hours to dig out of the mud. See pages 178–79.

FIGURE 16. Emigrant trail preserved in the mud flats. Looking east toward Floating Island. See page 179.

FIGURE 17. Wagon ruts preserved in the mud flats. Looking east toward Floating Island. See page 179.

FIGURE 18. Barrelhead. Dwight Kelly examines the remains of a barrelhead. Floating Island in the distance. See page 180.

FIGURE 19. Kelly Party Camp. On the east side of Silver Island, looking north. See page 184.

FIGURE 20. Dwight Kelly (left), Dan Orr (third from left), and Cummings Brothers at the base of Pilot Peak. The dark spot to the left of Dan Orr is the location of Donner Spring. See page 186.

FIGURE 21. Eugene Munsee. Munsee homesteaded one of the springs at Pilot Peak thirty years after the emigrants stopped there. See pages 186–89.

MAPS

Salt Desert Trails
and
The Hastings Cutoff

IDAHO

NEVADA

OREGON TRAIL

Snake River

GOOSE CREEK MTS.

CITY OF ROCKS

FORT HALL ROAD

PILOT PEAK

Wells

Halleck

Elko

Silver Zone Pass

PEQUOP MTS.

Victory High

Wendover

CLYMAN 1846

Humboldt River

South Fork

BIDWELL

RUBY MTS.

HASTINGS-DONNER 1846

Flowery Lake

TOANO RANGE

Ely

← SIMPSON — 1859

DEEP CREEK MTS.

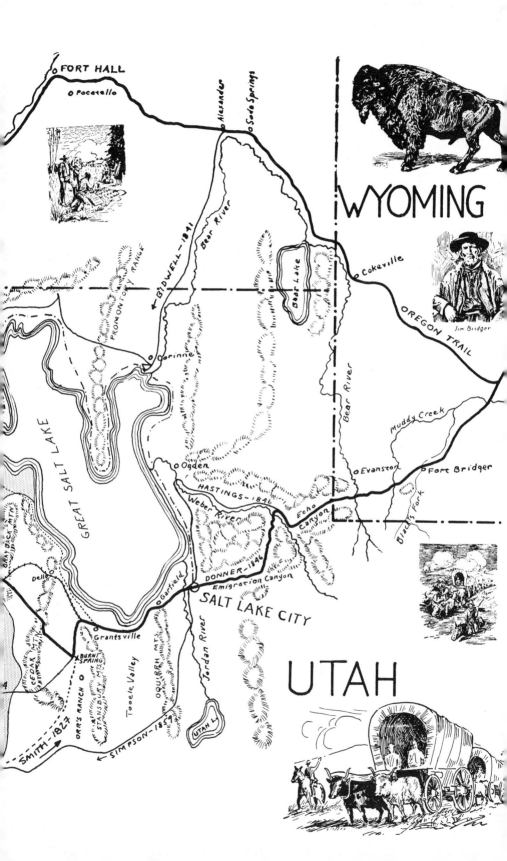

FORT HALL
o Pocatello

o Alexander
o Soda Springs

WYOMING

Bidwell—1841
Bear River

Bear Lake

o Cokeville

PROMONTORY RANGE

OREGON TRAIL

Jim Bridger

o Corinne

Bear River

Muddy Creek

GREAT SALT LAKE

o Ogden

o Evanston

o Fort Bridger

HASTINGS—1846

Weber River

Echo
Canyon

Blacks Fork

GRAY BACK MTN
DONNER—1846
Emigration Canyon

o Delle

o Garfield

SALT LAKE CITY

o Grantsville

CEDAR MTN
BURNT SPRING

STANSBURY MTS
ORR'S RANCH o

Tooele Valley

OQUIRRH MTS

Jordan River

UTAH

SMITH—1827

SIMPSON—1859

UTAH L.

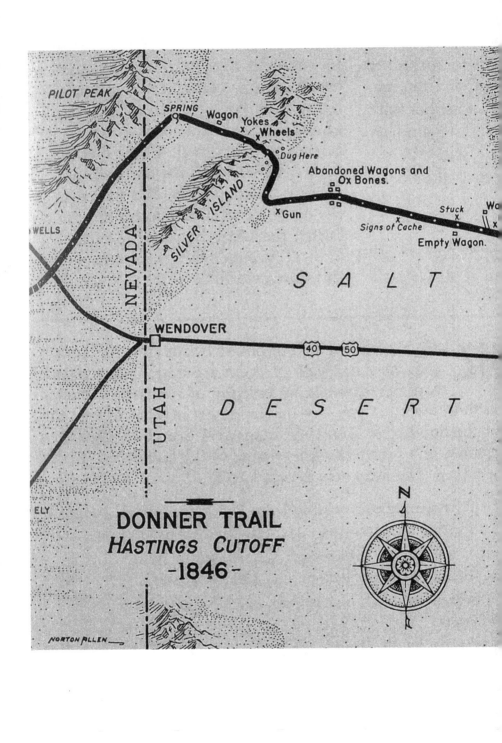

PILOT PEAK

SPRING Wagon Yokes
Wheels

Dug Here

Abandoned Wagons and
Ox Bones.

Gun

Stuck Wa

Signs of Cache

Empty Wagon.

WELLS

SILVER ISLAND

NEVADA

S A L T

WENDOVER

40 50

UTAH

D E S E R T

ELY

N

DONNER TRAIL
HASTINGS CUTOFF
-1846-

NORTON ALLEN

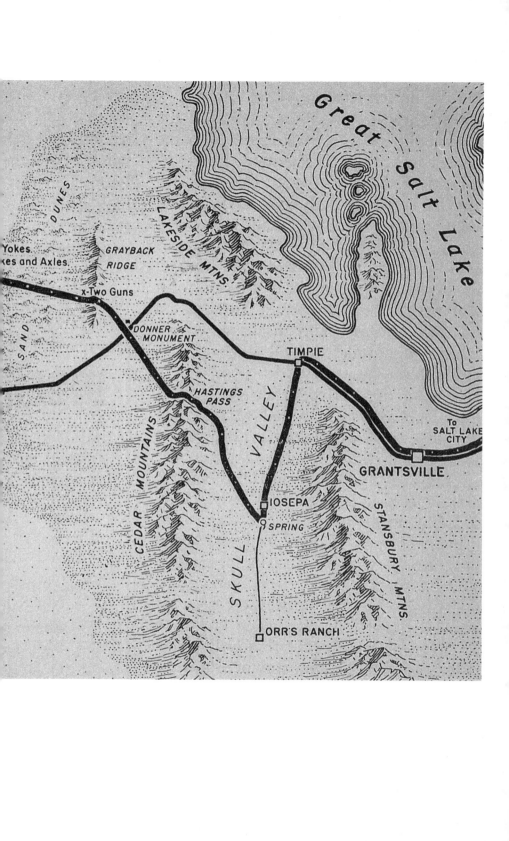

Preface (1930 Edition)

Much has been written in recent years about the old Oregon Trail, and many of the early travelers of that historic highway have left excellent descriptions of their journey. Several fine records of the California Trail, or the old Fort Hall Road have been preserved; but nothing has yet been published which deals directly with the Hastings Cutoff, the most dangerous stretch of desert trail between Independence, Missouri, and the Pacific.

Living near the mysterious Great Salt Desert, I became interested in the history of the Donner party, which met disaster there in 1846. In searching for information concerning this famous party of emigrants, I discovered that there had been several other crossings of the great desert both before and after 1846. The fragmentary records of these different expeditions, pieced together, make such an interesting record of early travel over this little known route, that I have brought them all together in this book, hoping that this information may prove of interest and value to students of pioneer history.

The story is as complete as I have been able to make it, but doubtless there are other documents preserved among treasured family records which would bring to light new and interesting facts, and the readers of this book are asked to cooperate with me in collecting in one volume all historical information which bears upon early emigration over the Hastings Cutoff.

Preface (1969 Edition)

When this book was first published in 1930 very little was known about the emigrant trails across the Great Salt Desert and documentary information was scarce and difficult to obtain. Since that time a large amount of new material has been discovered, mostly in the Bancroft Library at Berkeley, California, by Dale L. Morgan, Irene Paden and others, which makes it imperative that a new and much more complete edition be published.

Most readers of history are familiar with the story of the Donner party of 1846, many of whom perished in the snows of the Sierra during the winter of 1846–47, but few realize that the cause of that tragedy was the delay they experienced in trying to cross the

Salt Desert, through the foolish advice of Lansford W. Hastings, who was ambitious to become president of the Republic of California.

Living in Salt Lake City I became interested in the history of the various companies of emigrants who took the Hastings Cutoff in early days, and having discovered traces of their old trails, decided to follow them entirely across the Salt Desert, which I eventually did in 1929 and 1930, by car and on foot, finding many badly weathered relics of those early emigrant parties, which had not been disturbed since the emigrants passed. The tracing of this old trail was the greatest and most valuable experience of my life and I am fortunate in having done this research before anything had been disturbed.

ACKNOWLEDGMENTS

In gathering the information for this work, I have been assisted by a great number of friends, acquaintances and students of pioneer history. I wish to acknowledge my obligations to Mr. Clyde Wrathall, Delle, Utah, for first pointing out the old pioneer trail across the Salt Desert; to Mr. Frank Durfee and Mr. Dan Orr, of Grantsville, for their assistance in locating indistinct portions of the trail and also for much local early-day history; to Mr. Don Maguire of Ogden, for his personal memoirs of pioneer history; to Mr. Eugene Munsee, Wendover, for his story of the trail as he saw it fifty years ago; to the McKellar brothers and Cummings brothers at Pilot Peak, for valuable information and assistance; and to Mr. Hamp Worthington, Grantsville, for many interesting facts.

For documentary information I am under the greatest obligation to the great historian, Herbert Howe Bancroft, without whose wonderful collection of original documents this work would have been impossible; to Miss Edna Martin, of the Bancroft Library, who has done much valuable research work; to Miss Cristel Hastings, Mill Valley, California, for many valuable suggestions and personal interviews with pioneers; to Alice Riddle Jacobson, Manhattan, Kansas, and Mr. John Ellenbecker, Marysville, Kansas, for locating old landmarks; to William J. Hunsaker and Mr. Albert Spence, Los Angeles, for original information and for the only known photograph of Hastings; to Mr. Ferguson, Sacramento, for information on file in the California State Library; to Mr. Edgar M. Ledyard and

INTRODUCTION

Mr. J. Cecil Alter, Salt Lake City, for their co-operation and encouragement; to Margaret Shepard and Della Dye of the Utah State Historical Society; and to many others who have assisted me in gathering the facts for this record.

Charles Kelly
August 1968
Salt Lake City, Utah

1. LANSFORD W. HASTINGS

"**W**HISKEY!" SHOUTED A BRONZED and thirsty traveler to the man behind the bar.

"Yes sir," answered the bartender. But as he reached for a bottle, he paused.

"Say, aren't you Hastings, the famous temperance lecturer from Ohio?"

"Sure," replied the traveler, "and—well, by golly, if it isn't my old friend, the Reverend McDonald!"

Thus, in the year 1846 B. V.,[1] two men who had helped shape the destinies of the state of California renewed their acquaintance over the bar of Vioget's saloon in San Francisco. The bartender had formerly been a Methodist minister; his customer was California's first press agent.[2]

Lansford W. Hastings was a clever and very ambitious young lawyer from Mt. Vernon, Ohio, who had started for Oregon with an emigrant train in 1842, at the age of twenty-three. This company was composed of a number of settlers recruited by Dr. Elijah White, a missionary doctor who had been sent to the Oregon country a few years before, and who had returned east to recruit settlers for that fertile section. Dr. White's party consisted of one hundred and twelve emigrants, with all their worldly goods loaded in prairie schooners drawn by oxen.[3] Lansford W. Hastings was one of this party, and was elected to keep a record of the journey. This

---

[1] "B.V." stands for "Before Volstead." An act of Congress, the Volstead Act implemented the eighteenth amendment and outlawed the sale of alcoholic beverages from 1920–1933. The first edition of *Salt Desert Trails* was published during Prohibition, and this private joke probably expresses Kelly's opinion of the law.

[2] John Bidwell, "Life in California Before the Gold Discovery," *Century Illustrated Monthly Magazine* 41 (November 1890), 176.

[3] A. J. Allen, ed., *Ten Years in Oregon. Travels and Adventures of Dr. E. White and Lady* (Ithaca: Mack, Andrews, & Co., Printers, 1848).

record was published in 1845 as *The Emigrants' Guide, to Oregon and California*.[4]

Soon after the emigrant train left Independence, Missouri, the last outpost of civilization in 1842, Dr. White apparently began to make himself unpopular with the company, and a meeting was held at which Hastings was elected to act as captain, a post he occupied for the remainder of the journey. Dr. White naturally resented this loss of prestige and with a small company of friends detached himself from the main train until Fort Laramie was reached, where the two companies again joined for mutual protection against the hostile Indians.[5]

Reaching Independence Rock, a famous landmark along the trail, many of the emigrants stopped to carve their names on this desert register. Hastings and his friend A. L. Lovejoy, cutting their names with more than the usual care, were left behind when the train moved on. Suddenly they found themselves surrounded by yelling Indians, who stripped them and apparently intended to take their scalps. But a council was held and it was finally decided to return them to the company and ask a ransom. The negotiations were carried on by Thomas Fitzpatrick, famous old trapper and guide; Hastings and Lovejoy were released, but the Indians got little for their pains.

At Fort Hall the emigrants disposed of their wagons and pushed on into Oregon with their cattle and horses, over the Oregon Trail. Hastings seems to have discharged his duties as captain satisfactorily, and the company arrived at their destination safely.

The winter climate of Oregon, however, did not appeal to some of the newly arrived settlers, and so, in the spring of 1843, we find Hastings leading a party of thirty-six Oregon emigrants south into California,[6] their destination being Sutter's Fort, on the site of which Sacramento was later built.

The California country through which he passed evidently made a great impression on Hastings. At that time there were only

---

4. Lansford W. Hastings, *The Emigrants' Guide, to Oregon and California* (Cincinnati: George Conclin, 1845).

5. William J. Ghent, *The Road to Oregon: A Chronicle of the Great Emigrant Trail* (London and New York: Longmans, Green & Company, 1929).

6. H. H. Bancroft, *History of California*, 7 volumes (San Francisco: The History Company, 1884–1890), IV:389–92.

a handful of Americans in the territory, mostly around Sutter's Fort and San Francisco; but it seemed to him that such a marvelous country was ideal for settlement by emigrants from the east. The American settlers, and even some of the Spanish residents were very uncomfortable under the rule of Mexico, and hoped that there would soon be enough emigrants from the States to seize and hold the territory.

Hastings appears to have been a man of action as well as a man of vision. Opportunity seemed to be knocking at his door and he prepared to answer the knock. It occurred to him that if he would return to the States and bring out a large number of settlers, it might be possible for them, with himself as leader, to oust the Mexicans and hold the territory for themselves. As a reward for this leadership Hastings hoped to be elected president of California.[7] With this idea in mind he returned east in 1844, by sea to Mazatlan, overland to Mexico City, and to the States via Vera Cruz and New Orleans.

President of California! The more he thought about it, the more plausible it sounded. He could see no reason why the plan which had worked so successfully in Texas should not work equally as well on the Pacific coast. Fired with this ambition he wrote *The Emigrants' Guide, to Oregon and California*, in which he gave an account of his journey across the plains in 1842, and enlarged upon the wonderful advantages of California, hoping with the aid of this book to create enthusiasm for a large emigration. A paragraph will give a good idea of Hastings' own admiration for that section:

> ...in my opinion, there is no country, in the known world, possessing a soil so fertile and productive, with such varied and inexhaustible resources, and a climate of such mildness, uniformity and salubrity; nor is there a country, in my opinion, now known, which is so eminently calculated, by nature herself, in all respects, to promote the unbounded happiness and prosperity, of civilized and enlightened man.[8]

He paints a glowing picture of the time when:

---

7. Bidwell, "Life in California Before the Gold Discovery," 176.

8. Hastings, *Emigrants' Guide, to Oregon and California*, 133.

– 3 –

...genuine *republicanism*, and unsophisticated *democracy*, shall be reared up, and tower aloft, even upon the now wild shores, of the great Pacific; where they shall ever stand forth, as enduring monuments, to the increasing wisdom of *man*, and the infinite kindness and protection, of an all-wise, and overruling *Providence*.[9]

Not a bad effort for a young man of twenty-six! In this book Hastings, California's first press agent, sounded the keynote for all the boosters who were to follow in his footsteps; and if he sometimes soared beyond the bounds of exact truth, the residents of that great state will certainly not be anxious to cast the first stone.

Arriving in the east, Hastings could find no one who would finance the publication of his book; there was nothing to do but earn the price of publication himself Casting about for some quick means of raising money he fell in with the Rev. McDonald, a Methodist minister who was collecting funds for missionary purposes. Together they went about the country lecturing on the evils of intemperance, the dire need of the missionaries, and incidentally, the wonders of California. The wherewithal having shortly been secured by this means, the book was published at Cincinnati in 1845, and went through several editions. It seems to have excited a great curiosity among the pioneer farmers of Ohio, Illinois, Kentucky and Missouri, to see this marvelous country where wealth, health and happiness were to be had merely for the taking.

Strange as it may seem, the unhealthful climate of those eastern states was one of the principal reasons why so many decided to move to the far west between 1840–48. Nearly everyone was afflicted with periodic attacks of fever and ague, which made their lives miserable; hundreds of the early emigrants left their homes for no other reason. Nearly all early writers state that when the country began to be settled up and large acreages of sod broken, the ague appeared to be caused, as they believed, by decomposition of humus turned under by the plow but actually by mosquitoes.

Hastings organized a party of emigrants who were to return with him to California in 1845. But some were not able to settle their affairs in so short a time or dispose of their property; many delays occurred, and on account of the lateness of the season many others refused to start. He finally left Independence with only ten

---

[9] *Ibid.*, 152.

men, mounted on horses. It was then the middle of August, and those who knew the trail and the difficulties ahead tried to dissuade him from attempting to cross the Sierra so late in the season. The usual time for starting across the plains was in the early part of May, or as soon as grass was high enough to provide feed for the animals. Even then emigrants with wagons and oxen barely had time to cross the mountains before snow fell. Hastings, however, not being thus encumbered, thought they could get through safely. They traveled fast and furiously and succeeded in reaching Sutter's Fort on Christmas day. The season had been unusually late. Ordinarily snow fell on the Sierra in October, but they were lucky—so lucky that Captain Sutter declared that if they had been one day later they would have been caught in the snow and died in the mountains.

One man of this company of ten stood out from among his fellows—for two reasons. Dr. Robert Semple was 6 feet 8 inches in height, a giant of a man physically. He was also distinguished in many other ways, being founder of the *Californian*, the first newspaper in California; president of the Constitutional Convention in 1849; founder of the town of Benicia; owner of the first ferry on San Francisco bay; and prominent in nearly all of California's early activities.

While at New York in the spring of 1845, Hastings had met Sam Brannan, who, the next year, was in charge of the first party of Mormons to leave for the West, going to California by sea in the ship *Brooklyn*.[10] The records are not clear on what passed between Hastings and Brannan. We later find L. W. Hastings acting as agent of the Mormons in California. He selected a location for them at Montezuma, and confidently expected the whole Mormon colony to emigrate and settle there.[11]

Independence, Missouri, was then the starting place for all emigrant trains bound for the West. Emigration to California before the year 1846 had followed the Oregon Trail from Independence westward as far as Fort Hall, near what is now Pocatello, Idaho, where those going to California went southwest to the headwaters

---

[10.] Samuel J. Hastings of Boston tried to get a contract to move the Mormons to California.

[11.] Bancroft, *History of California*, III:778, V:548.

of the Humboldt, then west past the Sink and over the Sierra to Sutter's Fort.

This well-traveled route to California necessitated a long detour to the north to avoid Great Salt Lake and the Salt Desert west of it. It occurred to Hastings that if he could find a more direct route he would be able to divert a large number of Oregon emigrants to California, since by the time they reached Green River many were weary of the long journey and anxious to find a fertile country as quickly as possible. A shorter route would bring in a larger number of settlers, and the Republic of California would soon be a reality.

Acting on this theory he determined to explore a new route; so in the spring of 1846 we find him at Sutter's Fort preparing to return east as far as Bridger's to turn the tide of emigration.

The short-cut to California, which later came to be known as the Hastings Cutoff, passes through the center of the Great Salt Desert; and since the purpose of this narrative is to tell the story of the adventures which befell the emigrants who later attempted this route, we will now leave Hastings at Sutter's Fort while we make a short survey of the country over which they were about to pass— the most desolate stretch of desert in America.

2. THE GREAT SALT DESERT

Many thousands of years ago there existed in the Great Basin an immense fresh water lake which extended from southern Utah north into Idaho.[1] This lake, of which Great Salt Lake is an insignificant remnant, drained into the Portneuf, a tributary of the Snake River on the north. In the course of time, presumably at the end of the last glacial period, the lake tore out an immense drainage channel at its northern end, which in a very few years reduced the level of the lake 375 feet and left great terraces on the mountains where its shores had previously been. During subsequent geological periods the climate gradually changed until it became arid; rainfall was reduced and evaporation increased until the once great lake dwindled to its present size and became extremely salty on account of no longer having an outlet. Where Salt Lake City is now located the waters of old Lake Bonneville once stood a thousand feet deep.

Great Salt Lake in its present state extends seventy-five miles north and south, with an approximate width of fifty miles. To the west lies a great desolate expanse called the Salt Desert, with a length of one hundred miles and a width of seventy-five. This great level salt plain was in geologically recent times a part of Great Salt Lake, and even now lies only a few feet above high water mark. The Salt Desert is the floor of what was once the larger half of Great Salt Lake, into which no streams flow. Evaporation has removed the surface water, leaving only a great level expanse of mud and salt. No vegetation grows upon its surface, no fresh water enters it, and as far as the eye can see there is nothing but the apparently illimitable expanse of salt-plain.

[1.] Grove Karl Gilbert, *Lake Bonneville* (Washington, D.C.: Government Printing Office, 1890). U.S. Geological Survey, Monograph No. 1.

3. JEDEDIAH SMITH

The first white man to cross the Great Salt Desert was Jedediah Smith, an explorer and trapper, probably the most outstanding character of that first band of adventurers and trappers who explored the Great Basin under General Ashley in 1824-27.[1] Jim Bridger is given credit for the discovery of Great Salt Lake, but the honors should probably be divided among Bridger, Smith and Provost, who each independently discovered the existence of this great inland sea between the fall of 1824 and the spring of 1825.[2]

Jedediah Smith was born in New England and had been educated for the ministry; but to one of his temperament the ministry offered no attractions. Instead, he followed the call of the West and in 1824 we find him trapping on Bear River, a tributary of Great Salt Lake, even before the existence of that body of water was known.

The name Jedediah conjures up visions of the major prophets, and when we learn that he carried a Bible with him wherever he went the allusion seems perfect. We imagine him with a flowing beard and a voice like the trump of Gabriel. Yet the facts are that when he left home to seek adventure in the West he was still a very young man, and when he crossed the Salt Desert he was only twenty-eight years old.

Jedediah Smith did carry his Bible and his New England code of morals with him into the wilderness, where he quickly gained a reputation for shrewdness and sobriety. He was also one of the best shots in the fur business, an accomplishment which was an asset in a country full of grizzly bears and thieving savages. He carried his Bible in one hand and his loaded rifle in the other, trusting in the Lord, but taking good care that his powder did not absorb moisture.

---

[1] Harrison Clifford Dale, *The Ashley-Smith Explorations and the Discovery of a Central Route to the Pacific, 1822–1829* (Cleveland: Arthur H. Clark Company, 1918), 104, 158.

[2] J. Cecil Alter, *James Bridger* (Salt Lake City: Shepard Book Co., 1925).

In the spring of 1825, or more probably in the fall of 1824, a body of trappers were camped at their rendezvous on Bear River. One night a discussion arose around the campfire as to the probable destination of the river. On a wager Jim Bridger took his canoe and made his way alone down the river to settle the argument. He soon came to a large body of water which he discovered to be salt, and supposed it to be an arm of the Pacific Ocean.

When Jedediah Smith, who had been trapping on some of the streams tributary to the lake arrived at the encampment, he brought the news that he had discovered a great lake of salt water and had gone partly around it; he had viewed it from a high elevation and was the first to discover that it was in reality a lake and not an arm of the sea.

On August 22, 1826, Jedediah Smith, with a small company of trappers, left Weber River enroute to California with a load of furs, over a route approximating the Old Spanish Trail. Their route led past Utah Lake, a shallow body of fresh water which Father Escalante had discovered just fifty years before.[3]

When the party reached Los Angeles, they were forcibly detained by Mexican authorities for several weeks, but were eventually released after promising to return immediately over the trail they had just made. Smith, being a born explorer, did not relish the idea of retracing his steps. Besides, he had hoped to find the fabled Buenaventura River, perhaps a rich fur country. So, instead of retracing his steps he traveled north along the coast, trapping as he went, until far from any Mexican settlement. In this way he spent the winter of 1826–27, and in the following May tried to cross the Sierra Nevada on his return to the valley of Salt Lake. He failed in the first attempt, losing several animals; but in the second attempt, accompanied by only two companions, seven horses and one mule, he succeeded in crossing over on the hard-packed snow, somewhere in the vicinity of Mount St. Joseph, now called Lassen Peak. After eight days of strenuous travel from the eastern foot of the mountains, these three made their way across unexplored and unmapped deserts, approximately over the route later surveyed by Captain Simpson, and eventually reached Fish Springs on the western edge of the Salt Desert and headed across the salt flats to-

---

[3.] Dale, *The Ashley-Smith Explorations*, 187.

ward Skull Valley, traversing 30 miles of salty silt and another 30 miles of sage desert without water.

In a letter addressed to General William Clark, Superintendent of Indian Affairs, dated "Little Lake of Bear River, July 17, 1827," Jedediah Smith tells of his journey to California, and ends the letter with this short statement:

> After travelling twenty days from the east side of Mount Joseph, I struck the S.W. corner of the Great Salt Lake, travelling over a country completely barren and destitute of game. We frequently travelled without water sometimes for two days over sandy deserts, where there was no sign of vegetation and when we found water in some of the rocky hills, we most generally found some Indians who appeared the most miserable of the human race having nothing to subsist on (nor any clothing) except grass seed, grass-hoppers, etc. When we arrived at the Salt Lake, we had but one horses and one mule remaining, which were so feeble and poor that they could scarce carry the little camp equipage which I had along; the balance of my horses I was compelled to eat as they gave out.
>
> The company are now starting, and therefore must close my communication. Yours respectfully,
>
> Jedediah S. Smith, of the firm of
> Smith, Jackson and Sublette.[4]

Since this book was first published, Maurice Sullivan, a newspaper man of San Diego, California, discovered and published part of a journal kept by Jedediah Smith in which he tells in detail his experiences on this journey, together with a map of his route, all of which is too long to repeat here.[5] In Skull Valley he missed the spring at Orr's Ranch, which lies in the flat desert where no spring was expected to be, but found water beyond at the foot of a mountain and carried some back to his companion who had given out.

In *Hidden Heroes of the Rockies*, Isaac K. Russell makes the following statement:

[4.] *Ibid.*, 193–94.

[5.] Maurice S. Sullivan, *The Travels of Jedediah Smith; A Documentary Outline Including the Journal of the Great American Pathfinder* (Santa Ana: Fine Arts Press, 1934).

For years after Smith's journey the Piute Indians of Skull Valley, Utah, repeated the tradition that the first white men they ever saw were three who staggered, almost naked, in from the western desert, and were half crazy from breathing alkali dust.[6]

Russell obtained this information many years ago from trappers who still remembered the stories of early exploration in the Great Basin, and who were acquainted with the Indians of Skull Valley. I think we may consider it reliable.

This expedition of Jedediah Smith in crossing such a barren and desolate country for the first time, without any knowledge whatever of what lay before him, has never been fully appreciated by historians, due partly to the historian's lack of first-hand knowledge of the country over which he had to pass. Even today, with good highways and high-powered cars, the trip is not without danger due to the great distance between waterholes and the intense heat of the desert in summer. Smith, in crossing this country with only two companions and insufficient supplies, entirely ignorant of the dangers in his path, performed one of the most daring individual exploits in the whole history of western exploration.

*

The next crossing of the Salt Desert may have been by Isaac P. Rose in 1835. Rose came west with Nathaniel Wyeth and between trapping expeditions claimed to have been "white chief" of the Crow Indians. Among the trappers he was considered to be a treacherous and unreliable person and his story is not to be taken too seriously.

---

6. Isaac K. Russell, *Hidden Heroes of the Rockies* (Yonkers-on-Hudson: World Book Company, 1925), 158.

4. THE BARTLESON PARTY

No other attempt was made to cross the Salt Desert until 1841, when a party under Colonel Bartleson passed around the north end of the lake. While this party took a route never attempted before or since, part of their trail on the western edge of the desert coincides with the Hastings Cutoff, and the story of the Salt Desert would not be complete without their record.

These people were emigrants from Missouri, and the first to attempt to take wagons over the mountains into California. Their adventures are described by John Bidwell,[1] who was then only twenty-two years old, and whose last cent had been invested in a wagon, drawn by another man's oxen. Among the whole party of sixty-four emigrants there was less than one hundred dollars in cash. This party gathered at Sapling Grove, Kansas, and Colonel Bartleson assumed command, refusing to go unless he could act as captain. When ready to start it was discovered that none of them knew anything about the trail. Fortunately there arrived at the starting point Father DeSmet and all traveled together until they reached what is now Soda Springs, Idaho. Here DeSmet and Fitzpatrick went northwest into Montana, leaving the Bartleson party without a guide. Some chose to follow DeSmet as far as Fort Hall, but thirty-two of the original company were determined to try to get to California by going around the north end of the lake.

To learn something of the country which lay before them, four men were sent on to Fort Hall to get what information they could. They were unsuccessful in their efforts to obtain a guide, and the information they secured was very vague and practically valueless.

---

[1] John Bidwell, "The First Emigrant Train to California," *The Century Illustrated Monthly Magazine*, XLI (November 1890), 106–130; and John Bidwell, *A Journey to California, 1841*, Introduction by Francis P. Farquhar (Berkeley: The Friends of the Bancroft Library, 1964), from the only known copy of the first edition at the Bancroft Library. General John Bidwell became a capitalist, philanthropist and one of California's most prominent and useful citizens. He wrote the declaration of the "Bear Flag Revolution," drew up the contract between Sutter and Marshall for the building of the mill where gold was discovered in 1848, and was at one time a Prohibition candidate for President. During 1848–49, he took $100,000 in gold out of Bidwell's Bar.

In this party were the wife and small daughter of Benjamin Kelsey, the first woman and the first child to attempt a crossing of the desert, and the first to reach California over the Sierra. J. B. Chiles, also a member of this party, says:

It was considered almost rash for a woman to venture on so perilous a journey, but Mrs. Kelsey said: "Where my husband goes, I can go. I can better endure the hardships of the journey than anxieties for an absent husband." So she was received in the company and her cheerful nature and kind heart brought many a ray of sunshine through the clouds that gathered round a company [of] so many weary travelers. She bore the fatigues of the journey with so much heroism, patience, and kindness that there still exists a warmth in every heart for the mother and her child that were always forming silvery linings for every dark cloud that assailed them.[2]

Turning south at what is now Alexander, Idaho, the Bartleson party followed the Bear River several days to a point near the present town of Corinne, Utah. They were then near Great Salt Lake but could not as yet see its waters. From this point their course was northwest until they turned west around the north end of the lake. John Bidwell kept a remarkably accurate diary of this journey[3] and it might be well to let him tell his story:

W. 18th. [August, 1841]—Traveled but a short distance, when we discovered that a deep salt creek prevented our continuing near the river. In ascending this stream in search of a place to cross it, we found on its margin a hot spring, very deep and clear. The day was very warm and we were unable to reach the river, encamped on this salt creek and suffered much for water, the water being so salt we could not drink it, distance 15 miles.[4]

T. 19th. Started early, hoping soon to find fresh water, where we could refresh ourselves and animals, but alas! The sun beamed heavy on our heads as the day advanced,

---

[2] Doyce B. Nunis, Jr., ed., *The Bidwell-Bartleson Party, 1841 California Emigrant Adventure: Documents and Memoirs of the Overland Pioneers* (Santa Cruz: Western Tanager Press, 1991), 142–43.

[3] John Bidwell, *A Journey to California, 1841*.

[4] Near Corinne, Utah.

and we could see nothing before us but extensive arid plains, glimmering with heat and salt, at length the plains became so impregnated with salt, that vegetation entirely ceased; the ground was in many places white as snow with salt & perfectly smooth—the mid-day sun, beaming with uncommon splendor upon these shining plains, made us fancy we could see timber upon the plains, and wherever timber is found there is water always. We marched forward with unremitted pace till we discovered it was an illusion, and lest our teams should give out we returned from S. to E., and hastened to the river which we reached in about 5 miles.

A high mountain overlooked us on the East and the river was thickly bordered with willows—grass plenty but so salt, our animals could scarcely eat it; salt glitters upon its blades like frost. Distance 20 miles.

F. 20th. Company remained here while two men went to explore the country, they returned bringing the intelligence that we were within ten miles of where the river disembogued itself into the great salt lake. This was the fruit of having no pilot—we had passed through cash valley, where we intended to have stopped and did not know it.

S. 21st. Marched off in a N.W. direction, and intersected our trail of Thursday last, having made a complete triangle in the plain. At this intersection of the trails, we left a paper elevated by a pole, that the men, returning from Fort Hall, might shun the tedious rounds we had taken. Found grass and water which answered our purpose very well, though both were salt. Distance ten miles.[5]

S. 22nd. This morning a man (Mr. Bralaski) returned from the Fort....no pilot could be got at the Fort....near where we were encamped here, were a few Hackberry trees.

M. 23rd. Started, bearing our course west, in order to pass the Salt Lake—passed many salt plains and springs in the forenoon, the day was hot—the hills, and land bordering on the plains, were covered with wild sage....At evening

---

5. West of Corinne.

we arrived in full view of the Salt Lake,[6] water was very scarce. Cedar grows here both on the hills and in the valleys, distance 20 miles.

T. 24th. Cattle strayed this morning to seek water—late start—day was warm—traveled about 10 miles in a W. direction, encamped where we found numerous springs, deep, clear and somewhat impregnated with salt....[7] Here we procured salt of the best quality. The grass, that grew in small spots on the plains, was laden with salt which had formed itself on the stalks and blades in lumps, from the size of a pea to that of a hen's egg, this was the kind we procured, it being very white, strong and pure.

W. 25th. Remained here all day.

T. 26th. Traveled all day over dry, barren plains, producing nothing but sage, or rather it ought to be called, wormwood, and which I believe will grow without water or soil. Two men were sent ahead in search of water, but returned a little before dark unsuccessful.

Our course intersected an Indian trail, which we followed directly north towards the mountains, knowing that in these dry countries, the Indian trails always lead to the nearest water. Having traveled till about 10 o'clock P.M. made a halt, and waited till morning.—distance about 30 miles.

F. 27th. Daylight discovered us a spot of green grass on the declivity of the mountain towards which we were advancing. 5 miles took us to this place, where we found, to our great joy, an excellent spring of water and an abundance of Grass[8]—here we determined to continue, 'till the route was explored to the head of Mary's River and run no more risks of perishing for want of water in this desolate region.

---

6. Summit of the pass through Promontory Range, near Promontory, Utah. Camped at Cedar Springs just west of the pass, which has a very small flow.

7. Now called Salt Wells, between Promontory and Monument Point.

8. Pilot Spring, south of Snowville, and thirty miles north of Salt Wells.

S. 28th. Company remained here....

S. 29th. Capt. Bartleson with C. Hopper started to explore the route to the head of Mary's river, expecting to be absent about 8 or 9 days—the Company to await here his return.

[The company remained at this spring until the 5th of September.]

S. 5th. Grass having become scarce, we concluded to move on a little every day to meet Capt. B. & H. Traveled about 6 miles and encamped by a beautiful Cedar grove.[9]

M. 6th. Traveled about 7 miles.

T. 7th. Traveled about 7 miles, antelope appeared to be plenty.

W. 8th. Exceedingly cold; ice in our water buckets. Part of the Company remained on account of the cold—2 wagons with owners being contrary, went on.

T. 9th. The part of the Company that remained yesterday went on and overtook the 2 wagons. Capt. Bartleson & Hopper returned, bringing Intelligence that they had found the head of Mary's river—distant about 5 days travel, distance traveled today about 12 miles S.W. direction.[10] The Indians stole a horse—day cool.

F. 10th. Traveled about 15 miles and encamped without water.

S. 11th. Traveled about 15 miles and came to water, course W.

S. 12th. Mr. Kelsely [Kelsey] left his wagons[11] and took his family and goods on pack horses, his oxen not being able to keep up; distance today about 12 miles.[12]

[9.] Probably at Emigrant Spring.

[10.] Through Park Valley.

[11.] Probably at Owl Spring, eight miles east of Lucin. The route for the 10th, 11th and 12th is indefinite, but must have crossed Dove Creek, which was probably dry, and Muddy Creek, where they may have found water at what is now the Rosebud Ranch. They probably crossed Bovine Mountain through Emigrant Pass, west of the ranch, and then traveled directly to Owl Spring on the well-marked Indian trail. An iron boxing

M. 13th. Traveled about 15 miles south, between Salt plains on the E, and high mtns. on the W.[13]

T. 14th. Traveled about 25 miles and stopped about 9 o'clock at night, in the middle of a dry plain, destitute of water.[14]

W. 15th. Started very early, day was exceedingly warm, passed through a gap in a ridge of mountains, came into a high dry plain, traveled some distance into it, saw the form of a high mountain through the smoky atmosphere—reached it, having come about 15 miles—found plenty of water—our animals were nearly given out.[15] We were obliged to go so much further, in order to get along with the wagons: We concluded to leave them, and pack as many things as we could.

T. 16th. All hands were busy making Pack saddles and getting ready to pack....

F. 17th. About 11 A.M. all were ready to start; horses, mules, and 4 oxen, packed; proceeded south along the mtns. seeking a place to pass through. At length an Indian trail took us across into a dry plain, perfectly destitute of grass and water. Traveled 'till about midnight, having come about 17 miles. This plain was white in many places with salt, and the cool evening contrasting with the color of the salt on the ground gave a striking similarity to winter....

S. 18th. Morning found us on the East side of a Mountain not far from its base but there were no signs of water....

---

from the wheel of a linch-pin wagon was found at this spring, which may have belonged to the Kelsey wagons.

[12.] Camped at one of the springs along the base of Pilot Range, fifteen miles north of the McKellar Ranch at Pilot Peak.

[13.] Along the base of Pilot Peak. Camped on Pilot Creek, probably above the McKellar Ranch. Ten miles south of this camp Edwin Bryant saw the tracks of their wagons in 1846.

[14.] The valley between Pilot Peak and the Toano Range (Nevada).

[15.] The gap in the mountains is now called Silver Zone Pass; the high, dry plain is Steptoe Valley; the high mountain is Spruce Mountain; found water at the Johnson Ranch.

S. 19th....journeyed yesterday about 12 miles, did not travel to day.

M. 20th. Passed along one of the highest mountains we had seen in our whole journey [Ruby Mountains], seeking a place to scale it, as we wished to travel W. instead of S. being convinced, that we were already far enough South. At length passed through and descended into a beautiful valley, inclining towards the W. All now felt confident that we were close to the headwaters of Mary's river—distance 25 miles.

Traveling west through this valley they crossed another mountain and found themselves on the South Fork of the Humboldt which they followed to the main stream (then called Mary's River), and continued down past the Sink and into the Sierra Nevada.

In crossing these mountains, the Bartleson party experienced the most terrible hardships. Their cattle were killed and eaten, then the mules suffered the same fate, and even a dog which was a great pet of the whole party was eaten. After that they lived on coyotes, wildcats, crows and any living thing they could find. After wandering many days in the mountains they finally reached the fertile lands on the western side and found game, eventually arriving at Marsh's Ranch in the most pitiable condition, minus everything they possessed except the rags on their backs and their rifles, but without the loss of a single member of the party.

The desperate chances taken by this first party of emigrants can be appreciated only by attempting to follow their old trail. All other wagon trains followed routes which had been previously explored by men on horses. The Bartleson party, entirely ignorant of the nature of the country, traveled from the mouth of Bear River around Great Salt Lake and Salt Desert over a route which had never before been traveled by white men. There were many long stretches of desert where no water was to be found, and the great wonder is that they found sufficient to preserve their lives. J. B. Chiles, a member of this party, brought two other wagon trains to California, but never again attempted to follow his trail of 1841.

Such were the experiences of the first party of emigrants to reach California. They were the first emigrants to see the Great Salt Desert, and brought the first wagons into the states of Utah and Nevada.

5. FRÉMONT'S EXPEDITION

Colonel John Charles Frémont, "The Pathfinder," had been exploring the western country for the government during the years of 1842–1844. Partly due to his reports, emigration to the West was rapidly increasing, most of which followed the Oregon Trail through Fort Hall.

In 1845 Frémont organized another exploring party to survey the Great Salt Lake and surrounding country. When the expedition was ready Kit Carson was sent for, and to guide Frémont he sold the ranch he had just bought and stocked, and made all haste to join the party. With him was his friend Owens, and Frémont's trusted friend, Godey. How highly Frémont regarded these three may be understood from his remark, "The three, under Napoleon, might have become Marshals, chosen as he chose men."[1]

Upon arrival at Great Salt Lake Frémont made camp and began explorations that occupied him for two weeks. On October 22 the party broke camp, and following the southern shore of the lake for two days, passed the place where the Garfield townsite is located. They then crossed Tooele Valley, stopped at the springs near what is now Grantsville, rounded the point of the mountain at Timpie, crossed Skull Valley, and laid their course across the middle of the Salt Desert.

On the far horizon, seventy-five miles to the west, rose a prominent peak, a landmark toward which they decided to make their way in as straight a line as possible. Here, on the eastern edge of the Salt Desert, Frémont camped and made his preparations. The mules were rested and fed; following his usual course in such cases, a scouting party was sent on ahead of the main body. This party consisted of Kit Carson, Auguste Archambault, Maxwell, and one other man in charge of a pack mule. The four set out in the night and were instructed to light fires if water was found.

Consultations had been held previously as to the best way to cross the desert, but neither Carson nor Joseph Walker knew anything of the route. Walker, one of Bonneville's trappers, had ex-

---

1. Jesse Benton Frémont, *Memoirs of My Life, by John Charles Frémont*, Volume 1 (Chicago and New York: Belford, Clarke & Company, 1887), 427.

plored a route from Bear River to California in 1833, having been the first to take the route followed by the Bartleson party as far as the north point of the lake. From there Walker had gone northwest to the headwaters of the Humboldt, followed that river to the Sink, and crossed the Sierra in the vicinity of what is now Yosemite National Park.[2] Joseph Walker had been employed by Frémont for his knowledge of the country beyond, but he had never crossed this desert. Indians living in the vicinity claimed that no one had ever crossed before, and that to attempt it was sure death. One Indian, however, was at last persuaded to accompany the party, for a consideration, although he claimed no knowledge of the route.

Two hours before sundown on the day following the departure of the scouts, Frémont and the balance of his party began their march across the most desolate expanse of desert in America. The advance party had already been on their way about fifteen hours. Striking for the distant peak to the west they traveled as fast as was consistent with the going and when night fell they continued with no halt for refreshments.

The Salt Desert under a scorching sun is forbidding enough, but the Salt Desert by moonlight is absolutely uncanny. There is neither bush nor tree nor blade of grass, there is no sound of bird or insect, there is apparently nothing ahead, nothing behind, nothing to the right nor to the left. The desert stretches out before, white and interminable, where one seems to be walking in a treadmill, constantly moving, yet never arriving anywhere. Even these hardy explorers, accustomed as they were to the unusual, were affected by the eerie silence. Little wonder then that the Indian who had accompanied them became so frightened that his knees rattled together and he was unable to speak. On account of his terror he was useless as a guide, so Frémont gave him his wages and he vanished into the night like a frightened rabbit, never looking back.

The care which had been given the mules now began to pay dividends and the party made excellent time, continuing their march until well toward morning, when they camped near a low

---

[2.] Dr. W. F. Wagner, ed., *Leonard's Narrative: Adventures of Zenas Leonard, Fur Trader and Trapper, 1831–1836* (Cleveland: The Burrows Brothers, 1904).

ridge which rose from the plain and built a fire with some sage-brush which grew upon it. Before daybreak, however, Archambault rode up with the news that water had been found on the opposite side; so without waiting for sunrise the party saddled up and continued their journey. Late the next afternoon they reached [Donner Spring], a spring flowing a short distance from the foot of the mountain toward which they had been traveling. Frémont called this mountain Pilot Peak, an appropriate name which it still bears.

After recruiting their animals at the spring the party pushed on to California, having marked out a shorter route which was afterward followed by several parties of emigrants and later came to be known as the Hastings Cutoff, although Kit Carson was its original discoverer.

Frémont does not mention the loss of any animals on this part of the journey across the Salt Desert, but one of his men states that ten or fifteen horses and mules gave out and had to be abandoned.[3]

In such going a horse could make thirty-five or forty miles in a day of hard riding. Oxen, drawing heavily loaded wagons, were compelled to travel much more slowly and averaged only about fifteen miles a day. Frémont reported to Washington that this new route was much preferable, being shorter, with more pasturage, and well watered. But in view of the difficulties later encountered by emigrants at tempting to use this route, his statement seems to have been just a bit more than the truth.

Almost immediately after his arrival in California, Frémont got into difficulties with the Mexican authorities. The American settlers around Sutter's Fort and Coloma were hopeful that he had come to seize California for the United States, and were impatient to see this accomplished. Historians have enlarged upon an incident called the "Bear Flag Revolution," which was merely a gathering of Americans attempting to organize themselves against the time when they might be called upon to lend Frémont their assistance. At this meeting John Bidwell drew up the "constitution,"

[3.] Howard Stansbury, *Exploration and Survey of the Valley of the Great Salt Lake of Utah* (Philadelphia: Lippincott, Grambo & Co., 1852), 111.

and a man by the name of Todd, nephew of Mrs. Abraham Lincoln, painted the "Bear Flag," which is still preserved.

When a rumor reached Sutter's Fort that Frémont might need assistance, James Clyman, an old trapper, wrote Frémont a letter in which he offered to raise a company among the emigrants he had brought in from Oregon and those who had just arrived from the States. This offer Frémont declined, stating that with the small force at his command he deemed a retreat over the mountains as the only course open to him at the time. He was soon to change his mind.

In the meantime Clyman had started on his way east over the mountains, bound for St. Louis, acting as guide for several emigrants who had become dissatisfied with the country. Accompanying this eastbound party was our old friend, Lansford W. Hastings, whom we left at Sutter's Fort, and James M. Hudspeth who had come west with Hastings in 1842.

6. JAMES CLYMAN

James Clyman had been one of the company of trappers and adventurers employed by General Ashley between 1823 and 1827, having acted in the capacity of clerk. He was one of the party which discovered South Pass, through which traveled all emigrant wagons bound for Oregon and California.[1]

In the fall of 1823 he was with a party under Jedediah Smith near the Black Hills, when Smith was attacked and nearly scalped by a grizzly. Clyman sewed up the wounds and probably saved Smith's life. He was also one of the party which explored the Great Salt Lake in bull-boats in 1826. Returning to the east in 1827 after having made considerable money in the fur trade, Clyman took up the first land on which the city of Milwaukee was later built. In 1844, after numerous adventures, he decided to visit the West again, for the benefit of his health. He joined an emigrant train at Independence in the spring of that year, acting as treasurer of the company until they reached Oregon City. Here he met Dr. Elijah White, who had been displaced by Hastings as captain of his wagon train in 1842. Dr. White was then Indian agent for Oregon, and enlisted the good services of Clyman in an effort to obtain an appointment as governor of the territory.

Among those whom Clyman had brought to California from Oregon was James W. Marshall, a wagon maker and carpenter, who later built a sawmill near Coloma for John Sutter. It was in the millrace of this structure that gold was first discovered by him in 1848.

Clyman spent the winter of 1844–45 around Sutter's Fort and San Francisco. On a trip through Napa Valley, where he later settled, Clyman stopped over night at the hunting camp of Benjamin Kelsey, who with his wife and daughter had crossed the Sierra with Bartleson and Bidwell in 1841.

The party now traveling east with Clyman, in April, 1846, consisted of eighteen men (nineteen including Hastings' Indian servant), three women and three children, all mounted on horses or mules. Old Caleb Greenwood, over 80 years of age, who had

---

[1.] Charles L. Camp, ed., *James Clyman, Frontiersman*, Second Edition (Portland: Champoeg Press, 1960), 25.

guided the first wagons over the Sierra in 1844, was also a member of this party, together with two of his sons.

Leaving Sutter's Fort in April, they crossed the Sierra over a most difficult pass where they saw the trail of the wagons which Greenwood had piloted the year before.[2] Continuing east they followed the Truckee River until it turned north, then struck across the desert to the Humboldt, which they followed northeast for several days. When they had traveled as far as the South Fork they found the place where Talbot's division of Frémont's party had intersected the Fort Hall Road after crossing the Salt Desert the previous autumn.[3]

Hastings had heard of this new route and was anxious to explore it, hoping it would shorten the distance between Fort Bridger and the Humboldt and thereby assist him in his ambitions. A long consultation was held here, as to the merits of the route, but after much argument the party decided to follow this trail toward the Salt Desert.

The decision reached here was a momentous one for the emigrants who were later to follow this cutoff; and if Clyman and Greenwood, who were old mountaineers, had been more persistent with their objections, many lives might have been saved and untold suffering avoided.

Some of the party decided, however, to follow the trail of Frémont's men, while Greenwood, his sons and a few others continued on the trail to Fort Hall. In a few days the Hastings group stood on the summit of the Toano range,[4] looking eastward over an expanse of salt-plains which extended as far as the eye could reach. From here they made their way toward Pilot Peak,[5] which stood on the western edge of the salt-plain, and following the eastern side of the mountain, camped on Pilot Peak creek, where they found good water and grass.[6] After resting their horses the party

---

[2.] The Bonney party. Greenwood had been sent to Fort Hall by Captain Sutter to induce Oregon emigrants to come to California. See Fred Lockley, "Recollections of Benjamin Franklin Bonney," *Oregon Historical Quarterly* 24 (March 1923), 36–55.

[3.] Near Halleck, Nevada.

[4.] West of Wendover, Utah, just over the Nevada state line.

[5.] Twenty-two miles north of Wendover, Utah.

[6.] McKellar's ranch.

started east across the Salt Desert. Clyman describes this part of the trip as follows:

[May] 28 [1846]—Left our camp at the Snowy or more properly the spring Bute [Pilot Peak]...and took the Trail East and soon entered the greate salt plain   the first plain is 6 or 7 miles wide and covered in many places three inches deep in pure white salt   passed an Island of rocks [Silver Island] in this great plain and entered the greate plain over which we went in a bold trot untill dusk when we Bowoiked [bivouacked] for the night [at Grayback] without grass or water and not much was said   in fact all filt incouraged as we had been enformed that if we could follow Mr Fremonts trail we would not have more than 20 miles without fresh water   In fact this is the [most] desolate country perhaps on the whole globe there being not one spear of vegitation and of course no kind of animal can subsist and it is not yet assertained to what extent this immince salt and sand plain can be south of whare we [are now]   our travel to day was 40 miles

29 As soon as light began to shew in the East we were again under way   crossed one more plain (to cross) and then assended a rough low mountain [Cedar Mountain] still no water and our hopes ware again disappointed Commenced our desent down a ravine   made 14 miles and at length found a small spring of Brackish water[7] [in Skull Valley] which did not run more than four rods before it all disappeared in the thirsty earth   but mean and poor as the water was we and our animals Quenched our burning thirst and unpacked for the day after our rapid travel of about 20 hours and 30 hours without water. [8]

The next day Skull Valley was crossed, where they found many salt springs. Near where Grantsville now stands they found a number of deep holes full of good water which were later called "Twenty Wells" by the emigrants who stopped there. The water in these holes seemed to well up out of the ground, but did not flow

---

[7.] Redlum Spring in Skull Valley, at the foot of Cedar Mountain, east side of the pass. This small spring almost disappears later in the season.

[8.] Camp, *James Clyman*, 215-16.

away. The ground was hard all around the hole, and the water ran in from below as fast as it was dipped out.

From "Twenty Wells" the party followed the shore of the lake to Salt Lake Valley. Clyman says that the lake appeared to be only half as large as when he first saw it in 1826. An island (Stansbury) which had been miles from shore was then a part of the mainland, and he wondered if the whole lake would not dry up entirely.

Salt Lake Valley was very marshy and grown up with tall grass and tulles along what is now called the Jordan River, and in making their way through this marsh, Hastings, who seems to have taken over the leadership of the party, lost Frémont's trail. Crossing the valley toward the mountains they went too far south; instead of following the foot of the Wasatch range as Frémont had done, they struck into the mountains through what is now called Emigration Canyon, went down the opposite slope probably on an old trapper trail, and eventually came out on the Weber River three miles below Echo Canyon. Their route after leaving the valley had been very difficult on account of the dense growth of brush and aspen trees, and even without wagons they had trouble in getting through. From the Weber River to Fort Bridger the country was familiar to Clyman, and the party arrived there in due course.

Here Clyman waited for the emigrants from Oregon who were returning east on the Fort Hall Road; all then proceeded on their way to St. Louis. They were the first to travel the trail eastward that year.

Hastings and Hudspeth had come to Fort Bridger to intercept the emigrants who were bound for Oregon and guide them to California instead. Proceeding fifty or sixty miles farther east they made camp on the Sweetwater River where they awaited arrival of the first trains.

Hastings had now decided to guide wagon trains over the route he had just traveled. In his unbounded enthusiasm and determination to get a large number of settlers into California as quickly as possible, he seems to have overlooked the fact that oxen drawing heavy wagons travel very slowly. He had crossed the Salt Desert in about twenty hours of hard riding, without undue suffering, and it apparently did not occur to him that oxen could not cross as easily. He wrote letters recommending his cutoff as being three hundred miles shorter and perfectly safe for wagon trains; he gave these letters to a lone traveler[9] with instructions to deliver them to any emigrant trains he might meet on his way east.

[9.] Wales Bonney, who emigrated to Oregon in 1845, was returning east alone to bring out his family. See Edwin Bryant, *What I Saw in California* (New York: D. Appleton & Co., 1848), 127.

7. THE WILLIAM H. RUSSELL PARTY

Among the first wagon trains to leave Independence in the spring of 1846 was one under the leadership of Colonel William H. Russell, a gentleman who had been in the legislature of Kentucky, and was a friend of Henry Clay. Colonel Russell's party left Independence on May 5, and was joined a few days later by Edwin Bryant.[1] On May 19 nine wagons from Illinois under the leadership of George and Jacob Donner and James F. Reed joined this train, making 46 wagons in all. Samuel C. Young and George Harlan were also invited to become members of this party, but declined, stating that it was already too large; they traveled by themselves a few days in advance. The Donner brothers were moderately wealthy farmers; James F. Reed (whose Polish name was Reednoski) was a veteran of the Black Hawk war, having served in the same company with Abraham Lincoln and James Clyman. Jesse Boone, a grandson of Daniel Boone, and Judge J. Quinn Thornton, later a supreme judge of Oregon, were also members of this train.

Unlike the emigrants of 1841, the majority of these people were supplied with everything necessary for the journey and carried surplus goods for trade in California; their equipment was of the best. Reed had built a very large and comfortable wagon having a double deck for sleeping quarters. It had two side entrances, unlike the ordinary prairie schooner, and was equipped with a cook stove and every convenience for traveling. Reed's step-daughter Virginia later called it the "Pioneer Palace Car."

An idea of the equipment necessary for a journey across the plains might be of interest here, and the following from Judge Thornton's *Oregon and California in 1848* will give the reader an excellent invoice of what these wagons contained:

All persons...ought to use great caution in forming their connections. No partnership by which the rights of property are mingled, ought to be made, if it can be avoided.

[1.] Lieutenant in Company H, California Volunteers, under Captain Jacob, his traveling companion. Appointed alcalde of San Francisco by General Kearny, serving from February until May, 1847. Author of *What I Saw in California*.

If this can not be avoided, at least, those with whom such connections are formed, should be well known to be persons of principle; for it is certain that the toils and everyday occurrences of the way, will furnish the severest tests of character—tests so thorough and searching, that every thing, but the genuine gold, will be consumed in the furnace. These remarks, and others of a like character, are made with a view to practical usefulness.

Emigrants ought to procure strong, well ironed, light wagons, made of *thoroughly* seasoned timber. The tongue should be a *falling* one, and the hounds should be *thoroughly* braced, above, below, and at the sides, with iron. The bed should be made of three-quarter inch plank, and be also well ironed, having strong shoulders on the underside to prevent it from becoming displaced in ascending and descending steep mountains. Each wagon ought to have at least four yokes of strong, healthy, well-broken oxen, with long straight legs, and from four to six years old....Their yokes should be strong, but not unnecessarily heavy, and they ought to work easily upon the neck. They should also be provided with iron bow-keys, secured to the yoke by means of a light chain. Each wagon ought to be provided with about one dozen extra bows, made of hickory....

Too much caution can not be observed in the weight of the load. No furniture, and but few cooking utensils ought to be taken. The table ware should be tin, and the camp kettles should be made of sheet-iron. These ought all to be made in sets, so as to fit into each other, for the purpose of economizing space. Little else ought to be taken, than bed-clothing (without the beds, but buffalo-robes instead), an abundance of ordinary wearing apparel for use in the country, but buckskin for use upon the journey; and a *circular* tent. This tent is preferable to any other form, because it can be put up with one pole....

To this should be added, for each adult:—100 pounds flour; 100 pounds butter crackers; 100 pounds bacon sides—no hams; 50 pounds dried beef; 50 pounds kiln-dried corn meal; 20 pounds rice; 25 pounds beans; 1 light rifle, having a percussion lock, and carrying about 40 balls to the pound; 1 revolving, or Colt's pistol; 25 pounds lead; 12 pounds best rifle powder; 1 butcher-knife; 1 small tomahawk—with the nerve to use them, not rashly, but effectively, when necessary. Green goggles should be provided, to protect the eyes from the otherwise almost intolerable dust....

The provisions should be stored in half-inch pine boxes, of a uniform height, and corresponding in length with the width of the wagon-bed. Wearing apparel, bed clothing, etc., ought to be stowed in sacks (waterproof, if possible), to avoid the unnecessary and often fatal weight of boxes and trunks.

To each wagon there ought to be an ax; a drawing knife; a handsaw; a set of augers...; a gimlet; a hammer; about four pounds of assorted wrought nails; about forty pounds of tallow; and fifteen pounds of black lead.[2]

Thornton has also left a very vivid picture of Independence, Missouri, gathering place for all emigrants bound for Oregon, California or Santa Fe. He says:

The town of Independence was at this time a great Babel upon the border of the wilderness. Here might be seen the African slave with his shining black face, driving his six-horse team of blood-red bays....In one street, just driving out of town, was an emigrant, who, having completed all his preparations, was about entering upon the great prairie wilderness; whistling as though his mouth had been made for nothing else....

Here might be seen the indolent dark-skinned Spaniard smoking a cigar as he leans against the sunny side of a house. He wears a sharp conical hat with a red band; a blue round-about, with little brass buttons; his duck pantaloons are open at the side as high as the knee, exhibiting his white cotton drawers between his knee and the top of his low half-boots.

Santa Fé wagons were coming in, having attached to them eight or ten mules, driven by Spaniards, some by Ameri-

---

2. J. Quinn Thornton, *Oregon and California in 1848*, 2 volumes (New York: Harper & Brothers, Publishers, 1849), II:258–61.

cans resembling Indians, some by negroes, and others by persons of all possible crosses between these various races; each showing in his dress as well as his face some distinctive characteristic of his blood and race—the dirty poncho always marking the Spaniard. The traders had been out to Santa Fé, and having sold their goods in exchange for gold dust, dollars, and droves of mules, were then daily coming in; the dilapidated and muddy condition of their wagons, and wagon-sheets, and the sore backs of their mules, all giving evidence of the length and toil of the journey they had performed and were now about to terminate.

Merchants were doing all in their power to effect the sale of supplies to emigrants. Some of the emigrants were hurrying to and fro, looking care-worn, and many of them sad, as though the cloud had not yet passed away, that had come over their spirits, as they tore themselves from friends and scenes around which had clustered the memories of the heart. One was seen just starting, calling out to his oxen, and cracking his whip as though the world was at his control. Although some four or five children were in the wagon crying in all possible keys, he drove on, looking cheerful and happy, as though he was perfectly sure that he was going to a country where the valleys flowed with milk and honey. Behind the wagon, with her nose almost over the endboard, an old mare slowly and patiently stepped along, evincing as much care as though she knew that she was carrying "mother" and "the baby," and therefore must not stumble on that account.[3]

All the country west of the Mississippi was then Indian land. No white men attempted to cultivate it, except a few acres at the Shawnee Mission. For several days the westbound emigrants traveled the Santa Fé Trail, which for a considerable distance was identical with the Oregon Trail. The Kansas River was crossed on a ferry, operated by a Frenchman and his half-breed wife. From that point on there were no more ferries, and no white habitations of any kind until Fort Laramie was reached.

[3.] Thornton, *Oregon and California in 1848*, I:14–16.

At the crossing of the Big Blue River, just above its junction with the Little Blue, near what is now Schroyer, Kansas, the water was found to be very high, and the emigrants decided to wait a few days until it was safe to cross. While camped here, Mrs. Sarah Keyes, mother of Mrs. James F. Reed, for whom the big comfortable wagon had been built, was taken sick and died. She was buried near the trail, on a knoll under a large oak tree, and the grave marked with a headstone. The ancient oak has since disappeared, but the location of the grave was still remembered by the late Mr. J. G. Ellenbecker, a pioneer resident of Marysville, Kansas.

A half mile or so from this spot the emigrants found a beautiful spring breaking out from the side of the rocky creek bed, which they named Alcove Spring, carving that name in the rock, where it may still be seen. James F. Reed also carved his name and the date on a rock above the spring.

Many others left their names at this place, but erosion has since caused part of the ledge to fall, carrying with it these records, which now lie broken and scattered along the stream.[4]

Crossing the Big Blue, the emigrants followed the Little Blue to the Platte River. Hastings had represented the road to California as being plentifully supplied with water and grass for the sustenance of cattle enroute, and depicted the ease with which buffalo might be killed to supply meat. J. Quinn Thornton says:

> Lansford W. Hastings, who, if an opinion may be formed of him from the many untruths contained in his *Emigrant's Guide to Oregon and California*, is the Baron Munchausen of travelers in these countries, says, at page 8 of his book, "Having been a few days among the buffalo... and their horses having become accustomed to these terrific scenes, even the '*green-horn*' is enabled not only to kill the buffalo with expertness, but he is also *frequently seen driving them to the encampment, with as much indifference as he used formerly to drive his domestic cattle about his own fields, in the land of his nativity.* Giving the buffalo rapid chase for a few minutes, they become so fatigued and completely exhausted that they are driven from place to place with as little difficulty as our common

---

4. Grave and spring located in 1929 by Alice Riddle of Manhattan, Kansas, through the assistance of the late John G. Ellenbecker.

cattle. Both the grown buffalo and the calves are *very frequently* driven in this manner to the *encampment* and slaughtered.[5]

But the emigrants soon found that the great shaggy beasts of the plains were not quite so easily captured. The first buffalo were sighted soon after the train reached the Platte, and oxen and wagons were left unguarded on the prairie while the excited men raced after the half dozen animals which had been seen in the distance, expecting to accomplish their slaughter in a few moments. Some of the men were not able to return until the next day, having lost their way and worn out their horses.

James F. Reed had brought with him a racing mare which he prized very highly. Considering himself a "green-horn" he did not follow the buffalo on the first day, but remained with the wagons to observe the success of the other hunters, some of whom had had previous experience. The following letter written by him to his brother-in-law and printed in the *Sangamo Journal* on July 30, 1846, gives an interesting account of his experiences hunting buffalo:[6]

South Fork of the Nebraska, Ten Miles from the Crossings.
Tuesday, June 16, 1846.

To-day, at nooning, there passed, going to the States, seven men from Oregon, who went out last year. One of them was well acquainted with Messrs. [William B.] Ide, and [Robert] Cad[d]en Key[e]s,—the later of whom he says went to California. They met the advance Oregon caravan about 150 miles west of Ft. Larimere, and counted in all for California and Oregon (excepting ours), four hundred and seventy-eight waggons. There is in ours forty waggons, which make 518 in all; and there is said to be twenty yet behind.

To-morrow we cross the river, and by our reckoning will be 200 miles from Fort Larimere, where we intend to stop and repair our waggon wheels; they are nearly all loose, and I am afraid we will have to stop sooner if there can be found wood suitable to heat the tire. There is no wood

---

5. Thornton, *Oregon and California in 1848*, I:83.
6. This letter was carried east by James Clyman.

here, and our women and children are now out gathering "Buffalo chips" to burn in order to do the cooking. These "chips" burn well.

So far as I am concerned, my family affairs go on smoothly, but I have nothing to do but hunt, which I have done with great success. My first appearance on the wilds of the Nebraska as a hunter, was on the 12th inst., when I returned to camp with a splendid two year old Elk, the first and only one killed by the caravan as yet. I picked the Elk I killed, out of eight of the largest I ever beheld, and I do really believe there was one in the gang as large as the horse I rode. We have had two Buffalo killed. The men that killed them are considered the best buffalo hunters on the road—perfect "*stars*." Knowing that Glaucus could beat any horse on the Nebraska, I came to the conclusion that as far as buffalo killing was concerned, I could beat them. Accordingly, yesterday I thought to try my luck. The old buffalo hunters and as many others as they would permit to be in their company, having left the camp for a hunt, Hiram Miller,[7] my self and two others, after due preparation, took up the line of march. Before we left, every thing in camp was talking that Mr so and so, had gone hunting, and we would have some choice buffalo meat. No one thought or spoke of the two Sucker hunters, and none but the two asked to go with us.

Going one or two miles west of the old hunters on the bluffs, and after riding about four miles, we saw a large heard of buffalo bulls, great [?] for choice young meat, which is the hardest to get, being fleeter and better wind—On we went towards them as coolly and calmly as the nature of the case would permit. And now, as *perfectly green* as I was I had to compete with old experienced hunters, and remove the *stars* from their brows; which was my greatest ambition, and in order too, that they might see that a Sucker had the best horse in the company, and the best and most daring horseman in the

---

7. From Springfield, Illinois. Crossed the Sierra with Edwin Bryant before snow fell. Returned to rescue the survivors of the Donner party.

caravan. Closing upon a gang of ten or twelve bulls, the word was given, and I was soon in their midst, but among them there was none young enough for my taste to shoot, and upon seeing a drove on my right I dashed among them, with Craddock's pistol in hand—(a fine instrument for Buffalo hunters on the plains)—selected my victim and brought him tumbling to the ground, leaving my companion far behind. Advancing a little further, the plains appeared to be one living, moving mass of bulls, cows and calves. The latter took my eye, and I again put spur to Glaucus and soon found myself among them, and for the time being defied by the bulls, who protected the cows and calves. Now I thought the time had arrived to make one desperate effort, which I did by reining short up and dashing into them at right angles. With me it was an exciting time, being in the midst of a herd of upwards of a hundred head of buffalo alone, entirely out of sight of my companions. At last I succeeded in separating a calf from the cows, but soon there accompanied him three large bulls, and in a few minutes I separated two of them. Now having a bull that would weigh about 1200 lbs., and a fine large calf at full speed, I endeavored to part the calf from the bull without giving him Paddy's hint, but could not accomplish it. When I would rein to the right where the calf was, the bull would immediately put himself between us. Finding I could not separate on decent terms, I gave him one of Craddock's which sent him reeling. And now for the calf without one pistol being loaded. Time now was important—and I had to run up and down hill at full speed loading one of my pistols. At last I loaded, and soon the chase ended—and I had two dead and a third mortally wounded and dying.

After I had disposed of my calf I rode to a small mound a short distance off to see if Hiram and the others were in sight. I sat down, and while sitting I counted 597 buffalo within sight. After a while Miller and one of the others came up. We then got some water from a pond near by, which was thick with mud from the buffaloes tramping in it. Resting awhile the boys then wanted to kill a buffalo themselves. I pointed out to them a few old bulls about a mile distant. It was understood that I was not to join in the chase, and after accompanying the boys to the heights where I could witness the sport, they put out at full speed. They soon singled out a large bull, and I do not recollect of ever having laughed more than I did at the hunt the boys made. Their horses would chase well at a proper distance from the bull. As they approached he would come to a stand and turn for battle. The horses would then come to a halt, at a distance between the boys and the buffalo of about 40 yards. They would thus fire away at him, but to no effect. Seeing that they were getting tired of the sport and the bull again going away, I rode up and got permission to stop him if I could. I put spurs to Glaucus and after him I went at full speed. As I approached the bull turned around to the charge. Falling back and dashing towards him with a continued yell at the top of my lungs I got near enough to let drive one of my pistols. The ball took effect, having entered behind the shoulders and lodged in his lungs. I turned in my saddle as soon as I could to see if he had pursued me, as is often the case after being wounded. He was standing nearly in the place where he received the shot, bleeding at the nostrils, and in a few seconds dropped dead. I alighted and looped my bridle over one of his horns. This Glaucus objected to a little, but a few gentle words with a pat of my hand she stood quiet and smelled him until the boys came up. Their horses could not be got near him. Having rested, we commenced returning to the place where I killed the last calf. A short distance off we saw another drove of calves. Again the chase was renewed, and soon I laid out another fine calf upon the plains. Securing as much of the meat of the calves as we could carry, we took up the line of march for the camp, leaving the balance for the wolves, which are very numerous. An hour or two's ride found us safely among our friends, the acknowledged hero of the day, and the most successful buffalo hunter on the route. Glaucus was closely examined by many today, and pronounced the finest nag in the caravan. Mrs. R. will accompany me in my next buffalo hunt, which is to come off in a few days.

The face of the country here is very hilly, although it has the name of "plains." The weather rather warm— thermometer ranging in the middle of the day at about 90, and at night 41.

The Oregon people tell me that they have made their claims at the head of Puget Sound, and say that the late exploration has made the northeast, or British side of the Columbia, far superior to the Willamette Valley, in quality and extent of territory.

Our teams are getting on fine so far. Most of the emigrants ahead have reduced their teams. The grass is much better this year throughout the whole route than the last.

Respectfully your brother, James F. Reed.

Jas. W. Keys, Esq.[8]

The following letter from Mrs. George Donner, also printed in the *Sangamo Journal*, July 23, 1846, gives an interesting description of the daily life of the emigrants:

Near the Junction of the North and South Platte,
June 16th, 1846.

My Old Friend:—

We are now on the Platte, 200 miles from Fort Larimere. Our journey, so far, has been pleasant. The roads have been good, and food plentiful. The water for a part of the way has been indifferent—but at no time have our cattle suffered for it. Wood is now very scarce, but *"Buffalo chips"* are excellent—they kindle quick and retain heat surprisingly. We had this evening Buffalo steaks broiled upon them that had the same flavor they would have had on hickory coals.

We feel no fear of Indians. Our cattle graze quietly around our encampment unmolested. Two or three men will go hunting twenty miles from camp;—and last night two of our men laid out in the wilderness rather than ride their horses after a hard chase. Indeed if I do not experience

---

8. From the *Sangamo Journal*, courtesy Illinois State Historical Library. Reprinted in Dale L. Morgan, ed., *Overland in 1846*, 2 volumes (Georgetown: The Talisman Press, 1963), I:274-77.

something far worse than I yet have done I shall say the trouble is all in getting started.

Our waggons have not needed much repair, but I cannot yet tell in what respects they may be improved. Certain it is they cannot be too strong. Our preparations for the journey, in some respects, might have been bettered. Bread has been the principal article of food in our camp. We laid in 150 lbs. of flour and 75 lbs. of meat for each individual, and I fear bread will be scarce. Meat is abundant. Rice and beans are good articles on the road—cornmeal, too, is acceptable. Linsey dresses are the most suitable for children. Indeed if I had one it would be comfortable. There is so cool a breeze at all times in the prairie that the sun does not feel as hot as one would suppose.

We are now 450 miles from Independence. Our route at first was rough and through a timbered country which appeared to be fertile. After striking the prairie we found a first rate road, and the only difficulty we had has been crossing creeks. In that, however, there has been no danger. I never could have believed we could have travelled so far with so little difficulty. The prairie between the Blue and Platte rivers is beautiful beyond description. Never have I seen so varied a country—so suitable for cultivation. Everything was new and pleasing. The Indians frequently come to see us, and the chiefs of a tribe breakfasted at out tent this morning. All are so friendly that I cannot help feeling sympathy and friendship for them. But on one sheet, what can I say?

Since we have been on the Platte we have had on one side, and the ever varying mounds other—and have travelled through the bottom lands from one to ten miles wide with little timber. The soil is sandy, and last year, of the dry season, the emigrants found grass here scarce. Our cattle are in good order, and where proper care has been taken none has been lost. Our milch cows have been of great service—indeed, they have been of more advantage than our meat. We have plenty of butter and milk.

We are commanded by Capt. Russel—an amiable man. George Donner is himself yet. He crows in the morning, and shouts out "Chain up, boys! Chain up!" with as much authority as though he was "something in particular." John Denton is still with us—we find him a useful man in camp. Hiram Miller and Noah James are in good health and doing well. We have of the best people in our company, and some, too, that are not so good.

Buffalo show themselves frequently. We have found the wild tulip, the primrose, the lupine, the ear-drop, the larkspur, and creeping holy-hock and a beautiful flower resembling the bloom of the beech-tree, but in bunches large [?] as a small sugar loaf, and of every variety of shade to red and green. I botanize and read some, but cook a "heap" more.

There are 420 waggons, as far as we have heard, on the road between here and Oregon and California.

Give our love to all enquiring friends—God bless them.

Yours truly,

Mrs. George Donner.[9]

A majority of the wagons in Colonel Russell's train traveled together until they reached Fort Bernard, near Fort Laramie. Here Edwin Bryant and a party of nine, including Colonel Russell himself, decided to trade their wagons and oxen for mules to make better time, and from then on the train was known as the Donner party, under the leadership of George Donner.

Slight mention is made by any of the members of the Donner party of the incidents surrounding the "horse trade" at Fort Laramie. But it so happened that Francis Parkman, a young man just out of college and yearning for adventure, arrived at the fort just after the trade had been consummated. His story of the occasion contains some illuminating details:

> ...pushing through a noisy, drunken crowd, I entered an apartment of logs and mud, the largest at the fort: it was full of men of various races and complexions, all more or

---

[9]. From the *Sangamo Journal*, courtesy Illinois State Historical Library. Reprinted in Morgan, ed., *Overland in 1846*, II:561–63. Mrs. George Donner was among those who starved to death later at Donner Lake.

less drunk. A company of California emigrants, it seemed, had made the discovery at this late day that they had encumbered themselves with too many supplies for their journey. A part therefore they had thrown away or sold at great loss to the traders, but had determined to get rid of their very copious stock of Missouri whiskey, by drinking it on the spot. Here were maudlin squaws stretched on piles of buffalo robes; squalid Mexicans, armed with bows and arrows; Indians sedately drunk; long-haired Canadians and trappers, and American backwoodsmen in brown homespun; the well-beloved pistol and bowie-knife displayed openly at their sides. In the middle of the room a tall, lank man, with a dingy broadcloth coat, was haranguing the company in the style of the stump orator. With one hand he sawed the air, and with the other clutched firmly a brown jug of whiskey, which he applied every moment to his lips, forgetting that he had drained the contents long ago. Richard formally introduced me to this personage; who was no less a man than Colonel R(ussell), once the leader of the party. Instantly the Colonel seizing me, in the absence of buttons, by the leather fringes of my frock, began to define his position. His men, he said, had mutinied and deposed him; but still he exercised over them the influence of a superior mind; in all but the name he was yet their chief. As the Colonel spoke, I looked around on the wild assemblage, and could not help thinking that he was but ill qualified to conduct such men across the deserts to California. Conspicuous among the rest stood three tall young men, grandsons of Daniel Boone. They had clearly inherited the adventurous character of that prince of pioneers; but I saw no signs of that quiet tranquil spirit that so remarkably distinguished him.[10]

Some time after leaving the train Bryant saw a letter sent with a Mr. Bonney, by Hastings, stating that he had just surveyed a new

---

[10.] Francis Parkman, Jr., *Prairie and Rocky Mountain Life; or, the California and Oregon Trail*, Third Edition (New York: George P. Putnam, 1853), 156–57. This took place, not at Fort Laramie proper, but at a smaller private trading post eight miles east, called by various names.

route which shortened the distance to California by two or three hundred miles and was much superior in every way to the Fort Hall Road. The letter also spoke of opposition which might be encountered from the Mexican authorities and suggested that the emigrants cross the mountains in a large body.

The last newspapers Bryant had seen at Independence carried stories of General Zachary Taylor's operations against the Mexicans in the south, and the emigrants were naturally anxious about the reception they might receive upon their arrival. Hastings' letter, therefore, was timely and the advice seemed good. Circumstances were favoring his plan, conceived years before, and he hoped that the good will of the emigrants now enroute would soon assure him the presidency of California. His book had evidently accomplished the desired results and there were hundreds of wagons on the trail rolling toward the Pacific.

On July 17, Bryant's party camped with Hastings and Hudspeth near Black's Fork, where Hastings was awaiting the wagon trains. Bryant, however, was unfavorably impressed with their description of the new route and wrote letters to his friends in the rear warning them not to attempt the new Hastings Cutoff.

Joseph R. Walker, who had crossed the desert by that route with Frémont the year previous, passed Bryant near Hastings' camp driving a large drove of California mules which he hoped to sell in St. Louis. He strongly advised against the new route.[11] But after considering the matter for a day or two, while recruiting his mounts, Bryant decided to make the attempt in spite of his belief that it was unsafe for wagons and oxen, and engaged Hudspeth to guide him part of the way.

Led by Hudspeth,[12] Bryant and eight companions pushed forward, and after many difficulties in getting down Weber Canyon[13]

[11.] Bryant also passed Taplin, Reddick and two other returning members of Frémont's party, who were coming east by the Fort Hall Road, probably considering it much safer than the Salt Desert route which they had traveled westward the year previous.

[12.] Accompanied by Ferguson, Kirkwood and Minter, three young men belonging to the Young and Harlan party.

[13.] Instead of following his own trail over the mountains and down through Emigration Canyon, Hudspeth guided Bryant directly to Salt Lake Valley through Weber Canyon, a nearer but much more difficult route, and a route of which he knew absolutely nothing.

and into Salt Lake Valley, eventually reached Frémont's old camp of the previous year, on what is now called City Creek, where Salt Lake City stands. Crossing the valley and the Jordan River (then called the Utah Outlet), they followed the shore of the lake as Frémont had done, and on August 1 crossed Skull Valley and camped at the foot of the trail which Frémont had taken over Cedar Mountain, on the eastern edge of the Salt Desert.

Here, at the foot of the ridge, they found damp sand in the bottom of the gully, and scooped out a hole. Enough water seeped into this hole to supply their immediate wants, but it was very brackish, and there was not enough for the mules. Their precautions for crossing the seventy-five miles of salt desert which lay before them were very simple. A small powder keg holding three or four pints, the only vessel in the whole party which would hold water, was filled with coffee made from the brackish water of the spring. This was the emergency supply for nine men.

Being now ready for the attempt they arose very early the next morning and climbed the ridge. Arriving at the summit, Hudspeth pointed out the way they were to take, and after advising them to "ride like hell," returned to Skull Valley to explore a route farther south. From here on the party was without a guide, and the valley was so full of smoke from fires in the mountains that they could not see Pilot Peak on the opposite side.

Bryant states that so far as he knew, this route had only been taken twice previously, referring to Frémont and Hastings. He had not heard of Jedediah Smith's crossing, and he did not remember the Bartleson party until after crossing the Salt Desert.[14] After parting with Hudspeth, Bryant's party descended the ridge and struck a little north of west across the Salt Desert, finding traces of Frémont's trail here and there.

Edwin Bryant was a keen observer and an entertaining writer, and his description of the Salt Desert is the best to be found anywhere. He says:

> ...we had a view of the vast desert-plain before us, which, as far as the eye could penetrate, was of a snowy whiteness, and resembled a scene of wintry frosts and icy desolation. Not a shrub or object of any kind rose above the

---

[14.] Smith crossed farther to the south; Bartleson circled the northern end, then turned south to Pilot Peak.

surface for the eye to rest upon....It was a scene which excited mingled emotions of admiration and apprehension.

...a narrow valley or depression in the surface of the plain, about five miles in width,[15] displayed so perfectly the wavy and frothy appearance of highly agitated water, that Colonel Russell and myself...both simultaneously exclaimed—"We must have taken a wrong course, and struck another arm of the Great Salt Lake."...but soon, upon a more calm and scrutinizing inspection, we discovered that what represented so perfectly the rushing waters was moveless, and made no sound! The illusion soon became manifest to all of us, and a hearty laugh at those who were first to be deceived.

...we now entered upon the hard smooth plain we had just been surveying with so much doubt and interest....Beyond this we crossed what appeared to have been the beds of several small lakes, the waters of which have evaporated, thickly incrusted with salt, and separated from each other by small mound-shaped elevations of a white, sandy, or ashy earth, so imponderous that it has been driven by the action of the winds into these heaps, which are constantly changing their positions and their shapes. Our mules waded through these ashy undulations, sometimes sinking to their knees...creating a dust that rose above and hung over us like a dense fog....

The mirage...here displayed its wonderful illusions, in a perfection and with a magnificence surpassing any presentation of the kind I had previously seen. Lakes, dotted with islands and bordered by groves of gently waving timber, whose tranquil and limpid waves reflected their sloping banks and the shady islets in their bosoms, lay spread out before us, inviting us, by their illusory temptations, to stray from our path and enjoy their cooling shades and refreshing waters. These fading away as we advanced, beautiful villas, adorned with edifices...and surrounded by gardens, shaded walks, parks, and stately

---

[15.] Just west of Grayback Mountain, a low volcanic ridge; this plain is now covered with a growth of stunted greasewood.

avenues, would succeed them....These melting from our view as those before, in another place a vast city, with countless columned edifices of marble whiteness, and studded with domes, spires, and turreted towers, would rise upon the horizon of the plain, astonishing us with its stupendous grandeur and sublime magnificence. But it is vain to attempt a description of these singular and extraordinary phenomena. Neither prose nor poetry, nor the pencil of the artist, can adequately portray their beauties. The whole distant view around at this point, seemed like the creations of a sublime and gorgeous dream, or the effect of enchantment.

About eleven o'clock we struck a vast white plain, uniformly level, and utterly destitute of vegetation or any sign that shrub or plant had ever existed above its snow-like surface. Pausing a few moments to rest our mules, and moisten our mouths and throats from the scant supply of beverage in our powder-keg, we entered upon this appalling field of sullen and hoary desolation. It was a scene so entirely new to us, so frightfully forbidding and unearthly in its aspects, that all of us, I believe, though impressed with its sublimity, felt a slight shudder of apprehension. Our mules seemed to sympathize with us in the pervading sentiment, and moved forward with reluctance, several of them stubbornly setting their faces for a countermarch.

For fifteen miles the surface of this plain is so compact, that the feet of our animals...left but little if any impression for the guidance of future travelers....A cloud rose from the south soon afterwards, accompanied by distant peals of thunder, and a furious wind, rushing across the plain and filling the whole atmosphere with fine particles of salt, and drifting it in heaps like newly fallen snow. Our eyes became nearly blinded and our throats choked with the saline matter, and the very air we breathed tasted of salt.

During the subsidence of this tempest, there appeared upon the plain one of the most extraordinary phenomena, I dare to assert, ever witnessed....I had dismounted from my mule...and was walking several rods in front of the party....Diagonally in front, to the right, there appeared the figures of a number of men and horses....Some of these figures were mounted and others...appeared to be marching on foot. Their faces...were turned towards us, and at first they appeared as if they were rushing down upon us. Their apparent distance...was from three to five miles. But their size was not correspondent, for they seemed nearly as large as our own bodies, and consequently were of gigantic stature. At first view I supposed them to be a small party of Indians....I called to some of our party...to hasten forward, as there were men in front, coming towards us. Very soon the fifteen or twenty figures were multiplied into three or four hundred, and appeared to be marching forward with the greatest action and speed. I then conjectured that they might be Capt. Fremont and his party...returning to the United States....I spoke to Brown, who was nearest me, and asked him if he noticed the figures of men and horses in front? He answered me that he did, and that he had observed the same appearances several times previously, but that they had disappeared....It was then, for the first time, so perfect was the deception, that I conjectured the probable fact that these figures were the reflection of our own images by the atmosphere, filled as it was with fine particles of crystallized matter....but this phantom population, springing out of the ground as it were, and arraying itself before us as we traversed this dreary and heaven-condemned waste, although we were entirely convinced of the cause of the apparition, excited those superstitious emotions so natural to all mankind.[16]

About five o'clock Bryant dropped behind the balance of the party, looking for water along the foot of what is now called Silver Island, a rocky ridge projecting into the salt plain. Returning about dark after an unfruitful excursion, he came upon the pack mule which carried all their provisions, with her pack hanging under her belly. Rearranging the load he proceeded as fast as the mules would farther, and after dark, came upon Buchanan, whose mule had refused to go on. In company with the other two, however,

---

[16.] Edwin Bryant, *What I Saw in California*, 173–78.

the exhausted animal was persuaded to move slowly forward until ten o'clock, when they reached Pilot Peak and found the rest of the party encamped on a small stream flowing from a spring.

It would seem that one's first impulse upon finding fresh water after such a journey, would be to drink immediately and to excess. Bryant says that some hours previously he had suffered the extreme agonies of thirst, but that the craving for water had by this time become dulled so that he first unsaddled his mule and led it to water and grass before he thought of drinking himself. Worn down by the hard day's travel, there was no thought of cooking or eating, and they all threw themselves on the ground and immediately slept the sleep of the exhausted.

After resting one day at the spring, the party resumed their journey. Bryant says:

> We took a southwest course along the slope of the range of mountains under which we had encamped [Pilot Peak].

> After traveling about ten miles we struck a wagon-trail, which evidently had been made several years. From the indentations of the wheels, where the earth was soft, five or six wagons had passed here. The appearance of this trail in this desolate region was at first inexplicable; but I soon recollected that some five or six years ago an emigrating expedition to California was fitted out by Colonel Bartleson, Mr. J. Chiles, and others, of Missouri, who, under the guidance of Captain Walker, attempted to enter California by passing round the southern terminus of the Sierra Nevada; and that they were finally compelled to abandon their wagons and everything they had, and did not reach their destination until they had suffered incredible hardships and privations. This, it appeared to me, was evidently their trail; and old as it was, and scarcely perceivable, it was nevertheless some gratification to us that civilized human beings had passed here before, and left their mark upon the barren earth behind them. My conjectures, above stated, have been subsequently confirmed by a conversation with Mr. Chiles.

Following this old trail some two or three miles, we left it on the right....[17]

Bryant's account confirms the record contained in John Bidwell's diary, under date of September 13, 1841, where he speaks of traveling between "Salt plains on the E. and high mts. on the W." But Bryant has confused Chiles' first and second expedition. With Bartleson and Bidwell, J. B. Chiles passed Pilot Peak in 1841, making the trail which Bryant found there. Joseph Walker, however, was not a member of that expedition. Walker was hired by Chiles in 1843 to guide his wagons by the Raft River route to California through Walker Pass in the Sierra, and by taking that route did not come within sight of Pilot Peak.

Bryant and his party were without a guide, and it seems strange he did not follow the Bartleson wagon trail. Instead, he went farther south, paralleled the wagon trail across the next wide valley, and apparently never saw it again, although he certainly must have crossed it once more. If he had followed it for a day's travel, he would have found the abandoned wagons of the Bartleson party at the foot of Spruce Mountain on the western side of Steptoe Valley.

Crossing the Toano Range through Silver Zone Pass, Bryant and his friends reached the Humboldt River over the same route Lt. Talbot of Frémont's party had taken, which was also Hastings' eastbound route. Following the river they eventually reached the Sierra, which they crossed to Sutter's Fort, arriving there on September 1, 1846—the first to reach California that year.[18]

*

To Bryant's excellent description of the desert it might be well to add some further facts, so the reader will have a better idea of what the emigrants had to contend with. Aside from the great beds of solid salt, four feet thick, which were not discovered by these early emigrants, the desert consists chiefly of gray mud to an unknown depth, highly impregnated with salt. The moisture which

---

[17.] Bryant, *What I Saw in California*, 185–86.

[18.] Other members of the Bryant party were: John C. Buchanan, Bryant's secretary while alcalde of San Francisco; Richard T. Jacob, Captain of Company H, California Volunteers, 1847; William H. Russell; Hiram O. Miller, member of the second Donner relief party; James McClary; William H. Nuttall; A. V. Brookie; and W. B. Brown.

falls here during winter and early spring is absorbed by this mud. When the hot winds of summer blow across these salt flats, evaporation sets in, but each particle of evaporated water leaves its particle of salt on the surface. Soon a crust is formed which retards further evaporation, and the balance of the moisture is "sealed" in the mud below. Even in the very driest seasons the greater part of this desert is still soft beneath the crust. The heavy narrow-tired wagons of the emigrants cut deeply into this mud, but since the surface is absolutely level, there was no erosion, and the ruts were gradually filled with the finer sediments deposited by occasional storms, leaving the surface perfectly smooth. The old wagon tracks are still plainly visible after more than eighty years, as parallel lines of lighter colored sediment.

Nearly every year Salt Lake City experiences a "salt storm," which leaves every window and every automobile covered with a thin coating of salt. This is said to be caused by a high wind passing over the lake, which picks up salt water and drops it again on the city. The real cause, however, is more simple. When evaporation sets in on the Salt Desert in summer, the wind heaps up some of the fine particles of salt brought to the surface. When high winds preceding a storm strike this loose salt, it is carried up into the atmosphere in an immense white cloud. Rain, falling through this cloud of fine salt, brings it down again, often many miles away. Bryant's description makes this easy to understand.

8. THE YOUNG AND HARLAN PARTY

Having seen Bryant and his friends safely across the desert, we will now return to Hastings' camp on Black's Fork and follow the adventures of the emigrants he intends to guide in person across his newly discovered cutoff. Most of those who arrived at his camp preferred the comparative safety of a well-known road, heeding the advice of Clyman and Walker. Several parties, however, were persuaded to attempt the shorter route across the Salt Desert, on Hastings' assurance that it was safe and that they would save two or three hundred miles thereby.

In his book published the year previously, Hastings had said:

Those who go to California, travel from Fort Hall, west southwest about fifteen days, to the northern pass, in the California mountains; thence, three days, to the Sacramento; and thence, seven days, to the Bay of St. Francisco...The California route, from Fort Hall to the Sacramento river, lies through alternate plains, prairies and valleys, and over hills, amid lofty mountains....The Indians are....entirely inoffensive. Wagons can be as readily taken from Fort Hall to the Bay of St. Francisco, as they can, from the States to Fort Hall; and, in fact, the latter part of the route, is found much more eligible for a wagon way, than the former. The most direct route, for the California emigrants, would be to leave the Oregon route, about two hundred miles east from Fort Hall; thence bearing west southwest, to the Salt lake; and thence continuing down to the bay of St. Francisco, by the route just described.[1]

It was the route described in the last sentence which Hastings was now about to take; but a few facts should be noted in connection with this description. Hastings had taken Dr. White's company to Oregon in 1842; he had made a hurried trip with ten men on horses in 1845 over the Fort Hall Road, but had never been over the latter route with wagons. He had just come east from Califor-

---

[1.] Hastings, *The Emigrants' Guide, to Oregon and California*, 135, 137–38.

nia, but had taken the cutoff across the desert, on horses, and had therefore no experience with wagons over either of the routes when the book was written. Many of the emigrants now coming up to Hastings' camp carried copies of his book, and a copy carried by the Donner party is now in the Bancroft Library, Berkeley, California. As far as Fort Bridger, information in *The Emigrants' Guide* had been more or less reliable, since he had actually been over that part of the road with wagons; it was probably for this reason that so many now took his advice about the cutoff, particularly as he offered to guide them in person.

The usual fee charged by mountain men engaged in guiding emigrant trains was ten dollars for each wagon. There is no record whatever that Hastings charged any fee for his services from this point to Sutter's Fort. The emigrants were not aware of his personal ambitions, presuming that he in some way benefited from the sale of supplies at Fort Bridger. Such, however, was not the case, since Bridger had no idea that Hastings was coming east across the desert, and the fort was deserted when Clyman and Hastings arrived there.

When Hastings finally left Black's Fork, a week before the arrival of the Donner party, he was at the head of four companies of about ten families each, eighty wagons in all. Among these were the parties of Samuel C. Young and George Harlan.

Since this emigrant train was the first to enter Salt Lake Valley by any route, and since so little has been published in regard to these people, it might be well to set down here all the available information.

Samuel C. Young was a native of eastern Tennessee, and was the father of three sons, who accompanied him across the plains. Outside of this we know little about him.

Of George Harlan, however, we know considerably more. His paternal ancestor had come to America with William Penn. Somewhat contrary to the principles of Penn, Harlan had spent his life up to 1812 in fighting the Indians who were finally conquered by General Harrison. After peace had been declared he soon became lonesome for the war-whoop, no longer heard in Indiana, and moved to Missouri, near what is now Lexington. Here he was called upon to deal with the red men again, but his experience and good judgment saved much bloodshed. He was accompanied across the plains by his wife, Elizabeth Duncan Harlan, and two sons, Joel and Elisha, the latter of whom then eight years old, had been thrown from a wagon and run over, receiving an injury from which he suffered for many years. There was also Miss Minerva Fowler, who afterwards married Joel Harlan, and an Eliza Fowler, who later married Jacob W. Harlan, nephew of George.

Polly Harlan, a daughter, had married Peter Wimmer when the latter was a neighbor of the Harlan family in Indiana. The young couple had been bitten by the pioneer bug, like most early settlers, and had moved from place to place, eventually landing in Missouri where the elder Harlan had lately settled. Here Polly Garlan Wimmer died with the ague and Peter Wimmer later married Elizabeth Cloud Bays, a young widow, who as a girl had dug placer gold with her father and former husband in Georgia. When George Harlan decided to emigrate to California, Peter and his new wife joined the Harlan wagon train.

Some others associates with Harlan's party of whom we have no record other than the names were: John Hargrave, John Spence, Arthur Caldwell, John McCutcheon, Mr. Buchalass, John and Ira Van Gordan, Duncan Dickerson, Mr. Hooper, Jacob Russ, Simpson, McMonagill, and George McKinstry, nearly all with families. "Mr. Buchalass" may have been Benjamin R. Buckelew, who later became editor of the *Californian*.

Leaving the encampment on Black's Fork the combined company now under Hastings followed the trail to Fort Bridger, where they stopped a few days as one of their number, John Hargrave, was very sick and was not expected to live.

Leaving Fort Bridger Hastings led his company westward toward Great Salt Lake, passing Bridger's Butte, crossing the Little Muddy and Bear rivers and the divide into Echo Canyon, where no wagon had ever gone before.

Emerging from Echo Canyon they struck the Weber River, which here flows through a wide valley with high mountains on either side. When the advance parties reached the Weber, Hastings was with the lagging wagons. Instead of following the route they had taken in coming to Fort Bridger, Hudspeth now decided, for reasons unknown, to take the wagons down Weber Canyon, knowing that the river emptied into the lake, but having no knowledge whatever of the possibility of getting wagons through. The river bottom here was wide and level, although filled with dense brush and in places made marshy by old beaver dams. In a few miles, however, the walls of the canyon closed in, rising sheer from the bed of the stream, and the only way to get the wagons through these places was either to build a roadbed along the edge of the stream, or go over the mountains. Both of these methods seem to have been used at different points. But read their own story as compiled by Allen and Avery in the *California Gold Book*:

[At Hastings' camp]...information was received which determined some of the band to attempt a new route.... Captain Harlan had been assured that a long distance could be saved by...crossing the divide into Echo canyon. His information gave no hint of unusual difficulties in the way, and certainly none which could not be surmounted in a small part of the time which would be saved by taking the new route....Few difficulties, greater than those heretofore experienced, were met with until the divide had been practically crossed and the pioneers entered Echo [Weber] canyon, Here trouble began. The canyon is scarcely wide enough to accommodate the narrow river which traverses it, and there was no room for roads between its waters and the abrupt banks. In many places great boulders had been rolled by the mountain torrents and lodged together, forming an impassable way....Three such obstacles were encountered, and only about a mile a day was averaged for more than a week. The sides of the mountain were covered by a dense growth of willows, never penetrated by white man. Three times spurs of the mountains had to be crossed by rigging the windlass on top, and lifting the wagons almost bodily. The banks were very steep, and covered by loose stones, so that a mountain sheep would have been troubled to keep its feet, much more an ox-team drawing a heavily loaded wagon. On the 11th of August, while hoisting a yoke of oxen and a wagon up Webber mountain, the rope broke near the windlass. As many men as could surround the wagon were helping all they could by lifting at the wheels and sides. The footing was untenable, and before the rope could be tied to anything, the men found they must abandon the wagon and oxen to destruction, or be dragged to death themselves. The faithful beasts seemed to comprehend the danger, and held their ground for a few seconds, and were then hurled over a precipice at least 75 feet high, and crushed in a tangled mass with the wagon on the rocks at the bottom of the canyon.[2]

Emerging at last into Salt Lake Valley, the emigrants believed their troubles were over. A celebration was held at which Minerva and Ann Eliza Fowler, who were good violinists, did their bit to revive the spirits of the company. Wagons were repaired and their disordered contents carefully repacked. Following the foot of the Wasatch mountains, the train moved south, skirting the lake, until opposite the hot springs once known as the Municipal Baths, crossed the Jordan River, and proceeded directly toward the point of the Oquirrh mountains at the site of Garfield, near Magna, Utah.[3]

Now came the saddest incident of the trip. John Hargrave had taken cold after a day of extra trying labor in the mountains, and it had fastened upon his system and developed into typhoid pneumonia. His sickness affected every member of the band....He was too sick to travel, and no one thought of moving a rod until he was well again. The delay troubled them not a bit, but sorrow at the serious illness of Hargrave grieved every one of his comrades. From day to day he became worse, until at last he died, and a fearful gloom settled upon the camp. His grave was made on a knoll near the river Jordan, and no one ever had a more sincere hand of mourners to lay him away. His last resting place was a bower of flowers placed by loving hands....

The route of the band was on the south side of Salt Lake, and skirting the mountain so as to be sure of water. When the edge of the real desert was reached, which was readily recognized,...preparations were made for crossing the desolate wastes. Provided with an ample supply of water, and thoroughly rested, the train started across, and was two days and nights almost uninterruptedly moving on

---

[2] W. W. Allen and R. B. Avery, *California Gold Book* (San Francisco and Chicago: Donahue & Henneberry, 1893), 62–63.

[3] These were the first wagons to reach the site of Salt Lake City. William Clayton, Mormon pioneer, found their trail west of the hot springs in 1847.

before safety for the stock from thirst and starvation was reached. Then there was another rest. Soon after starting a mountain was reached, which the members of the band called Backbone mountain, and skirting which brought them to the Thousand Springs valley, and from thence across to the little Humboldt, and down this to Mary's river, now the Humboldt. They passed down that to the Basin and Sinks, and across the desert to the Truckee river, which takes its rise in the Sierra Nevada mountains. Reaching the head waters of the Truckee, the windlass and ropes were again necessary to lift the wagons and oxen over the rocks. Here the party were treated to a general snow-storm, which gave them the impression that there was a mistake somewhere in styling this the land of perpetual summer.[4]

This account gives a very good description of Weber Canyon and the difficulties encountered there, but passes over the more dangerous crossing of the desert. We are fortunate, however, in having another account in the obituary of Samuel C. Young, which gives a very vivid description of that part of the journey. Writing of the emigrants who had traveled together from Missouri:

When they arrived at Fort Bridger they divided up again, some going to Oregon others to California, by the Fort Hall route, while still another party took the unfortunate route called the Hastings' Cut-Off. Hastings had made them believe that his route was three hundred miles nearer to the head of the St. Mary's River than any other route, and that they would get there three weeks ahead of the Fort Hall emigrants.

There were four companies formed at this place, of about ten families to a company, to travel the Hastings Cut-Off. They travelled along together until they arrived at Weber Canyon; here the male portion of these four companies spent four days clearing the boulders out of the way, and then they could make but one and a half miles per day. To give an idea how bad this canyon was to take wagons through, when the Donner Party came on afterwards and examined it, they would not attempt to go through.

---

4. Allen and Avery, *California Gold Book*, 64–66.

Hastings had made them believe that the desert was but forty miles across. When they arrived there[5] they made every preparation that the country and their circumstances would allow; they filled all their vessels full of water, procured all the grass they could take with them, to feed and sustain their stock; and when they had finished their preparations, they began their perilous journey in the evening and travelled all night, stopping now and then to rest and give the stock a little hay. Morning came at last; and such a sight! The sun rose in full splendor, reflecting his rays on this vast salt plain, as white as snow and as far as the eye could reach not a thing to be seen, not a spear of grass or a drop of water, and the end could not be detected by the eye. The stock was showing great signs of fatigue; a little hay and some water revived them, and a cup of coffee and a cold snack had as good effect on the emigrants. It was a blessing that they were ignorant of what was in store for them. They were led to believe that they would reach water and grass by noon; full of hope they again started their jaded and trusty teams. They travelled until noon; the stock showing great distress, they stopped to feed them some grass and give them a little water, which comprised nearly all they laid in. The emigrants by this time had become very much discouraged. The eye could not detect the end of the plain. But no time was to be lost, so they started again, in the midst of the glare of the sun at noon-day, upon this still vast, white salt plain. Every mile travelled that evening produced its effect; oxen gave out and lay down, some to rise no more; others from extreme thirst, became crazy and nothing could be done with them and finally they would become exhausted and drop down dead. From the middle of the evening, one disaster after another happened nearly every step of the way. Wagons were abandoned; such of the oxen as could travel were taken out and driven along, others would give up and lie down, even after the yoke was taken off, and neither persuasion nor the whip could make them budge. These misfortunes continued and in-

---

5. Skull Valley.

creased during that evening, until it seemed as if all were lost. But night came at last; that at least shut off the reflection of the sun. In the midst of all but despair they stopped to give the last pound of grass to the surviving stock, and a few favorites got a little water, and such as had wagons left went to them and got out and ate and divided with others their frugal meal. At last they started on their long night-tramp, hoping to get to water and grass before morning. On they travelled, every mile so full of disaster that the recital would fill pages; but they struggled on through that long, dark and lonely night, still praying for water and grass, but morning was again ushered in with the sun's reflection upon the white, salt plains, with no signs of the end. The loss of stock through the night could now be realized. A halt was ordered, a little rest was taken, with a morsel to break the fast, and the order was given to make the last effort to get through. From this until noon more stock was lost than during the last twenty-four hours. At noon they reached water and grass in a most worn-out and despondent condition. Some of the teams were left; some as far back as thirty miles. Water and grass were hauled back and some of the stock saved and some of the wagons were brought in; others were abandoned and it took many days to collect everything together and get ready to start again. Here was eighty-two miles of desert these emigrants had passed over, instead of forty. Volumes could be written, on the sufferings of man and beast that occurred during this eighty-two-mile march across the desolate wastes. At last they reached St. Mary's River with the loss of most of their stock, worn out and greatly discouraged—to find the Fort Hall emigrants had passed on three weeks ahead of them, posting notices of that fact.[6]

Considering the amount of work which they must have done on this trail, it would seem that much of it would still be visible. But extensive railroad construction and the building of both the old and new motor highways have apparently obliterated all traces

---

6. "Biographical Obituary. Samuel C. Young—A Pioneer of 1846," *San Jose Pioneer*, November 9, 1878. Courtesy Bancroft Library.

of it except at one point, called Devil's Gate. Here the old Hastings trail is still visible [in 1969] where it crosses over a point of the mountain which nearly chokes up the canyon. Certainly at this point it must have been necessary to use the windlass both in raising and lowering the wagons. Below this place a roadway was built at the foot of the rocky bluff in the edge of the river. Above Devil's Gate an ancient trail has been cut in the side of the mountain high above the stream, some parts of which are still wide enough for wagons; but it is impossible to conceive of wagons having passed some of the rocky points on this dizzy trail, and if this is actually the old Hastings road those first pioneers must be given credit for more sheer labor and perseverance than most historians are willing to admit.[7]

Neither Samuel C. Young nor Harlan seemed to be particularly bitter toward Lansford W. Hastings, the man who was responsible for their close squeak with disaster and death.

[7.] Thomas W Abbott, late resident of Farmington, came to Utah in 1848, at the age of 15 years. Some cows had been left near Fort Bridger by the Mormons that year, and Abbott and some other young men were sent back to herd these cows through the winter and to make butter for passing emigrants the next spring. He left Ogden and passed up Weber Canyon; had great difficulty in getting through on horseback, but remembered seeing several places where the Hastings party had cut down the banks of the river in order to cross their wagons. In some places they had been compelled to travel down the stream bed.—A. O. Kennedy, Ogden.

9. THE LIENHARD JOURNAL

Since this book was first published two new sources of information have been discovered. The first is by Heinrich Lienhard who was traveling with a German friend and joined the Harlan-Young party, probably at Fort Bridger. Lienhard kept a daily journal, written at the time and on the spot, which furnishes in detail the daily happenings on the desert, and is the only known daily journal. This was translated from the German by Dale L. Morgan and published by the Utah State Historical Society in *West from Fort Bridger*.[1]

The other source is a map of the emigrant route across the plains drawn by T. H. Jefferson and published by the California Historical Society.[2] Jefferson did not keep a journal so far as known, but did make some notes on the section of map dealing with the Great Salt Desert. He invented his own names for landmarks along the trail, not knowing that most of them had already been named, but they are easily identified.

*

Beyond Fort Britcher [Bridger] there are two roads, the old one past the so-called Soda Springs and Fort Hall, and a new one called Captain Hastings' Cutoff which is said to be much shorter and passes by the Great Salt Lake. Many companies ahead of us already had chosen Hastings' Cutoff as their route, and we, too, thought it preferable.

On July 26 we finally broke camp again and entered upon the new road past the Fort, leaving the Fort Hall road to our right. After following the road through a rapid ascent we came to a dry valley, and having passed the rising ground found it again to descend

---

1. J. Roderic Korns and Dale L. Morgan, eds., "West from Fort Bridger: The Pioneering of the Immigrant Trails Across Utah, 1846-1850; Original Diaries and Journals Edited and with Introductions," *Utah Historical Quarterly*, Volume 19 (1951). Revised and Updated by Will Bagley and Harold Schindler(Logan: Utah State University Press, 1994).

2. T. H. Jefferson, *Map of the Emigrant Road From Independence, Mo., to San Francisco, California.* New York: Berford & Co., 1849. Published with Author's Accompaniment and an Introduction by George R. Stewart (San Francisco: California Historical Society, 1945).

a little. On the right, by the side of the road, scarcely 6 miles from the Fort, we came upon an ice-cold spring flowing out of the ground near a thicket. We passed yet another spring into the right near the road, but camped by a brook, approximately 6 miles from the first spring and about 12 miles from the Fort. The stream [the Big Muddy] contained only a little water, but on the other hand we found enough grass for the draft animals here.

On the 27th, our road led through many hollows between rocky hills, whereby we passed several springs of water, of which a few had an unpleasant taste of mineral salts. Around one of these springs the surface of the ground had taken on a rust color, from which it would appear that the water contained iron. In these narrow, deep little valleys through which the road wound, grass springs up everywhere that water exists, but the grass was coarse in spots, like rushes. In the evening, near sunset, after having traveled about 18 miles, we reached the Bear River, where we camped. In the afternoon Captain Hastings met us; he turned back again with us and remained overnight in our camp. The weather continued as it had for several days, quite even. The morning was cool; during the day it was sunny but rather windy.

On the 28th when I went out in the morning to drive our cattle to the wagons, I scared up in the thicket along the river bank a short-legged animal which at first I took to be a young gray bear. I had with me no other weapon than my usual walking-stick, but even so I would not suffer the animal to escape. I immediately engaged it and administered to it as it ran a few vigorous blows with the stick, whereupon it suddenly wheeled about to offer resistance, and showed me at close range a mouth full of splendid, sharp teeth, with which it did its best to seize me by the legs. So furious became the onslaught that for a short time I thought it would succeed in seizing me. I struck as rapidly as possible at the head of the animal, which must have observed a small hole in the ground; it sought to back into this and in fact succeeded in doing so, but the hole was so shallow that the head remained outside. This gave me a better opportunity; after two or three heavy blows over the eye. all at once it lay dead and I had knocked out an eye. The animal proved to be a fine fat badger rather than a young bear; it had flesh much resembling that of a bear, which by all was heartily relished.

We now had always on our left the Uinta Mountains; in that direction conifer forests appeared to exist. In the valley of this river, the water of which was clear and good, there were a few trees resembling red fir, but cottonwood trees and willow thickets were the most characteristic feature of the Bear River Valley here where we crossed it. The Bear River is not entirely insignificant; it must deliver the greatest amount of water to the Great Salt Lake; however, in flowing to the lake it makes a great bend and during its course several considerable affluents empty into it. To the right and in front of us there was no real mountain but only rocky hills, which here and there were sparsely overgrown with miserable cedars. Yesterday we went through a growth of giant sagebrush which often reached a height of more than 4 feet and grew so close together that one could scarcely go between them.

Today the sagebrush fields made room over the hills for a scanty growth of some kind of grass. After we had gone about 7 miles, we camped near the channel of a nearly dry brook, where however we found a spring of excellent water, together with sufficient grass for our cattle. The 52 wagons traveling ahead of us here had taken two different routes, and Hastings had shown us still another which he considered the better way, and which we thought to put to the test. Hastings left us in the evening to overtake a company in advance of us.

On the 29th we remained at the same camping place while some gave needed repairs to their wagons, others mended their footgear or clothing, and yet others washed. The last two nights the still water was covered with a thin crust of ice; the days however were bright and warm. Yesterday morning we had intended to proceed on our journey, and taking his rifle and hunting knife Ripstein set off to look out the way—or rather, went ahead in the direction our road would lead us in the hope of shooting an antelope. It was only after he had gone that we found that repairs to our wagon were absolutely necessary before we could pursue our onward journey. We feared that this had occasioned Ripstein some inconvenience, for of course he supposed that he would meet us on the way, not that we would remain at yesterday's camp. Evening came, but Ripstein had not returned; where he could be, nobody knew.

After breaking camp on the 30th, our way led up a long, moderately steep slope, thence rapidly down through a hollow between the hills, passing a spring about 3 miles from the last campsite, and soon afterwards reaching the dry channel of a brook, which we followed until we had gone about 14 miles from our previous camp, where again we found water and grass, our two prime necessities. Ripstein still had not returned and we were seriously concerned about him.

Most of the day, July 31, we followed this watercourse and its windings. To our right rose spike-rocks (conglomerate) of a reddish color, several of them from 3 to 4 hundred feet high; to our left were various knolls and hills, at times quite rocky, then again overgrown with scanty grass and small underbrush. The narrow gorge led us entirely to the south [southwest] and became ever more constricted, so that we were very often compelled to cross the bed of the stream, and finally had to cut the road through a dense willow thicket. Here we found an abundance of red, black, and yellow currants, which to us was an agreeable state of affairs, for it was not every day that we came upon enjoyable fruit. In this little valley we came upon oaks again, which though small were the first we had seen. This evening, as we were making our camp, crowded close to the bed of the brook in a place where we found grass and water, Ripstein came back to us, and just when we had given him up as wholly lost, for he had been missing three days and two nights. He was at first quite incensed with us, in view of the arrangements we had made for him to keep in mind when he should turn toward camp. He had shot an antelope and subsequently had carried it a considerable distance to where he hoped to meet us; when however he did not find us, in the belief we must already have gone far ahead, he proceeded rapidly on, leaving the antelope behind and hastening forward until he came up with a company far in advance of us, only to learn that we were still behind. He then turned back again several miles along the road. The first night he attempted to spend under a rocky ledge, but the prairie wolves [coyotes] would not let him sleep; a small pack of these animals watched him incessantly, and when he rebelled and set off from the spot, they escorted him like a pack of dogs, only a few paces behind. He had shot a badger, but he had lost his knife while occupied with the antelope; accordingly it was not possible with anything he had at hand to cut off a piece to roast. He had therefore been obliged to fast until he fell in with the other company, when he was enabled to appease his hunger.

On the 1st of August we took up our journey again, still through this narrow valley, which some had given the name Willow

Canyon. All along the brook we found many springs of water, so that the stream channel no longer remained dry as it had been farther back. The road was, however, if possible even worse than on the previous day; it had the same serpentine sinuosity, and often we were obliged to enter into alliance with the ax itself to carry the road through the densely grown wood.

In one place we found in bushes exceeding 8 to 12 feet in height the Juneberry [elderberry] tree (*juni Beeren*), extraordinarily full of the sweet, grape-like clusters of fruit. We halted a short time to gather of them, all helping themselves to hearts' content, for they were fully ripe and tasted amazingly good. We concluded that Master Bear must enjoy himself here also, from the evidence of the many broad tracks in the here damp and somewhat softened ground, and the broken branches left dangling.

After proceeding for perhaps 12 miles through various windings the ravine opened suddenly before us upon a valley with a beautiful little river of clear water flowing through it. This stream was known as the Weber River; it flows through a rather pretty little valley in a northeasterly [northwesterly] direction at the southeasterly foot of the high Wasatch Mountains, which this valley enters from the Salt Lake. We followed down the windings of the little river, past high hill promontories which often looked like castle ruins. Thomen supposed Father Noah must have come this way with his Ark, and abandoned part of the same. Traveling on about 5 miles farther along the banks of the Weber River, we camped on a high embankment near the river. Some among us, desiring to bathe in the clear water, discovered in the shallows an abundance of crayfish. At once we took ourselves, armed with forks, down into the waters and soon had a sufficient number of crayfish to provide us with the greater part of our evening meal.

On the slopes of the Wasatch Mountains rising above us grew some firs, a few groves of cedars, and sundry bushes. In the valley, on the other hand, willows and cottonwood trees were the principal growing things; we also found some maples, oaks, and alders, the last over 20 feet high. In the valley there were a number of narrow places, which often forced us to cross from one side of the river to the other.

On the 2nd day of August, we took up our journey on through the valley, now a little wider without the road being much better than on the previous day, for it proceeded through brush, across the bed of the river, and through a wood for a distance of 5 1/3 miles. Then the valley opened up again. We bore somewhat to the right and the river to our left, where two small brooks flowed into it. We proceeded from this place about 1 1/2 miles farther down the valley and then camped. The mountains on both sides of us had a beautiful appearance. In consequence of the very long-continued dry weather, the thriving grasses in the gravelly soil were nearly all dry. Great smoke clouds were indicative of grass fires which probably originated through the negligence or thoughtlessness of careless travelers.

On the 3rd of August as we were making our way down along the river in a northerly [northwesterly] direction, and after we had traveled about 5 miles, we encountered Captain Hastings, who had returned to meet us. By his advice we halted here. He was of the opinion that we, like all the companies who had gone in advance of us, were taking the wrong road. He had advised the first companies that on arriving at the Weber River they should turn to the left which would bring them by a shorter route to the Salt Lake; this advice they had not followed, but trusting to their luck had taken the road down the river. We thereupon turned our wagons around and went back about 2 miles, where we encamped. This day for a while was overcast, with a little rain, after which we again had warm sunshine.

On the 4th we remained in camp. A few of the company endeavored to seek out a better route but returned to camp without having effected their object.

On August 5 we again set out, not however up the valley but down it, to where the so-called bad places of the Weber River commence. Kyburz, the Barbers, and we stopped and encamped, while the other part of our company made the passage of the dreaded places without any particular difficulty. Instead of flowing to the north [northwest] as hitherto, the Weber River here had taken a westerly course; the worst place, properly speaking, was 5 miles long. The Weber River had broken through the steep, high Wasatch Mountains; it was a deep cleft through which the waters foamed and roared over the rocks.

On August 6 we ventured upon this furious passage, up to this point decidedly the wildest we had encountered, if not the most dangerous. We devoted the entire forenoon and until fully one o'clock in the afternoon to the task of getting our four wagons through. In places we unhitched from the wagon all the oxen except the wheel-yoke, then we tied one drove at both hind wheels, and the rest steadied the wagon; we then slid rapidly down into the foaming water, hitched the loose oxen again to the wagon and took it directly down the foaming riverbed, full of great boulders, on account of which the wagon quickly lurched from one side to the other; now we had to turn the wheels by the spokes, then again hold back with all the strength we had, lest it sweep upon a low lying rock and smash itself to pieces. In going back for each wagon we had to be very careful lest we lose our footing on the slippery rocks under the water and ourselves be swept down the rapid, foaming torrent.

When I began the journey, I had three pairs of boots and one pair of shoes. Today I was given the last service by the one remaining pair of boots, for the heels near the foot had raised up sidewise and upside down. Henceforth I must manage to make my own footgear. When the first company came through, they of course found no road whatever, and it was only by much toil that they were enabled to get through; we had, in comparison, relatively little trouble.

After leaving to our right the Weber River, which empties itself in the Salt Lake not far from this place, we proceeded on south about 3 miles over good wild meadowland, the Wasatch Mountains now on our left, and encamped in a small grassy vale with a sufficiency of good water. The weather was very warm.

On the 7th we reached the flat shore of the magnificent Salt Lake, the waters of which were clear as crystal, but as salty as the strongest salt brine. It is an immense expanse of water and presents to the eye in a northeasterly [northwesterly] direction nothing but sky and water. In it there are a few barren islands which have the appearance of having been wholly burnt over. The land extends from the mountains down to the lake in a splendid inclined plane broken only by the fresh water running down from ever-flowing springs above. The soil is a rich, deep black sand composition [loam] doubtless capable of producing good crops. The clear, sky-blue surface of the lake, the warm sunny air, the nearby high mountains, with the beautiful country at their foot through which we on a fine road were passing, made on my spirits an extraordinarily charming impression. The whole day long I felt like singing and whistling; had there been a single family of white men to be found living here, I believe that I would have remained. Oh, how unfortunate that this beautiful country was uninhabited! I did not then foresee that within perhaps two or three weeks of our passing, this solitude would be filled with hundreds of civilized men intending to remain, and yet it was so, the Mormons followed on our heels in the vain hope that here in this wilderness they would forever be permitted to live as they pleased. Since then hardly 29 years have passed, and the Mormons undoubtedly have understood for a long time that their cherished dream of independence is coming to an end.

Our road had taken us for the most part along the lakeshore through luxuriantly growing bulrushes. After traveling about 20 miles, I should say, we again pitched camp, having reached a small river, the Uta, the water of which was a little warm, but otherwise of good quality. The grass was poor and fuel scarce. The Wasatch Mountains were high. In several of the ravines we could see a few small conifers, but the country as a whole appeared to be scantily wooded.

On August 8 we left the Wasatch Mountains to our left or to our rear and set out in a southwesterly direction toward another reddish-brown mountain [the Oquirrh Mountains], which in the exceedingly bright and clear morning air appeared to be hardly 6 miles away, though before this day was over we could testify that it was fully twice that distance. Ten miles on across a plain brought us to a swampy section, where bulrushes and a little rank marsh grass grew, through which the road yet took us. The water was salty and unpalatable, so that the stock refused it. Two miles farther on, we arrived at the foot of the mountain, where a large, crystalline spring, somewhat warm and a little brackish, welled out of the ground. We halted here a short time, so that our stock might gain a little rest. Where the spring broke out of the ground, it formed a beautiful basin, in which, not even taking off our clothes, several of us bathed. In the vicinity of this spring stood an immense, isolated, rounded rock under which was a cave, and those going into it found a human skeleton. During the forenoon's travel we had again caught up with the advance division of our company, and the reunited train continued their journey together. We passed along the occasionally marshy shore at the south end of the Salt Lake and camped finally at a large spring at the foot of the mountains, the water of which was slightly brackish. An expanse of swampy meadowland here separated us from the lake. We must have made about 6 miles this afternoon.

On August 9 we continued our journey westward, to round the south end of the lake. Ripstein, an American named Bunzel, and I walked some distance ahead of our wagons and came to a place where the road passed close to the lake. The morning was so delightfully warm and the quick clear water, without any animal life, so inviting that we soon resolved to take a salt water bath. The beach glistened with the whitish-gray sand which covered it, and on the shore we could see the still-fresh tracks of a bear, notwithstanding which we soon had undressed and were going down into the salty water. We had, however, to go out not less than a half mile before the water reached our hips. Even here it was still so transparent that we could see the bottom as if there were no water whatever above it, yet so heavy that we could hardly tread upon the bottom with our feet; it was here no trick at all to stand even on tiptoe. I confidently believe that one who understood only a little of swimming could swim the entire length of the 70-mile-long lake without the slightest danger of drowning. I was a poor swimmer, Ripstein none at all, and he could lay himself on his back, so that fully half of his body emerged above the clear salt brine. Had I not known that in ordinary water I sank lightly beneath the surface, I would have supposed that I had become an absolutely first-rate swimmer, for I could assume every conceivable position, without the least danger. I could in a sitting position swim on my side, swim on my back, and I believe one could make a competent somersault without special effort, for by giving only a slight push with the foot against the bottom, one could leap high up. Since my hair was thick, hanging down to my shoulders, when I lay on my back, I had to hold high a great part of my body before my head came under water. For learning to swim, no water in the whole world is so well adapted as the Salt Lake; here, at the mouth of an in-flowing fresh water stream where one could choose gradually lighter water, one could safely learn how to be a perfect swimmer. I swam nearly the whole distance back, yes, one could easily swim in water which was hardly more than 1½ feet deep. Only a single feature had the swimming in this lake that was not conducive to pleasure; this consisted in the fact that when one got a little water in one's eye, it occasioned a severe burning pain; and after we reached the shore and dressed ourselves without first washing in unsalted water, being desirous of hastening on, we soon experienced an almost unbearable smarting or itching over the whole body where the salt water had filled up all the crevices of the skin with an all-enveloping deposit of salt.

Nearly the whole day the road led past the foot of the mountains close to the shore of the lake in a westerly direction; thereby we passed other large springs of water, of which most, however, were salty. At one of these springs, which was a little fresher, and where also we found grass for our cattle, we made our camp; the lake lay back from the road, separated from it by an expanse of marshland.

On the morning of August 10 we found nearly exhausted, in one of the deep holes of spring water, an old ox belonging to Mr. Hapy [Hoppe]; he must have fallen in during the night and was unable to keep himself from being drowned, for he died soon after we helped him out.

We had reached a broad valley or cove, where there were many deep but happily salt-free springs; we found, as well, much good grass, and a grove of trees was not lacking. Three [?] other companies were here in camp beside us, and since it was known that we would soon have hard work for our cattle, it was necessary to allow a thorough rest, that the cattle might be in very good condition. Hastings had ridden back to a company remaining behind, in case it should be necessary to point out the way; a few wanted to wait for his return before again taking up their journey. The rather high mountains surrounding the broad cove were but sparsely wooded; only a little brook [North Willow Creek] rising from several small springs carried some water toward the valley, which after reaching the valley soon exhausted itself in the sandy, even pebbly soil a half mile above our location, afterwards reappearing as deep springs here where the companies had been encamped.

Since we left Fort Bridger, where we encountered so many Indians, of the Sioux tribe I believe, we had seen no more until yesterday; these last were dark, poorly clothed, not thin but undersized fellows, belonging to the Uta tribe. Those we came upon living here were the so-called Digger Indians, a tribe which had a reputation of being treacherous and cunning, and not averse to murdering white men when by craft they can do so without fear of punishment. "Digger" is the equivalent of the German "Gräber," and this name is applied to nearly all the tribes dwelling between this point and the settlements in California, because they all live on various roots which they dig with sharpened sticks. The Indians whom we met from here on called themselves Sho sha nee, or "*Schoshanie*," by which name only are they properly called. Of wild game we had seen for a long time nothing but occasional tracks, but these tracks gave evidence of the presence of bear, elk, deer, and the large mountain sheep, and showed that they at times frequented this region.

On August 11 we remained in camp resting. Two of the companies which had been encamped near us left this place to pursue their onward journey; in one of the other companies which was still encamped nearby, a man died who had been ill only a short time.

On the 12th of August also we remained at the same place, having to wash and mend our shoes and clothing. Mr. Hastings had returned; he was of the opinion that we should give our cattle more opportunity to recruit. The man who died yesterday in the company encamped nearby was buried today, whereupon they likewise left us to continue on their journey.

Again on the 13th we remained at the same camping place. Our stock, which at the time of our arrival had been badly worn down, had begun to recover their strength very satisfactorily; today it appeared as though they would commence a dance among themselves; they made all sorts of antic leaps, more in keeping with the demeanor of young goats than of old and large oxen. For our part, we had nothing against their being so light-hearted; on the contrary, we rejoiced in their revelry. The weather the last few days had been not unpleasant, although the sky was often cloudy.

On the 14th of August we at last went on again. At no other place, with the exception of the Platte, where we had to remain a few days for the purpose of obtaining buffalo meat, had we remained so long; we stayed here this length of time chiefly because our enfeebled cattle must soon undergo a long journey without grass and water, and their strength had to be renewed. Our road led along the base of the mountains in a northerly direction a distance of ten or 12 miles, then we bent again to the left around the point of the mountain, thus leaving the Salt Lake to our right and gradually receding from it. Along the way we came to more springs, passing them by because for the most part the water was quite salty.

The bowels of the mountains which bound the lake on the south most likely contain enormous deposits of rock salt, and the lake undoubtedly is composed in the main of salt. Since the lake has no known outlet, the large quantity of water flowing down into it from the rather sizable Bear River, the large Weber, and the perhaps nearly as large Uta River must evaporate during the summer time. The salt content of the many fairly large salty springs is likely to increase each year, for the salt itself does not evaporate.

Late in the afternoon, in another cove of these mountains, we came finally to another spring, the water of which, though somewhat salty, we could drink, and which provided also sufficient grass for our cattle. John Barber brought us a scorpion about 2 1/2 inches long, without, however, knowing that he had such a thing. The insect was dead; had it been alive, he would probably soon enough have learned his mistake. John had supposed it to be a new species of crayfish, for he had taken it out of a spring. I told him, however, that had it been a live scorpion he would very soon have let it go. Thus the catching of new crayfish appeared henceforth to have been spoiled for him.

Early on the 15th of August we arrived at the last fresh water springs, of which there were several, and fortunately we found also a great abundance of grass. Here again we overtook the last immigrant company in advance of us, including the Harlans and Weimer, with whom we had begun the journey from Indian Creek.

On the next day, August 16, this company again started on. The first wagon was already in motion when from the hindmost wagon a bundle of clothes was thrown out, belonging to the well-known, fat, fair-haired Miss Lucinda. The owner of this bundle one would as little or even less want to keep in one's wagon as the bundle itself. The bundle had flown from one of Mr. Harlan's wagons, into which Miss Lucinda twice already had been admitted; they had again become disgusted, and had probably thrown out the bundle of clothing as the best means of getting rid of the ever eager-for-marriage Lucinda. Had we not long been well-acquainted with the character of this worthy individual, we would have regarded this action of the Harlans as exceedingly heartless; as it was, some of us now considered that although Mr. Hoppe had twice already put her out, she would never have left the settlement except that he took her along, and thus he was the one to take again into his wagon the bundle and the speciously tearful Lucinda. There was a good deal of talking back and forth, as everyone sought to impose the burden on someone else, until at last we came generally to the opinion that as we could not abandon this piece of human flesh in the wilderness, Mr. Hoppe's family *must* take her in again, which view Hoppe unwillingly accepted.

We remained on the 16th of August here where the stock found the abundant fresh grass as good as the excellent water. We ourselves spent the time in preparing as well as possible for entering on the morrow upon a long stretch of from 70 to 90 miles without grass and water. With our pocket knives we cut as much grass as we could, binding it in bundles to carry with us. Every receptacle that would hold water was placed in readiness for our departure by being filled with this indispensable fluid, and we would have been happy had we possessed four times as much to take along.

The 17th of August dawned with our stock lying here and there in the grass, contentedly chewing their cuds. The carefree time now past, each of us was occupied loading into the wagons the prepared grass and the small, water-filled receptacles, and that with all possible care, so that under no circumstances should any be lost. The oxen we led once more to water, for now they could drink all they might desire, but this would not be the case hereafter. It was 9 o'clock by the time we set off. Before us lay a broad salt plain or valley [Skull Valley], where grew only a very little thorny, stunted vegetation; indeed, the ground was often a salt crust. Our direction was northwesterly, in a straight line to the mountain opposite [Cedar Mountains]. After a time the road began to ascend a hill, and about half-past 1 o'clock we reached a spring rather high on the mountainside. We halted here solely that our stock might drink; however, the water, although attractive to look at, was quite salty and the stock were not yet thirsty enough to drink it. Similarly, the small supply of coarse grass in no wise served, for they were not hungry enough to eat it.

According to report, the immigrants who had gone in advance of us had dug a well near the road on the west side of these hills, 15 or 20 miles from here. We decided among ourselves that four of us should go ahead until we came to the supposed well, and there await the arrival of our wagons. Big Bunzel, Zins, Thomen, and I were to search for the well, even though night should fall before we reached it. The wagons were to continue on the way as long as possible, but if they met with some especial difficulty, they should wait for the next day. After a rest of 1½ hours, we again set off on our journey, going ahead as above-mentioned, but without taking any firearms with us, each having only his walking stick. We traveled at first for several miles at the foot of a high range of hills [Cedar Mountains], proceeding along the lower slope in a northerly direction, and came finally to the place where the road climbed upward over very steep hills [Hastings Pass]. We were sure that our wagons would camp here tonight, for in order to surmount the acclivity the teams would have to be at least doubled, if not trebled.

By the time we had attained this high summit and bent our steps toward the wide, desolate valley below, the great, dark-red disk of the sun already had reached the northwestern edge of a boundless flat plain lying before us, an oppressive solitude as silent as the grave. The soil was composed of sand and gravel, from which nothing but small, thorny shrubs, *greasewood*, perhaps 1 1/2 feet high, eked out a miserable existence. Neither wolf nor antelope nor any other animal was to be seen or heard; however, lying scattered over the ground were the bones and gigantic horns of fallen mountain sheep and a few elk. The longer we continued on over the dusty, sandy road down toward the desolate plain, the darker it became. No sound was perceptible except our own muffled footfalls in the loose sand, which had been made unstable by the wagons and the hoofs of the livestock in advance of us. One behind the other, like so many recruits learning to march, we strode along without speaking. It was perhaps 10 o'clock when at last Bunzel suggested that we lie down by the side of the road, since under these conditions we could not expect to find the well. We scarcely replied to him but continued on as before. Bunzel was a big, strong man, but we all regarded him as lazy. He would not willingly stay behind by himself, so he followed along. After we had marched on perhaps another half hour, Bunzel broke the stillness of the night by saying that we must stop, for we had found no water and he was tired and sleepy, but we paid no more attention to him than before, so that at length he actually remained behind. The other three of us pursued our onward way until about midnight, when we too began to feel fatigued; to this time we had scarcely distinguished our sleepiness from the everlasting monotony of the darkness. We laid down on the gravel-strewn earth a few paces to the left of the road, but the night was quite chilly, and although previously we had run almost a sweat, we felt the cool night air not a little. Thomen had matches with him, and we attempted to gather a quantity of the half-dry bushes, *greasewood*, in the process injuring our hands to no small degree. We had no particular difficulty in kindling a fire, but it was of such a character that it soon went out, these plants not being woody enough to make a lasting fire. We dug holes in the sand and in these sought to shelter ourselves somewhat against the cold night air, in which, however, we scarcely succeeded. We made a fire again, and again laid down, until the gray light of day [August 18] appeared, when Bunzel once more caught up with us.

We had with us nothing either to eat or to drink, but the need to eat did not torment us especially. As the sun rose toward the zenith, however, its effects became ever more difficult to endure; there was then nothing which provided any shade at all, and if we threw ourselves on the ground, we felt the heat all the more, so that we longed for the return of the night.

Some 2 miles ahead of us we could see a rocky hill [Grayback Mountain] which rose about 70 feet above the plain, and over which the road led. Thomen, Zins, and Bunzel decided to go on that much farther and there await the arrival of our wagons, while I preferred to wait where I was, that I might the sooner obtain water when the wagons should come. Ever more insupportable grew my thirst and I scarcely turned my gaze from the place where I anticipated that the wagons must appear from the distant hill over which we had come last night. At length I saw a little dust arising, but it soon proved to be only a solitary horseman coming from that direction; on his reaching me, I found him to be a little old fellow from Baden, Müller, who was traveling with Hoppe. He had come ahead on horseback with two small kegs and was to go on till he should reach fresh water, when he was to fill them and turn back again, Müller informed me that the company had remained overnight at the foot of the steep hill and had gotten over it early this morning only with considerable difficulty. He thought they must soon be seen coming down out of the hills, and rightly; there where I had seen the first dust cloud arising, another now ascended on high, and like a snake the wagons wound down into the plain. To me they seemed long in coming; however come they did, and I had quenched my thirst by the time we reached the rocky hill before us. At this hill we made a mid-day halt and rested for an hour. We gave each head of stock about a gallon of water, together with a little of the grass we had brought with us, of which, indeed, they ate, but more gladly would they have had additional water. It was probably fully 3 o'clock when we resumed our journey and proceeded down from the hill again into the plain, soon coming to a small Sahara desert. The wind blew strongly from the northeast and drove the whitish-yellow sand before it as our wagons wound their way among numerous sand hills from 10 to 12 feet high; the air was darkened so that we could scarcely perceive the sun; one might have supposed that already twilight had come, although it was yet too early; this flying sand perhaps most resembled a very heavy snowstorm. Fortunately, this Sahara was not so great in extent as that of Africa; it could not have been more than 4 or 5 miles wide here where we crossed it. When we had left it behind, the wind died away almost entirely.

We had now reached a totally barren plain where not the slightest sign of plant life was to be seen. In this heavy twilight it had become so dark that we could just make out the ground on which we were now traveling, a sand mixture infused with salt so as to form a grayish clay, which had a very considerable resemblance to the bottom of the salt lake itself. Either this locality at times stood under salt water, perhaps in the rainy season, or the plain had formerly been a part of the salt lake, or possibly it was here connected with it. On reaching this plain, we halted and again gave each head of cattle a little water and grass. Taking a little refreshment ourselves, we then recommenced our onward journey, hoping that by the next morning we would have arrived at the expectantly watched-for freshwater springs and their attendant good grass.

Zins and I remained with the wagon, while Ripstein, Diel, and Thomen went on ahead intending to go on until they should arrive at the freshwater springs. Step by step we continued over this gray waste in the increasing darkness of the night. Here and there the ground was a little soft, additional evidence that not long since water must have been standing here. We went on without ceasing until about 1 o'clock in the morning, when suddenly our three comrades spoke to us; a short distance from here they had come upon a man who had remained behind to take care of several wagons; from this man they had learned that the distance to the nearest freshwater springs and grass was at least 24 miles. We soon came up to the wagon in which this man was staying, and from him we learned that those ahead of us had left many wagons behind and driven the cattle ahead to the springs, there to recover strength, after which they would come back for the wagons. Up to this time our cattle appeared to be in passable condition; the night was cool, and the level plain excellent to travel on, with the exception of a few somewhat wet places. In the far-off it was gradually growing lighter; some distance to our right we could perceive in the dawning light a chain of very steep-sloped mountains; a little to our left, almost in front of us, we could make out a few other mountain-tops [Silver Island] which rose almost perpendicularly from the gray, dead plain, and there we hoped to find the longed-for water. When the sun came up, slowly rising like a great, round, red disk from the apparently limitless plain that stretched before us, we had come to within a few miles of this last high mountain. Up to this time we had passed 24 wagons which had been left behind; now we made a halt. Our oxen all appeared to be suffering; the whole of their bowels appeared to cry out, an incessant rumbling which broke out from all; they were hollow-eyed, and it was most distressing to see the poor animals suffer thus. We could give them no more water, having only a little for ourselves, and the grass we gave them they would hardly touch. However, we could not remain here, we had to go on, and the poor cattle had to drag the wagons along behind them. Presently we came upon abandoned cattle, a few already dead, while others yet moved their ears; they could be saved only by others coming back bringing water for them.

The lofty, precipitous mountains [Silver Island] rising from the plain now loomed up on our left as we approached their north end. On them, however, grew no vegetation; they appeared reddish-brown, as if burned; at the foot of these mountains it was perfectly dry, without a sign of moisture. In front of us, near these mountains, rose a pebbly knoll; surely we must now be near the water, so we hoped, but alas, when we reached the summit we saw, over a 10-mile-wide valley, through the bluish haze, another high mountain beyond [Pilot Peak], and we realized that we would have to reach this before we should have completed the crossing of the endless plain.

The valley between us and the haze-shrouded mountains in the distance looked like a wide, large lake, the apparent surface of which here and there mirrored a deceptive semblance of the mountains and hills; we knew, however, that this was only a mirage, having already experienced several illusions of the kind. Straight through the seeming expanse of water, from the opposite shore, a black monster moved toward us like a frightful, giant snake, in a long, sinuous line. We all stared a long time at this puzzling apparition; it separated into detached parts, and we then supposed it must be a band of Indians. However, as we traveled slowly down the hill to meet them, we realized that what we saw was neither a monstrous snake nor friendly Indians, but a considerable number of men with oxen, a few mules, and horses, who were going back into the barren desert to recover their abandoned wagons.

We had taken but one short rest since sunrise, at which time we drank the last of our warm water. Not only our cattle but all the members of the company were now suffering from thirst. We found the returning teamsters supplied with water, carried in small kegs on the backs of some of the oxen or mules. At our request they willingly gave each of us a drink, but they could spare none for our cattle and we asked none for them. The sun shone burningly hot, as it did each day when not obscured by clouds, and we were seriously afraid that our cattle would not be able to get across this wide valley, for they appeared to be suffering terribly.

Our wagon was the second in line, but our leading yoke of oxen every instant were in danger of breaking their horns off in the wheels of the wagons ahead of us, for they continually tried to pull up to it so that they might remain a while in its shade, in this way continually getting between the wheels. In an effort to avert this, Zins drove while I walked ahead of them; soon, however, I received quite a thrust from the horns, since each of the two foremost oxen sought to profit by my small shadow, and to push the other away. Eager as I was to alleviate as much as possible the sufferings of the poor devils, in this way they very soon cured me of my enthusiasm for going ahead of them.

In this valley there was a great quantity of the finest salt, often in a 2-inch-thick crust. Here and there flowed, a few inches deep, crystal-clear water which, however, was as salty as salt itself, and the poor cattle, tormented by their dreadful thirst, tried constantly to drink of it, only to shudder in consequence. Slowly we were nearing the huge, common camping place where a small village of wagons stood. To this point not a single head of our cattle had given out, and we were coming ever closer to the green grass when suddenly first one and then the other ox of our leading yoke fell, scarcely a quarter of a mile from the grassy ground. Zins and I had considerable difficulty getting them to their feet again, but after this was accomplished, we went slowly on until we arrived at the grass-covered ground, and scarcely had the oxen reached there than they began to run as rapidly as though they were not at all tired. On arriving at the lower end of this wagon village we stopped and freed the poor animals from their yokes. Fortunately the spring was so hedged about by the wagons that the cattle could not gain free access to it, and it was therefore necessary for them to satisfy their thirst slowly from the water that flowed over the ground and gathered in their own footprints. A full two hours passed before they seemed to get quite enough, after which their first need appeared to be rest.

The spring [Pilot Spring] was a fine one about 4 by 6 feet across, and from 4 to 5 feet deep, the water fresh and good, and entirely free from any saline or mineral taint. The Kollog [Kellogg] brothers had a fine, large, black hound which they had brought along with them to this point, and which probably was extremely thirsty by the time it arrived here; it had jumped into the spring, immersing itself and drinking, but when it came out upon the grass again, it had suddenly fallen down, and shortly afterward it died.

Although Mr. Hoppe was not always our captain, our party was known as Hoppe's Company. We were told that the companies which had gone in advance of us had been generally of the opinion that our party would suffer most in crossing this long desert, to the point, perhaps, of perishing altogether. Here we were, however, the only company which had had to leave behind neither a wagon nor an animal, at which they were not a little amazed.

The journey from the last good water to this point had taken from 9 o'clock in the morning of the 17th to about 4 o'clock in the afternoon of the 19th of August, and during this time only on the first night had the cattle actually enjoyed rest, without, even then, being freed from their yokes. Otherwise, all the stops we made put together could hardly have amounted to more than 4 hours, and apart from this it was continuous driving until our arrival at these springs. During that time, all the water we could give to each head of cattle could scarcely have exceeded 1½ gallons. To be sure, we had spared our cattle as much as we could under the circumstances, but we had reason to congratulate ourselves that we had made this crossing without suffering the slightest loss.

In spite of long-sustained fatigue everyone was animated and happy; the young girls gathered together and sang, while the young Americans danced to the squeaky sounds which a man named Roadies coaxed from his old fiddle, so that the dust eddied up in clouds; in short, one might have supposed the whole journey completed.

On the 20th we of course remained here; again there was washing and mending to do while the cattle were given the rest and recuperation they so much needed. They seemed to relax very well indeed, except that the grass had become very short in consequence of the number of the cattle and the long stay here. Today two hunters came into our camp, Frenchmen if I am not mistaken, as also two or three Sho Shawnee Indians, with whom the hunters could carry on a somewhat halting conversation. As provision, the Indians carried with them in a leather bag a brownish mass which the hunters said was prepared from an edible root the Indians dug from the ground—the very same for which we called them Diggers (*Gräber*). One of these hunters, on leaving one of their camping places, had recently left behind a revolver which was found by a Shoshawnee. Not knowing whether the gun was loaded, or how to handle it, he had played with it aimlessly until suddenly, and to the great surprise of the Indian, the gun went off, thereby occasioning a slight injury. Thereafter the Indians had regarded the revolver as a mysterious object and went almost in fear of it, regarding the discharge of the same as a sign from the *Manito* (great spirit) that the object would bring nothing but harm should they keep it. They had very cautiously picked it up from the ground, and having observed which direction the hunters went, had concluded to carry this weird gun to them and hand it over, lest *Manito* take some other vengeful action. The hunters did not attempt to put an end to the superstition of the Indians; on the contrary, they sought to strengthen it yet further; to this state of affairs they owed it that they again had the revolver; such a firearm lost in the wilds is a loss that one cannot immediately replace.

Today most of the wagons which had been left on the desert were brought into camp, and everyone was in good spirits. Stories were told, and there was singing and dancing. At one spot the young maidens had gathered together, and among them, like the devil among angels, Miss Lucinda also had taken her place, although, to be sure, without having been invited; we could easily enough see that Lucinda's presence among them was not very agreeable to the others. Such a thing, however, she would not perceive. The young men stood in a circle around the singing girls. Alfred, Lucinda's [former] ten-hour-husband, stood at my left close beside me, and like most of the rest of us was listening to the songs when all at once Lucinda hurled a short piece of wood at him—without, however, hitting him; the piece of wood grazed the hair of both of us. Had it actually struck Alfred, he might well have been injured, for Lucinda was a healthy specimen of two-legged animal. This new heroic deed of Lucinda's was too much for the people to stomach, and the elder Kellogg came up to Alfred to ask, "Are you going to let such behavior pass unnoticed?" In his simplicity, the young fellow answered that he was but a poor follower and did not know whether he even had a friend. Kellogg told him that we were all his friends, and he should, were he in Alfred's place, by no means permit the insulting behavior of this person to pass unnoticed. Although the girls had all moved away from her and all showed by their scornful glances the regard in which they held Lucinda, this in no way induced her to leave the place.

With respect to this person, I wish to have done with her, so I will here relate the rest of what I know about her. Lucinda had begun the journey with Hoppe's family, sought and found admission by the Harlans, and had from among them married the young fellow, Alfred, after failing of marriage with Zins, but during the night quarreled with him so that by the next morning they parted and would have absolutely nothing more to do with one another. She returned again to the Hoppes and cast an eye, if not two, on the large, good looking man, Mike, who drove the other wagon. He, however, no doubt to put an end to these pressing attentions, left Hoppe's employ the day after he shot the buffalo with my carbine. Hoppe had then written a letter purporting to be from Mike to Lucinda, which had allegedly been found on the road. Since Lucinda could not herself read the letter, Mr. Hoppe himself had the kindness to read it aloud in the presence of many belonging to the company. The letter consisted of an ardent declaration of love, such that the hearers, Lucinda excepted, had been much amused.

Lucinda, however, hugged the excessive love letter to her breast after Hoppe handed it over, and had sighed, "*Oh—my dear Mike, I wish you was here,*" etc. Miss Lucinda soon after returned to the Harlans again, with whom she remained till the beginning of the long desert known under the name, "*the long trip*" [i.e., "the long drive"]. Here, as already set forth, they had thrown her bundle of clothes out of the wagon as a means of ridding themselves of her, and only with great difficulty, by threatening him, almost, was Hoppe finally prevailed upon to take her again into his wagon. No sooner had we all arrived at this place where we, the Harlans, and the greater part of the whole company were gathered, than she again found shelter with the Harlans.

It is said that when Lucinda had hardly reached the first settlement in California she married a hefty young man; this fellow, however, soon turned sickly and died! In the autumn of 1847, while I was acting as superintendent at Sutter's Fort, I had the opportunity of seeing Lucinda again single, shortly after her "*dear, dear husband*" died and was buried. At the Fort, she felt most comforted when people said to her, "Lucinda, you are still very young and you will surely find another man." Her usual reply was, "*Do you think so?*" However, the people in the Fort did not well accord with her love's desire, for with the exception of a rather thin Irishman named Pray [Edmund Bray] nobody would have anything to do with her, and Bray himself shortly appeared to be doubtful whether upon taking her as his wife, he would be able to fulfill his duties as a husband. In view of such doubts it seemed that his first ardent desire to be married suddenly cooled and he decided that he preferred to continue a while longer in his proud bachelorship. At all events, Lucinda evidently at last became convinced that there was no fishing in the Fort. She left this region to rejoice with her presence Pueblo de San Jose (the village of the holy St. Joseph), which is situated near the southern end of the Bay of San Francisco. On arriving there, she reportedly put an end to her widowhood by marrying a sailor. This experiment, according to persons who knew and had seen her, she repeated three times within six weeks. It is well that I have no further particulars of Lucinda's history to relate, for it has been difficult enough to conclude this one story about her.

On the afternoon of August 21, toward evening, we forsook this camping place, the grass having become scant, and went on 2 miles south, where water equally good, and grass undoubtedly better were to be found, although many others were there.

On the 22nd we remained in camp here, since our cattle were in need of still more rest; moreover, we faced a long stretch of road on which we should find neither grass nor water. On this day I found two small scorpions. Around us there were many small springs, and as far as the water moistened the ground, the vegetation was green and beautiful; however, the water soon oozed away in the sandy ground, and beyond, all was the same everlasting dry monotony.

Again on the 23rd we remained here, yearning however to move on. The weather was clear and quite warm; toward evening a warm west wind arose.

On August 24th we *five German Boys* broke camp, leaving the rest of the company behind. It appeared to us as if the zeal of our company to press on had relaxed. We still had a long and difficult drive before us, after which the cattle again would have to be allowed to recruit, hence no time should be wasted. Our way led at first in a southwesterly direction, through the salt plain, past several springs, some of which were salty and others fresh, with very little grass. After traveling perhaps 6 miles we climbed gradually through a gorge between rocky cliffs [Silver Zone Pass], a so-called *Gap*, whereby our course bent ever more to the west. On both sides of the gorge were high, overhanging rocks; in this gorge, so it was said, was a well which had been dug by immigrants who had passed through two years earlier, and this well we were obliged to reach this evening. Although a pair of us were coming up the gorge ahead of the slowly moving wagons, too rapidly did the darkness of the night come over us to discover the indications of a spring. The oxen were tired and followed reluctantly in the track of those still in advance of us. At last we decided to wait until daylight. We fastened our cattle with a small chain in a hasty fashion to a wagon wheel, took a little to eat, and lay down to sleep, with the understanding that we would rise very early the next morning. Ripstein today felt quite unwell, having fever and no appetite; he was carried in the wagon.

On the next morning, the 25th, scarcely had the day begun to dawn than Father Thomen woke up his sleepy comrades in accordance with the agreement. The cold morning air felt only too agreeable, and we just then were quite willing to sleep on a while longer. But Father Thomen this morning was so ready with his heartfelt *Donner* and *Wetter* that I for one began to have a dislike for our wagon box and to rub my sleepy eyes. The creaking of the wagon box afforded sufficient evidence to Thomen that I had heard him. He left, but again his battery of *Donnerwetter* opened up, to such effect that Zins began to roundly abuse him and tell him it was wholly unnecessary under the circumstances to make so much noise. In my case, however, the result had been that my feet were now hanging down from the wagon and I was attempting to yawn myself awake. A few more *Donnerwetters* and I was on the ground supporting Father Thomen in his endeavor. Since Zins now found himself in the minority, he as well as Diel finally roused up.

We found in our vicinity a little bunchgrass, "*sagegrass*," which we cut and gave to our oxen, who greedily devoured it. With our breakfast we were soon enough finished, after which we yoked up and again proceeded slowly on down through the gorge. We had gone scarcely 100 yards before we actually found near the road a spring hole perhaps 12 feet deep. We stopped, naturally, and equipping myself with a bucket and a small receptacle I forced my way the few steps down to the water. The water was clear, cool, and pleasant to the taste. Of course we quenched our own thirst first and set aside a little to carry along with us, after which our oxen got about 2 gallons to the head. Though insufficient, this was for the animals some slight alleviation. Had hostile Indians come near us last night, they could hardly have found a better place to surprise and massacre us than from behind the various detached rocks around camp; it would not have been difficult for them to have trapped and gathered us up as into a sack.

We at last reached the end of the gorge, and from it emerged out upon the table land. Although this valley had no salt flats, the quality of the soil was in other respects the same, pebbly and sandy. On our right we came upon a great circle of interwoven cedar branches with a wide opening. The ground there was the same sort of dry soil as elsewhere, and what the purpose of this circle could be was to us at first an enigma. Later on, I learned from old hunters that in this circle the Indians caught the swift-footed antelope, and this was the way they went about it: Perceiving an antelope near this circle. a group of Indians would seek, by naturally drawing closer, to drive the animal into the entrance to the circle. The closer the animal approached the opening in the circle, the greater care the Indians took that it should escape neither to the side nor behind them. Finding itself approached ever nearer to the side and behind by the advancing Indians, the antelope would elect to flee into the wide opening before it rather than to accelerate its flight alongside the enemy. As soon as the antelope was actually inside the circle, the Indians looked on the hunt as a success. The best bowmen placed themselves on both sides of the opening in the cedar branches, while others formed a ring, part in and part outside the circle, and then began the true hunting. Seeing the enemy approaching from all directions, the antelope would be afraid of the cedar-circle, but would see the wide opening by which it entered and hope to escape the same way. Scarcely would it emerge, however, than it would be shot from both sides, the arrows entering the body with such great force that when it was not immediately killed, it could not flee much farther and soon would be brought down by the pursuing Indians.

The great, gray wolf catches the antelope in a very similar way, and perhaps the Indians have learned their cunning stratagem directly from the wolf. At all events. if I may be allowed a few more words, I shall demonstrate its intelligence and powers of calculation.

To catch a healthy antelope, at least four wolves must associate themselves, not that a single wolf is afraid, but because they know that the antelope is much swifter than they are. When this respectable company of four or more large wolves has assembled, they creep up in such a manner that they form a large circle, the antelope of course being in the middle between them. Naturally, they seek to take the antelope upon an open plain. Now they gradually approach it, so that when the antelope perceives one and seeks to turn in another direction, it see one there also, ahead and behind; suddenly, to its alarm, it perceives that wherever it turns, the frightful enemy comes ever nearer. In its agitation the antelope loses its presence of mind and seeks to break out of the wolf circle anywhere possible, but the wolves come on warily, and rapidly closer. The antelope becomes blind with fear and suddenly it is seized by one of the wolves; soon afterward, the one which but a short time before was so swift-footed will perhaps have been wholly devoured.

We arrived at our new camping place about 11 o'clock in the morning, finding another company already encamped there. At this place, two years earlier, an immigrant company had camped; apparently they had suffered the loss of the greater part of their stock along the way, for they had abandoned their wagons here, burying in the ground what they could not carry with them. After they left, the Indians had burned the wagons; the travelers in advance who had recently arrived here had found what was left of the wagons. Ripstein today was quite ill; he had the true measles, which began to show on his skin. From our camp of last night we had traveled about 14 miles to this point. We had not found exactly a superabundance of grass here, but there was a tolerable supply, and the water was also good, so we decided to remain here the next day, August 26, and await the arrival of our company.

Although we caught sight of no Indians, during the night we could see their fires in the nearby mountains and hills; however, we were not molested in any way. Since our company had caught up with us again yesterday, we left our camp today together again. Our road led us in a direction almost straight south. After traveling 14 miles, we reached a place where we found sufficient grass and water [Flowery Lake]. There was, on the other hand, no great abundance of firewood, but we managed with the pieces of wild sage at hand. The nature of the valley bottom is the same as hitherto.

On August 27th we left this camping place and proceeded about 14 miles across the valley bottom almost directly south, where we again made a halt at a spring of good water, in the vicinity of which there was also a sufficiency of grass. Wild game we frequently came upon; I saw today at least 40 antelope.

On the 28th our road led almost wholly westerly across a depression in the mountain (gap) [Jasper Pass]. Emerging into a valley [Independence Valley] in all respects the same as the one we had left, we crossed it and after having traveled 14 miles once more camped at the foot of a mountain lying opposite, at a fresh water spring [Mound Springs] in the vicinity of which there was again a little grass. The nearby mountain [northern extension of Spruce Mountain] was smaller than the one [Pequop Mountains] we crossed today. The weather was clear, with a warm south wind at night. In this valley we today saw several sand-storms from 150 to 300 feet high, very rapidly turning or whirling about themselves, moving comparatively slowly as they moved along the valley from the south to the north.

On the 29th we resumed our journey directly up the mountain slope in a westerly direction, over a low place in the mountain, where a little water gave rise to some scattered grass, a few small cedars and several little white alder trees, and thence down into another dry valley [Clover Valley] across which the road led us to the mountainous region opposite [East Humboldt Mountains]. We found a spring at the foot of these mountains, and to the extent that the water moistened the ground, a scanty supply of grass. Of sage there was no lack. Our march this day again amounted to about 14 miles. [Not?] far off to the right from our camp, in several places, smoke mounted upward, evidence that Indians lived in this vicinity. The weather was the same as yesterday.

On August 30 we took up our journey again, starting off in a southwesterly direction. The low place where we crossed the mountains was rather steep. The valley [Ruby Valley] lying before us was again broad, in most respects resembling those crossed earlier. Our road during the day proceeded in a southwesterly direction across this flat valley; the mountains [Ruby Mountains] we were approaching rose from it high and precipitous. A large number of splendid, cold, freshwater springs broke out at the base of these mountains; we could perceive them at a distance, from the scattered timber which grew about them, and it did our eyes good to see the grass here growing. At one of these springs we encamped, finding there one of the companies which had gone in advance of us.

The Indians here were not so shy as those in the vicinity of our previous encampment. Some 30 Sho shannees made their appearance at our camping place, of which two were old, exceedingly ugly squaws, and the others adult men, ranging in age from perhaps 18 to 50-odd years. The two eldest Indians were fat old fellows, one of whom had hair perfectly red, the only red-haired Indian I have seen. His hair, by the way, was coarse, but in his whole bearing and figure he was like the rest of his companions. A sour, doltish Englishman was smoking his clay pipe. The Indians gave him to understand by means of signs that they would find it most agreeable to be permitted a few puffs also. The Englishman, however, rejected their pleas, answering that these filthy Indians should not smoke from his pipe. Although the Indians did not understand his words, they recognized his forbidding mien as unfriendly to them, and we could immediately perceive an unpleasant expression on their dark faces.

The unfriendly behavior of the Englishman, however, was also disapproved by his fellow travelers; we regarded his action as rude, and under the circumstances, very unwise. While we were in the country of these Indians, it was to the interest of each of us to make them our friends, for through rude, hostile treatment we could soon transform these children of nature into bitter, treacherous enemies who could find many ways to injure us if they so desired. An elderly American woman, the mother of five grown children, who like her husband were members of the company encamped near us, sought to allay the angry feelings of the Indians. Quickly filling her own pipe with tobacco, she lighted it and handed it to one of the fat old Indians. He accepted it with every sign of the greatest satisfaction, took 10 or 12 large puffs, letting the smoke escape through his nose with obvious pleasure, and then gave it to his equally fat companion at his side. He, after having gratified himself similarly, handed it on to the next, and so it was repeated, without exception, until the last had had his turn. All were highly pleased over the signal favor which had been bestowed on them by the white man's squaw, and though earlier they had favored the unkind, rude Englishman with malignant, vengeful looks, the countenances they turned upon the woman without exception were friendly and smiling. Had the American woman stayed on here, the red-haired chief would perhaps out of sheer gratitude have raised her up to be the "Lady Chief."

The two old squaws were frightfully ugly, having only a small piece of animal skin around their loins, which barely covered their bodies. With their big, wrinkled, dirty bellies, they looked much like old sows which had just been wallowing in mud, although I do believe that a half-way respectable pig would have exceeded them in beauty. These Indian women were amazed at the soft, smooth, nearly white, yellow hair of an attractive 6-year-old boy. Their loud laughter was very like a high-pitched, many-sided, sonorous screaming which distorted their faces in a repulsive manner. They could hardly look enough at the boy; they must continually point at him; and their gabble with each other sounded much like that of a number of magpies when by chance a cat or a fox approaches. These squaws did not sit with the men but off by themselves. Of young Indians there was not a sign, which showed that the Indians were afraid the white men would carry them off; so that we could not so easily take them away, the children must have been hidden in a few coverts in the high, precipitous mountains near us, to remain while the whites stayed on. Probably the men would not have objected had the white men carried off the two old squaws, since they were permitted to visit the camp of the whites. A few of the men were adorned with a necklace of large bear claws, but otherwise they were almost wholly naked. In complexion they were as dark as the Sioux, but they were not so large and stately, more resembling the California Indians.

On September 1 [August 31?] we remained here in camp.

On September 2 [1?] we traveled southward down this valley, not, however, making a very long day's journey. The road led for the most part over a pretty, grassy, gradually flattening plain. Several large springs made fertile a considerable area; nevertheless, the large springs soon exhausted themselves after reaching the flat valley, so that close by we could see another waste of barren earth.

On September 3 we took up our journey on southward and made our camp near a rocky projection at the southerly end of the mountains, so to speak, in the middle of several large and magnificent springs of the best fresh water. Were all these springs passed the last two days gathered together, they would form a not inconsiderable river, but here the water lost itself again in a scarcely half-mile-long stream. Several of the springs would have yielded water enough to drive a large mill. One of these springs, not far from our camping place, was particularly noteworthy. It formed a basin from 12 to 14 feet across and perhaps about as deep; it had the regular form of a stupendous, convex funnel. The water was crystal-clear; the sides were of an ash-gray color, and perhaps 5 or 6 feet beneath the surface, around the whole pool, there was a dark-colored band from 3/4 to 1 inch wide. From the bottom, exactly in the middle of the pool, the clear fluid welled upwards, driving small pieces of earth or mud a few feet high, which however, immediately sank back to the sides again. The basin was ringed around its entire circumference, the water flowing out only through a small opening in front. What made this spring even more interesting was that in it were perhaps a half dozen small fish, from 4 to 5 inches long, which played in this natural aquarium. Nowhere else, on the whole journey between Missouri and California, did we find so many beautiful springs, and such good water, as here.

In the evening, as dark was coming on, a few young Shoshanees came to our camp. We gave them a little food and signified to them that they should then leave our camp, which they willingly did.

On September 4 our way led past the above-mentioned rocky projection around to a southwesterly direction, whereby we came gradually if only slightly higher; there was again the same growth of small underbrush and sage, growing from the sandy, pebbly desert earth. Late in the afternoon we arrived at a small spring brook; with the good water there was also some grass, and we concluded to encamp here. After we had made our camp, I went down the brook a short distance and there found in it a human skull—whether this skull originated from a white man or an Indian, there was no means of determining. I brought it back with me to camp, but as nobody seemed to be especially pleased over my find, I carried it back to where I had found it.

One of the company had shot a large, strong vulture still smelling of carrion—a so-called Turkey Buzzard—and brought it to camp. It had, however, so strong a stench that we quickly flung it away. It was soon disposed of a second time, by a few Indian children; seeing that the bird was left unemployed, one of them asked through signs whether they might be permitted to take it with them with a view to eating it. Naturally, we granted this request most willingly.

On September 5 we set out in the same direction as the previous day, but as we came higher up, the road veered around more to the right. Arriving at the summit of the pass [Hastings Pass] toward noon, we made a noon halt there where sundry springs broke out. Continuing on, we passed through an isolated forest of white alders and also, if I am not mistaken, a few cedars. The road wound first to the northwest and finally wholly to the north, now going steadily down into the valley [Huntington Valley]. Late in the afternoon, on reaching a place where we found sufficient grass and water, we camped again. The high mountain, which for some days we had followed to the south, gone around, and finally climbed over, on its western side was not nearly so steep and precipitous as on its eastern, and must have been easy to climb, whereas the east side often rose nearly perpendicular. This range of mountains, and the three or four previously crossed, like the wide, flat, largely barren valleys lying between, extended nearly parallel with one another from north to south. The last range, I believe, is that called the Humboldt Mountains.

September 6. Last night was the coldest we had up to this time; this morning the ground actually was a little frozen. Still pursuing our onward journey, we came continuously lower down the valley, entirely in a northerly direction. Below us in the valley a few Indians were encamped. One of them rose up by me with one hand held high over his head, shaking it like an enthusiastic preacher, beginning at the same time to speak—or preach—in a somewhat ceremonious tone. Since I could understand no syllable of what he said, I left him standing amid his companions and went on past them.

Farther down the valley we came to a pretty little brook which took its rise from the west side of these high, in-part-gone-round, in-part-climbed-over mountains. In such a case as this, a high country from which mountains rise higher still, it is probable that the heights are wholly covered with snow until late summer, to which circumstance the many large, cold springs owe their existence. The westerly slope appeared to us to be but sparsely wooded.

In the afternoon I followed the road not far from the right bank of the brook, again in a northwesterly direction, going along a couple of miles in advance of our company. On both sides rose small mountains, through which the road and the brook directly proceeded, the little valley becoming ever more narrow ahead. Often in the road I found fresh tracks of Indians, despite which I carried no firearms with me. The heat in this little valley was great; there was no breeze at all, so that the sun shone down with full power. As I approached the mountains ahead, I could see only a deep notch from which the rock rose sheer on either side; thither the stream course wound, and our road with it.

To the left, near the road and on the bank of the thus-far quietly flowing, clear brook, not far from an immigrant, sat a dark Indian. I seated myself close to his left side and stroked his velvety back a few times, meanwhile exhibiting to him a friendly countenance and nodding approval to indicate my cordial feelings toward him. The Indian appeared to be neither frightened nor angry at my familiar behavior; on the contrary, he also nodded and smiled. We made no attempt to converse with one another through speech;

instead we resorted to all manner of signs and gestures. Recalling what I had heard of the edible roots, I took my stick in my hand and made a motion with it, as if I wished to dig something from the ground. My gaze then left off roving over the ground, and exhibiting a small finger, I put it into my mouth and then moved my jaws as if I were eating, after which I put my walking stick into the hand of my dark friend. The Indian had understood me perfectly; he knew that I wanted him to dig a few roots for me. He immediately sprang from his seat, searched near the road on the ground about us, dug in a few places, and after a few moments returned with a couple of small, yellowish roots. I signified that he should first eat thereof, which he did at once, then I bit off a small piece and cautiously tasted it. The taste, much resembling that of a parsnip, pleased me, and I ate the rest of the small piece with relish.

The Indian regarded my confidence in him as complete, now that I had put into my mouth the rootlet he had dug. He took my stick from my hand, went quickly off again, and zealously dug still more roots. As soon as he had a small number, he pounced upon a few large grasshoppers and brought the whole back with him. One of the largest grasshoppers he pressed with its long, thrashing legs against a piece of root, opened his mouth, and made a movement with his jaws as if to eat, without, however, actually doing so. Then he offered me the grasshopper, together with the root, about as one would hand buttered bread to a child. The Indian appeared surprised that this time I would not accept the offering. By way of showing me that he expected me to do nothing at all strange, he now himself bit off a part of the upper body of the grasshopper, together with its head and a piece of root, and chewed this flesh and its garnishing in a lively manner, thus showing me that it tasted exceedingly good. Considering that he had in this way perfectly convinced me, he offered me yet again this rare dish. I was, however, in spite of his artful effort at persuasion, not at all encouraged to emulate his good example, and he turned upon me a look as though he half pitied me, and I should not be at all surprised if he thought that this was a most stupid person who did not have the least idea of what was good.

The rest of the roots I left for the others to taste, and Thomen, who came along about this time, gladly ate of them, so that once more the Indian busied himself roundabout, bringing back a moderate quantity of the roots. Not wanting to go farther down the gorge this evening, we decided to camp at this place. We *five German Boys*, as usual, had baked from bread-dough and fat three cakes apiece, which with a little buffalo meat, together with tea or coffee, was a meal that we repeated on the journey two or three times a day. We desired to take our supper in our tent, and had seated ourselves on the ground inside when the tent opened again and without ceremony in came our Indian friend. Seating himself beside Thomen and me, he thereby indicated that he too now was ready to eat. It was up to us to laugh and make the best of the situation. We each gave him half a cake, and meat, and coffee, and our comrades also each gave him a piece of their cake. Our evening meal thus became a little scanty, but it sufficed, and the Indian seemed satisfied with his new evening meal, going away well pleased. The enjoyment of unfamiliar raw vegetable was followed for Thomen and even more for me, by severe abdominal pains and—diarrhoea, the result being that often during the night I wished that I had never seen this Indian parsnip. Toward morning, however, all again became well.

On September 7 six or eight Indians came to our camp, among whom was my friend of the evening before; he came up just as we were about to leave the camping place. My root-friend had both of his hands completely full of roots, which he wanted to present to me. However, the pains and the running about which these had occasioned me last night had perfectly disgusted me with them. The brown fellow seemed not quite to understand why it was that I would have no more roots, when yesterday evening I had signified to him my desire to eat them. Only through signs could I make him understand, so I bent forward, holding my belly with both hands, and groaned as though I had severe abdominal pains; then I produced with my mouth certain sounds such as at times escape entirely different human organs, at the same time making a gesture with my hands toward my rear. The Indian understood me perfectly and a veritable storm of laughter burst from their throats. My friend laughed if possible hardest of all and tossed his roots on my back. We of course laughed with them and parted, after all, as good friends.

Scarcely 200 paces from our camping place, we entered the deep gorge through which the river cut its way, and through which our road led. The mass of rock rose in several places nearly perpendicular, around which the stream twisted in several great bends, now to the right, now to the left, the gorge becoming more contracted. Often we believed the way completely obstructed until we closely approached the openings. In places we advanced through dense thickets principally made up of white alder and willows. If I remember aright, the passage through this gorge (Echo Canyon?) was six miles long. Each moment we had to recross the stream, the water often coming nearly as high as the wagon bed. As often there was a 3-, 4-, or 5-foot drop from the bank down into the river bed, and it was just as steep going out on the opposite side. In this way we had already crossed the river to and fro 13 times when, late in the afternoon, we arrived finally at the last crossing. Ripstein and Diel had gone ahead without the least concern for the wagon or the company, notwithstanding they had seen how difficult the road was.

Here, at the 14th and last crossing, the road on the right side was ominously high, as also on the left. The stream was wide, and it looked to us as if the water to our left were deep. The right ox of the leading yoke was called Ben; he was a large, lean fellow with very long horns, a little cross-eyed but for the rest a very good, obedient animal; however, there were times when he would have his own way, and thereby he displayed only too well his obstinate oxen nature. As we approached this last crossing, our Ben seemed not well impressed with the wide, deep-looking water to our left. He squinted and blinked at it, as if he thought, "This brook is by no means empty; herein go I not." More to the right the water was not so deep; it flowed over a pebbly place, and we could easily see the bottom. Ben's ox-understanding told him, probably, that an ox his size ran no risk of drowning in water $1\frac{1}{2}$ feet deep. We no sooner commenced the crossing than we found that Mr. Ben was not disposed to go straight down into the water; he turned aside to the right (Gee). Zins, who was driver today, fortunately stopped in time. Thomen remained at the rear of the wagon to keep it from upsetting, for it had a heavy list to the left. I fastened a small piece of rope to Ben's right horn and sought through hard pulling to draw the stubborn old fellow to the left, while Zins cracked his whip and shouted "Oh haw," but Ben would Gee and our right wagon wheel rose still higher, as a result of which our wagon inclined yet more to the left. With some difficulty we managed to stop the oxen again. I now placed myself on the right side of the ox Ben and shouted "Oh Haw" while I sought with all my power to shove him to the left, but when all the oxen together began to pull again, I was brushed aside by the squint-eyed fellow as easily as if I had been only a child. Thomen and Zins shouted together, and over toppled our wagon into water 4 feet deep, the bows together with the covering under water and the wheels appearing there where the bows should have remained. The bows of course were broken, and all our belongings lay in the water. I thought that my fine, double-barreled gun must now be broken and my books ruined, but nevertheless said not a word. Zins also was quiet, though angry. Thomen however let loose a huge volley of *Donner und Wetter* g—d d—m, g—d d—m, a veritable giant avalanche of the strongest expressions of anger, which he varied with the question, "What shall we do now?"—a question he asked several times in succession. Our silence Thomen could not understand, and he continually repeated his question.

"We can't long remain here, and if we all abuse one another like sparrows or like Thomen we will get nowhere," I replied to the last of his what-shall-we-do-nows. "I know what we will have to do; we will have to unhitch the oxen, drive them to the little island yonder, come back and carry our belongings over there too, right the wagon, draw it over to our belongings, load them in, hitch up the oxen again, and again drive on."

Thomen at these words became so irritated that his *Donnerwetters* fell upon one another as thick as hailstones, succeeded with a whole stream of G—d d—m's. Zins broke out finally into laughter, which however did not serve to silence Thomen. Zins said, "Exactly as Lienhard has said, so must we do; if the three of us just stand here and abuse and scold as you are doing, our situation will never be mended." Thomen, who was not yet able to control himself, replied that he had been angered not so much by my words themselves as by the cold-blooded manner in which I spoke of our extremely precarious situation, as though it were nothing.—As I had proposed, so we did. There were, to be sure, a few more small *Donnerwetters*—, especially when Thomen and I lifted his bedding out of the water and a small river gushed out of it. For the rest, we soon completed our labor, hitched up the oxen again, and drove on, leaving the place just as the first of the wagons that were following us reached this last crossing. We had traveled on only a few feet when Ripstein and Diel came back; they had learned from a man on horseback who had passed us while our belongings lay in the water what had befallen us. They commenced to abuse us, but we gave it back to them with interest, calling them rotten, unfeeling fellows who would be well advised to keep their mouths shut, and they were finally glad when we stopped bawling them out. The damage we suffered was not great. The bows were broken. of course, the cover torn, and nearly everything more or less soaked; however, the gunpowder remained almost completely dry.

We found a place to camp immediately beyond the gorge, where this stream joined Mary's [Humboldt] River, which was perhaps slightly larger than the river down which we had come. The wagons following us remained behind so long that we remarked jocularly among ourselves that several others must have upset their wagons in the same place, without, however, actually believing it. After a long while, they at last appeared, one after the other, and it turned out to be true—two other persons had upset their wagons in the same place, although in all the previous crossings only one such accident had occurred.

September 8 we made a day of preparation, our principal object being to dry out our things. In the nearby thicket I found a small bundle of Indian belongings hanging on a tree, among which was a bow shaped from two pieces of horn of a mountain sheep. I bound the things all together again and hung them up in the same place. In the afternoon several Shoshawnees came to our camp. One of them sought through signs, the sounds we made in driving our oxen, to make us understand that from still another direction wagons were coming up [down] Mary's River. His information was correct, for here the road from Fort Hall joined that by way of Hastings Cutoff (which might much better be called *Hastings Longtripp*). How much we had profited by this cutoff we soon enough learned through a small company which had taken the Fort Hall road. They had left Fort Bridger 12 or 13 days after we did, and were now just as far advanced as we.

*

Lienhard's journal covers the entire Hastings Cutoff from Fort Bridger to its junction with the Fort Hall Road. Lienhard has included many personal items and stories of travel on the emigrant trail which have been included to show conditions of early day travel by ox team. For the exact location of landmarks, see the extensive footnotes in West from Fort Bridger, *edited by Dale Morgan.*

This party of "German boys" usually traveled together and has been listed as part of the Harlan-Young party, although actually they did not always travel as part of that group, but probably a short distance behind them most of the time. After crossing the salt flats they seem to have moved in their own small group, sometimes behind and sometimes ahead of those being guided by Hastings.

10. THE JEFFERSON MAP

Very little is known about T. H. Jefferson, the maker of this rare map. He was listed in St. Louis newspapers as being one of the prominent persons starting west in 1846. His stay in California was short, since his map was published in New York in 1849 and was carried by some of the gold rushers of that year.[1]

This map is of particular value because it gives the date of every camp. The only part we are interested in here is the section from Fort Bridger to the Humboldt River and particularly the section covering the Great Salt Desert. While he has invented his own names for the various landmarks, they are readily recognized.

One strange thing about this map is that it shows a well located somewhere among the sand dunes just east of the salt flats. No other traveler speaks of any such well. However, there is a possibility that such a well existed even though most of the emigration did not find it. Sheepherders who have run sheep over these sand dunes claim that by digging down in the sand and placing a barrel with both ends knocked out in the hole to keep it from caving in, water can always be found. While it is somewhat brackish it is drinkable and readily used by sheep. In crossing these dunes on the emigrant trail I found no signs of such a well, but oddly enough just south of the railroad station of Knolls there is a well once used by Indians and now kept open by coyotes and jackrabbits, which substantiates the sheepherders' story.

This map was not available to me when I followed the old trail from Fort Bridger across the salt flats, but it is accurate in every respect wherever traces of the trail were visible. It will not be republished here but may be consulted from the reproduction in *West from Fort Bridger*.

---

[1] T. H. Jefferson, *Map of the Emigrant Road From Independence, Mo., to St. Francisco, California*.

11. THE DONNER PARTY

The Donner party, which had started from Independence with Col. Russell and Bryant, was a week behind the train which Hastings was guiding. Clyman met this party near Fort Laramie. James Clyman, James F. Reed and Abraham Lincoln had all been members of Captain Jacob Early's company during the Black Hawk war. Clyman says:

> [I] had known Mr. Reed previously in the Sauk war. He was from Springfield Illinois.

> Mr. Reed, while we were encamped at Laramie was enquiring about the route. I told him to "take the regular wagon track [by way of Fort Hall], and never leave it—it is barely possible to get through if you follow it—and it may be impossible if you don't." Reed replied, "There is a nigher route, and it is of no use to take such a roundabout course." I admitted the fact, but told him about the great desert and the roughness of the Sierras, and that a straight route might turn out to be impracticable.

> The party when we separated, took my trail by which I had come from California, South of Salt Lake, and struck the regular emigrant trail again on the Humboldt.[1]

Clyman strongly advised all who asked him about the route not to attempt the cutoff. But in spite of these warnings, and because of the lateness of the season, the Donner party decided to try the new route.[2]

Following Hastings' trail they arrived at the place where he had passed down Weber Canyon; but here they found a note posted probably by Hudspeth advising them not to attempt that canyon, as it was too difficult for wagons; he vaguely outlined a different route—the route by which he had come to Fort Bridger. The instructions, however, were not clear; there was considerable differ-

---

[1.] Camp, ed., *James Clyman*, 266.

[2.] C. F. McGlashan, *History of the Donner Party* (Truckee: Crowley and McGlashan, 1879); Eliza P. Donner Houghton, *The Expedition of the Donner Party and Its Tragic Fate* (Chicago: A. C. McClurg & Co., 1911); Bryant, *What I Saw in California*.

ence of opinion among the company, and it was finally decided to send Reed, Stanton and Pike ahead on horses to find Hastings and if possible bring him back to get them out of their troubles. After great difficulties Hastings was finally located near the southern end of Great Salt Lake. He refused to leave the party he was with, but took Reed to the summit of Big Mountain in the Wasatch Mountains and pointed out to him the route he must take to get the wagons down out of the mountains and across the Salt Desert. Reed returned to his party, blazing the trail as he went, leaving Stanton and Pike, whose horses had given out. They later returned, more dead than alive, after having been given up for lost.

Endeavoring to follow the route pointed out by Hastings, the emigrants cut their way down through Mountain Dell and over Little Mountain to what is now Emigration Canyon,[3] eventually reaching Salt Lake Valley, where they thought their troubles were over. As it turned out, their troubles had only just begun.

Crossing the valley, the Donner party camped near the southern shore of the lake.[4] It was now the third or fourth of September.

Luke Halloran, a consumptive who had come west for his health, died in George Donner's wagon while crossing the valley and was buried beside the grave of John Hargrave, one of the Hastings company, in what later became the Grantsville cemetery.

On the sixth of September they reached "Twenty Wells," now Grantsville, where they found plenty of good water and grass. Continuing the next day they found similar "wells" and plenty of grass all along the route, which was south in Skull Valley. Making camp at a good spring, they discovered fragments of paper lying about which were laboriously pieced together. It proved to be a note which read: "Two days—two nights—hard driving—cross desert—reach water." This had been fastened to a post near the spring, but the birds had picked it to pieces, and it was only with great difficulty that it was deciphered.

Hastings seems to have been entirely too impetuous and foolhardy to act as guide for emigrant trains, taking them over new

---

[3.] The tracks of these wagons where they emerged from Emigration Canyon were visible until 1960.

[4.] Near the springs at Lake Point.

and untried routes, and making many promises which he was unable to fulfill; it was probably Hudspeth who left the note.

While the Donner party is camped at the big spring at what is now called Iosepa in Skull Valley, let us see what James F. Reed has to say about his experiences in crossing the Great Salt Desert.

At the beginning of the journey in Independence, emigrant Hiram Miller began keeping a daily journal. He kept this record until he reached Fort Bernard where he traded his wagon for horses. At that place he turned his journal over to James F. Reed, who continued it from that place into California. In the part of the record kept by Reed he speaks of himself in the third person, as Miller would have done, but the handwriting is definitely that of Reed. This valuable record was first published by the Book Club of California.[5] It begins at Fort Bridger and is reproduced here as far as Pilot Peak using the version published in *West from Fort Bridger*. Since Reed said so little about his crossing of the Salt Desert, an account he wrote in 1871 supplements the diary. The section ends with Virginia Reed's moving account.

THE REED JOURNAL

Frid. [July] 31 [1846] We Started this morning on the Cut off rout by the South of the Salt Lake. & 4 1/2 miles from the fort there is a beautiful Spring Called the Blue Spring as Cold as Ice passed Several Springs and Encamped at the foot of the first steep hill going west making this day . . 12 [miles]

Sat. 1 Aug.ᵗ 1846—left Camp this morning early and passed through Several Valleys well watered with plenty of grass, and encamped at the head of Iron Spring Vall[e]y making 1515

Sund 2 this morning left Camp late on acct of an ox being missing Crossed over a high ridge or mountain with tolerable rough road an[d] encamped on Bear river making 16 on a little Creek abut 4 miles from Bear River we ought to have turned to the righ[t] and reached Bear Riv[er] in one mile much better road said to be

Mon 3 left our encampmt and traveled a tolerable rough Road Crossing Several very high hills and encamped at the head of a

---

5. Carroll D. Hall, ed., *Donner Miscellany: 41 Diaries and Documents* (San Francisco: Book Club of California, 1947).

larger Vall[e]y with a fine little running Stream passing by the edge
of of [sic] our Camp   Cattle plenty of grass Count[r]y appear more
hale west   Made this day 16

Tues 4   this day left our encampment about 2 oclock   Made
this day about 8   Our encamp was this day in red Run Valley
[three words interlineated:] fork of weaver

Wed 5   Started early and traveled the whole day in Red Run
Valley and encampe below its enterens [?] into Weavers Creek 15

Thur 6   left our encamp. about ten oclock and encamp above
the Cannon   here we turn to the left hand & Cross the Mountain
instead of the cann[o]n which is impassible although 60 waggons
passed through. this day made 10

Frid 7. in Camp on weaver at the mouth of Canon[6]

Sat 8   Still in Camp

Sond 9   Still in Camp

Mo 10   Still in Campe   James F. Reed this evening returned he
and two others having been sent by the Caravan to examine the
Canon and proceed after Mr Hastings, who left a Note on the on
the [sic] road that if we Came after him he would return and Pilot
us through his new and direct rout to the South end of the Salt
Lake Reed having examined the new rout entirely and reported in
favour, which induced the Compa[n]y to proceed

Tues 11   left Camp and took the new rout with Reed a Pilot he
having examined the mountains and vallies from the south end of
the Lake   this day made 5

Wed, 12   left Camp late and encampe on Bosman Creek on
New rout   made 2 [the numeral 3 over written with 2] [7]

Thur 13   Mad[e] a New Road by Cutting Willow Trees &
[encamped?] on Basman Creek   2 [again the numeral 3 is over-
written with 2]

Frid 14   Still on Basman Creek and proceeded up the Creek
about one mile and Turned to the right hand up a narrow valley to
Reeds Gap and encamped about one mile from the mouth making
this day 2 [Written in margin:] Spring of water

Sat. 15   in Camp all hands Cutting and op[e]ning a road
through the Gap.

---

6. Reed omits any mention of his experiences in meeting Hastings or
exploring the route ahead.

7. Beauchemin's Creek, now known as East Canyon Creek.

Son 16 Still Cl[e]earing and making Road in *Reeds Gap*.

Mon 17 Still in Camp and all hands working on the road which we finished and returned to Campe

Tus 18 this Morning all started to Cross the Mountain which is a Natural easey pass with a little more work and encamped making this day—5 J F Reed Brok[e] an axletree

Wed 19 this day we lay in Camp in a neat little valley fine water and good grass the hands ware this [day?] on the other on West Side of Small mountain, in a small Valley [Emigration Canyon] Clearing a road to the Vall[e]y of the Lake We have to Cross the outlett [Jordan River] of the Utah Lake on this Rout Nearr the Salt Lake

Thus 20 Still in Camp and hands Clearing road

Frid 21 this day we left camp and [this word crossed out] Crossed the Small mountain and encapd in the vally running into the Utah outlett making this day 4

Sat 22 this day we passed through the mountains and encampd in the Utah [Salt Lake] Valley making this day 2

Son 23 left Camp late this day on acct. of having to find a good road or pass through the Swamps of the utah outlet finally succeeded in and encamped on the East Bank of Utah outlett making 5

Mo 24 left our Camp and Crossed the plain to a spring at a point of the Lake mountain [Oquirrh Mountains] and 1½ miles from the road traveled by the people who passed the Cannon 12 [Written in margin:] Brackish Water [Written in margin still later:] It took 18 days to gett 30 miles

Tues 25 left Camp early this morning intending if possible to make the *Lower Wells* being fair water 20 which we made [Two words written in margin:] fair water and in the evening a Gentleman by the name of *Luke Halloran*, died of Consumption having been brough[t] from Bridgers Fort by George Donner a distance 151 miles we made him a Coffin and Burried him at the up[p]er wells at the forks of the road in a beautiful place. [8]

Wed 26 left Camp late and proceed^d to the upper wells One of them delightful water being entirely fresh the rest in No. about 10 all Brackish this day Buried Mr Luke Halloran hauling him in his Coffin this distan[ce] 2 which we only mad[e] and Buried heem

---

[8.] Grantsville. First burials in Grantsville Cemetery.

as above Stated at the forks of the [road] One Turning directly South to Camp the other West or onward.

Thur 27 left early this day and went west for half the day at the foot of the Lake [Stansbury] Mountains the latter 1/2 the day our Course S. W. to a No. of Brackish Wells making 16 *miserable water*

Frid 28 left Camp and glad to do, so, in hopes of finding fresh water on our way but without Success untill evening when it was time to Camp Came to a No of delightful fresh water wells   this Camp is at the Most Suthern point of the Salt Lake   20 miles North west we Commence the long drive   We are taking in water, Grass, and wood for the various requirements. 12

Sat 29 in Camp wooding watering and laying in a Supply of grass for our oxen and horses, to pass the long drive which Commence about [ ] miles   we have one encampment between but neither grass wood or water of sufficient quallety or quantity to be procured   water [one word written in margin:] *sulphur* Brackish, grass short and no wood—

Son 30   made this day—12 to a Sulpher Spring [Redlum Spring] in the mountain which ought to be avoidid   water not good for Cattle, emigrants Should keep on the edge of the lake and avoid the mountain entirely   here Commenced the long drive through the Salt dessert.

JAMES FRAZIER REED'S NARRATIVE OF 1871, DESCRIBING THE CROSSING OF THE SALT DESERT

We started to cross the desert traveling day and night only stopping to feed and water our teams as long as water and grass lasted. We must have made at least two-thirds of the way across when a great portion of the cattle showed signs of giving out. Here the company requested me to ride on and find the water and report. Before leaving I requested my principal teamster [Milford Elliott], that when my cattle became so exhausted that they could not proceed further with the wagons, to turn them out and drive them on the road after me until they reached the water, but the teamster misunderstanding unyoked them when they first showed symptoms of giving out, starting on with them for the water.

I found the water about twenty miles from where I left the company and started on my return. About eleven o'clock at night

[September 2] I met my teamster with all my cattle and horses. I cautioned them particularly to keep the cattle on the road, for that as soon as they would scent the water they would break for it. I proceeded on and reached my family and wagons. Some time after leaving the men one of the horses gave out and while they were striving to get it along, the cattle scented the water and started for it. And when they started with the horses, the cattle were out of sight, they could not find them or their trail, they told me afterward. They supposing the cattle would find water, went on to camp. The next morning they could not be found, and they never were, the Indians getting them, except one ox and one cow. Losing nine yoke of cattle here was the first of my sad misfortunes. I stayed with my family and wagons the next day, expecting every hour the return of some of my young men with water, and the information of the arrival of the cattle at the water. Owing to the mistake of the teamsters in turning the cattle out so soon, the other wagons had drove miles past mine and dropped their wagons along the road, as their cattle gave out, and some few of them reaching water with their wagons. Receiving no information and the water being nearly exhausted, in the evening [September 3] I started on foot with my family to reach the water. In the course of the night the children became exhausted. I stopped, spread a blanket and laid them down covering them with shawls. In a short time a cold hurricane commenced blowing; the children soon complained of the cold. Having four [five] dogs with us, I had them lie down with the children outside the covers. They were then kept warm. Mrs. Reed and myself sitting to the windward helped shelter them from the storm. Very soon one of the dogs jumped up and started out barking, the others following, making an attack on something approaching us. Very soon I got sight of an animal making directly for us; the dogs seizing it changed its course, and when passing I discovered it to be one of my young steers. Incautiously stating that it was mad, in a moment my wife and children started to their feet, scattering like quail, and it was some minutes before I could quiet camp; there was no more complaining of being tired or sleepy the balance of the night. We arrived about daylight [September 4] at the wagons of Jacob Donner, and the next in advance of me, whose cattle having given out, had been driven to water. Here I first learned of the loss of my cattle, it being the second day after they had started for the water. Leaving my family with

Mrs. Donner, I reached the encampment. Many of the people were out hunting cattle, some of them had got their teams together and were going back into the desert for their wagons. Among them Mr. Jacob Donner, who kindly brought my family along with his own to the encampment.

THE REED JOURNAL RESUMES

Mon [August] 31 in dessert

) drive of sixty miles 60

Tusdy Sepr 1 in dessert

Wed 2 in d[itt]o Cattl got in Reeds Cattl lost this night

Thusdy 3 in d[itt]o Some teams got in [last five words crossed out]

Fridy 4 in d[itt]o [these two words crossed out] lost Reeds Cattle 9 Yok[e] by Not driving them Carefule to water as directed by Reed—the rest of teams getting in and resting, Cattle all nearly given out [Six words written in margin:] Hunting Cattl 3 or 4 days

Sat 5 Still in Camp in the west Side of the Salt Dessert

Send 6 Started for Reeds waggon lying in the Salt Plains 28 miles from Camp Cached 2 waggs and other effects

Mon 7 Cam[e] in to Camp in the Night and the waggon Came in on Tuesdy morng

Tuesdy 8 Still fixing and resting Cattle

Weds 9 Mr Graves Mr Pike & Mr Brin loaned 2 Yoke of Cattle to J F Reed with one Yok[e] he had to bring his family waggon along

Thrs 10 left Camp and proceeded about [this word crossed out] up the lake bed 7

Frid 11 left the Onfortunate lake and mad[e] in the night and day– about 23 Encamped in a valley wher[e] the[re] is fine grass & water

Sat 12

Sond 13 left Camp and proceeded south in the Vally to fine sp[r]ing or Basin of water and grass—difficult for Teams Made this day 13

Mo 14 [this date written over the word "Sunday"] left the Basin Camp or Mad Woman Camp as all the women in Camp ware mad with anger and mad[e] this d[a]y to the Two mound Springs 14 [this figure written over an apparent 13]

Tus 15 left the 2 mound Sp[r]ings and Crossed the mountain

as usual and Camped in the West Side of a Vally and made this day about 14

Wed 16 left Camp Early this morig   Crossed flat mount[ai]n or Hills and encamped on the east sid[e] of a Rug[g]ed Mountain [Ruby Mountains]   plenty of grass & water   18   here Geo Donner lost little gray & his Cream Col. Mare Margrat—

Th 17 made this day South in the Mineral Vally about 16

Frid 18 this day lay in Camp

Sat 19 this day mad[e] in Mineral Vally 16 and encamped at a large Spring breaking out of from the and part of large Rock Stream la[r]ge enough to turn one pr [pair] Stone   passed in the evening about 10 Spring Branches Springs Rising about 300 Yds above where we Crossed

Son 20 this day made 10 up the Mineral Vally   passed last evening and this day 42 Beautiful Springs of fresh water

384 Miles from Bridger

Mon 21 Made 4 miles in Mineral Vally due South   turned to the west 4 miles through a flat in the mountain [Hastings or Overland Pass] thence W N W 7 miles in another vally [Huntington Valley] and encamped on a smal[l] but handsome littl[e] Branch or Creek [Huntington Creek] making in all 15 miles

Tues 22 Made this day nearly due North in Sinking Creek Val[le]y about ten miles owing to water   10

Wed 23 Made this day owing to water about Twelve 12 miles Still in Sinking Creek Valley—

Thrs 24 this day North west we mad[e] down Sinking Creek valley about 16 [this figure written over an apparent 17] and encamped at the foot of a Red earth hill   good grass and water wood plenty in the vallies Such as sage greace wood & cedar [?] 16—

Frid 25 September This day we made about Sixteen miles 16 for six miles a very rough Cannon a perfect Snake trail   encamped in the Cannon about 2 miles from its mout[h]

Sat 26 this day made 2 miles in the Cannon and traveleed to the Junction of Marys River   in all about 8

Marys River

Sond 27 Came through a Short Cannon and encamped above the first Creek (after the Cannon) on Marys River   6

Mond 28 this day after leaving Camp about 4 miles   J F Reed found Hot Springs   one as hot as boiling water   left the River

Crossed over the Mounta[in] to the west Side of a Can[n]. and encamp in Vally   12

Tus 29   This day 11 o.clock left Camp and went about 8 mil[e]s to the river a gain   2 graves   had 2 oxen taken by 2 Indians that Cam[e] with us all day

Wed 30 left Camp about 10 o clock and made this day 12 miles down the River

Thurs Oct 1 left Camp and made 15 miles down the River encamped on a Rich bottom   this night Mr Graves, lost a fine mare by the Indians

Fridy [Oct. 2] Still down the River   made to day 12 miles

Sat 3 left Camp early   made this day 10 miles

Son 4 Still—

[Here the diary closes. In the end pages are some calculations, appended to this chapter, evidently based on the mileages in the diary.]

EPILOGUE

Virginia E. B. Reed to her cousin Mary Gillespie
Napa Valley, California, May 16, 1847.

...o my Dear Cousin you dont [k]now what trubel is yet   a many a time we had on the last thing a cooking and did not [k]now wher the next would come from but there was awl wais some way provided   there was 15 in the cabon we was in and half of us had to lay a bed all the time   thare was 10 starved to death while we ware there   we was hadley abel to walk   we lived on litle cash a week and after Mr Breen would cook his meat and boil the bones   Two or three times we would take the bones and boil them 3 or 4 days at a time   Mama went down to the other cabin and got half a hide   carried it in snow up to her wast   it snowed and would cover the cabin all over so we could not get out for 2 or 3 days at a time   we would have to cut pieces of the loges in sied to make fire with. I coud hardly eat the hides   Pa stated out to us with provisions on the first of November and Came into the Great California Mountain, about 80 miles and in one of the Severest Storms Known for Years past, A raining in the Valley and a Hurrican of snow in the mountains   it Came so deep that the horses & mules Swamped So they could not go on any more   he cash his provision and went back on the other side of the bay to get a compana of men and the San Wakien got so hye he could not crose well thay Made up a Compana at Suters Fort and sent out   we had not ate any thing for 3 days & we had onely a half a hide and we was out on top of the cabin and we seen the party a coming

O my Dear Cousin you dont [k]now how glad i was, we run and met them   one of them we knew   we had traveled with them on the road   thay staid thare 3 days to recruet a little so we could go   thare was 20 started all of us started and went a piece and [8-year-old] Martha and [3-year-old] Thomas giv out and the men had to take them back   one of the party [Aquilla Glover] said he was a Mason and pledged his faith that if we did not meet pa in time he would come and save his children ma and Eliza James & I come on and o Mary that was the hades thing yet to come on and leiv them thar . . . did not now but what thay would starve to Death   Martha said well ma if you never see me a gain do the best you can   the men said thay could hadly stand it   it maid them all cry but they said it was better for all of us to go on for if we was to go back we would eat that much more from them   thay gave them a littel meat and flore and took them back and we come on   we went over great hye mountain as steap as stair steps in snow up to our knees   litle James walk the [w]hole way over all the mountain in snow up to his waist. . . . when we had traveld 5 days travel we met Pa with 13 men going to the cabins   o Mary you do not nou how glad we was to see him   we had not seen him for 5 months we thought we woul never see him again   he heard we was coming and he made some seet cakes the night before at his Camp to give us and the other Children withe us   he said he would see Martha and Thomas the next day   he went in tow day what took us 5 days   when pa went to the Cabins some of the compana was eating those that Died but Thomas & Martha had not ate any   Pa and the men started with 12 people   Hiram O Miller Carried Thomas and Pa caried Martha and thay were caught in a Snow Storm which lasted two days & nights and they had to stop   Two days it stormd so thay could not go and the Fishers took their provision and thay weer 4 days without any thing   Pa and Hiram and and all the men started [with] one of Donner boys Pa a carring Martha Hiram caring Thomas and the snow was up to thare wast and it a snowing so thay could hadly see the way   thay [w]raped the children up and never took them out for 4 days & thay had nothing to eat in all that time   Thomas asked for somthing to eat once

Those that thay brought from the cabins some of them was not able to come from the Starved Camp as it is called, and som would not come   Thare was 3 died and the rest eat them   thay was 10 days without any thing to eat but the Dead   Pa braught Thom and paty on to where we was   none of the men Pa had with him ware able to go back for Some people Still at the Cabins, there feet was froze very bad so thare was a nother Compana went and braught them all in   thay are all in from the Mountains now. . . . O Mary I have not wrote you half of the truble we have had but I hav Wrote you anuf to let you [k]now what truble is but thank god and [we were] the onely family that did not eat human flesh   we have left every thing but i dont cair for that we have got through with our lives but Dont let this letter dishaten anybody   never take no cutofs and hury along as fast as you can

*

The "Pioneer Palace Car" was left standing in the mud.[9] The others, after having been brought to Pilot Peak by friends, were abandoned. Jacob Donner and Keseberg also left one wagon each on the desert.

Recuperating their cattle here for several days, the company again set out on the sixteenth, traveling all day and until four o'clock the next morning before they found water. Here, at what is now called Flowery Lake, they made another cache of goods to lighten their loads and conserve the strength of their remaining cattle.

On account of the various delays they had experienced, the season was now so far advanced that they feared it would be impossible to get over the Sierra before snow fell in the mountain passes.

The numerous delays had also greatly diminished their supplies, and they were suddenly confronted with the fact that there would not be enough to last until they reached California. It was decided to send someone in advance of the party to try and obtain supplies from Captain John Sutter at Sutter's Fort.[10] Stanton and

---

[9.] Virginia Reed Murphy, "Across the Plains in the Donner Party," *The Century Illustrated Magazine*, 20 (July 1891), 409.

[10.] Miles Goodyear had built a stockade on the site of Ogden, Utah, in the fall of 1845, His ranch was not visible from the place where the emigrants emerged from the canyon. Goodyear took a pack train loaded with

McCutchen volunteered for this duty, and left immediately, reaching the mountains in time to cross with the stragglers of the Hastings' party. Stanton was young and unmarried, hence some feared he might not return; McCutchen left his family with the emigrants, and therefore they felt certain that he at least would not fail them. As it transpired McCutchen became ill and remained at Sutter's Fort, while Stanton, without any kindred in the company, finally made his way back through deep snow with supplies furnished by Sutter. He afterwards froze to death in a second attempt to reach Sutter's Fort.[11]

After numerous misfortunes, and after having many of their remaining cattle stolen or killed by Indians, the party reached the foot of the pass over the high Sierra. On account of the extremely emaciated condition of their cattle they failed to reach the summit at the first attempt, and returned to camp near what is now called Donner Lake. When they arose in the morning they discovered that the mountains were covered with snow. In spite of this, another attempt was made to cross, which again resulted in failure. On the third day three feet of snow fell at the camp, and the party was marooned, without supplies, for the winter.

The balance of this tragic story has been told so often that it will not be repeated here.[12] Attempt after attempt was made by different small parties on foot to get through to Sutter's Fort. Some of these remain the most heroic spectacles of all time. Women and small children braved thirty to fifty feet of snow in the dead of winter, without food of any kind, in an attempt to carry news of the plight of their comrades to those on the other side. Many of these died somewhere along the hundred miles of snow between Donner Lake and Sutter's Fort. Some few got through, more dead than alive, but although Sutter made heroic efforts and

---

deer and elk hides to Los Angeles in January, 1847, over the southern route discovered by Jedediah Smith and returned over the Hastings Cutoff in July.

11. The Bible which Stanton was carrying when he died was later recovered by George McKinstry and was recently discovered in the possession of a lady in Ogden, Utah.

12. McGlashan, *History of the Donner Party*; Houghton, *The Expedition of the Donner Party*.

time after time organized expeditions for their relief,[13] very few supplies ever reached them, and before relief finally came in the spring, they were compelled to eat the flesh of their dead companions. Only forty-four of those who started on the trek across the Salt Desert ever lived to see the land of promise.

During the winter which the Donner party spent at the foot of the snow-filled pass, but one Indian was seen. Toward spring this Indian passed near the camp. One of the men tried to get near enough to talk with him, hoping that the Indian could show them how and where to procure some sort of food. But the savage took fright and disappeared, after first leaving a few dried bulbs of some kind on the snow for the man who approached him.

The Indians who had harassed the emigrants on Truckee River, however, were not ignorant of the fate of those at the winter camp. Fortunately, the Indian story of their contact with the Donner party has been preserved by Sarah Winnemucca Hopkins, daughter of Chief Winnemucca, and granddaughter of Chief Truckee, in her book, *Life Among the Piutes*.

Sarah Winnemucca was born probably some time in 1841 or 1842. She was a very small girl when emigrants first began traveling the California Trail. The stories of these first white travelers were told and retold around the Indian campfires, and these she recounts briefly in her autobiography.

According to the Indian account, the Piutes were very anxious to be friendly with the white men who first came to Carson Valley, where they lived. The earliest emigrants avoided contact with the Indians, but later and stronger companies shot them down like rabbits, burning their rush dwellings and destroying their winter's food supply. For this reason the Piutes were hostile to all white men, in 1846, and it was their purpose to attack the trains when they could do so without danger to themselves, thus discouraging travelers from passing through their territory.

Speaking particularly of the Donner party Sarah Winnemucca says:

> This whole band of white people perished in the mountains, for it was too late to cross then. We could have saved them, only my people were afraid of them. We

---

13. George McKinstry, one of the Young and Harlan party under Hastings, was very active for their relief.

never knew who they were, or where they came from. So, poor things, they must have suffered fearfully, for they all starved there. The snow was too deep.[14]

Apparently the lone Indian who passed by the camp carried the news of what was happening there to Chief Winnemucca and old Truckee, his father. The Indians were dumbfounded when they heard that white men were actually eating one another, and fled to the mountains where they hid for a time, fearing that the white men would return and eat them. From that time on it was believed that white men were fond of killing and eating Indians, and little Sarah Winnemucca and other Indian children were constantly frightened into obedience by being told that if they were not good children the "white men would come and eat them up." This threat so thoroughly frightened the chief's little daughter that for a long time afterward, when emigrants came pouring through their country, she would run and hide with terror whenever a wagon train or a white man approached their camp.

This incident is a peculiar reversal of the old-time threat of white mothers, to the effect that if their children were not well-behaved "some bad Indian will get you." According to a legend of Winnemucca's people, they had at some time in the dim past exterminated a tribe of cannibal Indians who lived in a cave near the Sink. These Indians, so the story goes, were red-headed, and practiced cannibalism both on their own people and on captives. This practice so incensed the Piutes that, after many warnings, the tribe was finally besieged in a large cave and exterminated by fire and smoke. Strange to say, the ancient legend has proven to be true. Prof. Harrington, of the Southwest Museum, Los Angeles, discovered and excavated this same cave, near Lovelock, Nevada, in 1929.

*

Among those who started across the plains in 1846 was Captain Joseph Aram and family, accompanied by a few other emigrants, about twenty wagons in all. Captain Aram left Independence about the first of May; but he did not follow the regular trail taken by the majority of wagons that year. Instead, he struck the trail of the Mormons who had been ejected from Illinois

---

[14] Sarah Winnemucca Hopkins, *Life Among the Piutes: Their Wrongs and Claims* (Boston: Cupples, Upham & Co., 1883), 13.

early that year, and who were then encamped at Council Bluffs. Passing through the Mormon camp without being noticed, they pressed on, guided by Robidoux, and did not meet the Donner party again until they arrived at Green River. Captain Aram says:

Here we waited a few days. While there several emigrants arrived; the Donner party was amongst them. While there Captain Hastings arrived from California by way of Salt Lake. He advised us by all means to go that way, assuring us that we would save a month's travel, but our old pilot, Greenwood, who was familiar with the country, told us that it would be much safer to go by Fort Hall. After much talk many of the emigrants took Hastings' advice, particularly the Donner party. It was a fatal mistake for them. We had a very good road to Fort Hall, it being the advice of our pilot, Greenwood....

When we arrived at the point where the Hastings road would meet ours, as we were told by our pilot, we made a halt as there was plenty of grass. We rode one day's ride to see if we could learn anything of the Hastings party. All the intelligence we could get was from the Indians. They told us by signs that they were a long way off, and that they had lost many cattle.[15]

This story adds some interesting facts to the other narratives just reviewed. Old Caleb Greenwood had come east to the North Fork of the Humboldt with Hastings and Clyman, and at Fort Hall was engaged to guide Captain Aram's company; but Greenwood, who had guided the Bonney party over the Fort Hall Road in 1845, his second trip over that route, was fearful of trying to take wagons across the Salt Desert, and against the persuasion of Hastings, advised Captain Aram to take the well known trail, with the result that they passed on ahead of Hastings' party, instead of losing a month's travel, as had been predicted.

Arriving at the point where Frémont's trail intersected the Fort Hall Road, the place where Hastings and Clyman had turned off to cross the desert, Aram wrote that his party went back along that trail to see if they could hear anything of those who were crossing the desert. The Indians in that vicinity had seen nothing of Hast-

---

[15.] Joseph Aram, "Across the Continent in a Caravan," *Journal of American History* 1 (Fourth Quarter, 1907), 627–28.

ings' party, but news had already reached them that the emigrants had crossed the desert and lost many cattle. It is well that Captain Aram and Greenwood did not follow the trail farther, since as we have already seen, Hastings had turned south around the Ruby Mountains, and struck that river again below the place where Captain Aram stopped to look for him.

Aram's company eventually arrived at the Mission of Santa Clara, where the women and children were quartered while the captain and most of the other men joined Colonel Frémont's army of California Volunteers. On account of the dampness of the old deserted mission buildings, many died there that winter. Provisions were scarce, and when the emigrant volunteers returned from the campaign they were without their pay and practically destitute.

Before allowing Caleb Greenwood to pass out of this story, it might be well to insert here a short sketch of this mountain character given by Edwin Bryant in his *What I Saw in California*. After spending some weeks in California, Bryant and some companions started on October 30, 1846, to join Frémont at Monterey. Greenwood, by this time, had arrived with Captain Aram's company, and had then gone on a hunting expedition with his family. Bryant and his friends got lost in the mountains and valleys somewhere between Sutter's Fort and Monterey, and wandered around for some time. Then he says:

Descending into the valley, we travelled along a small stream two or three miles, and were continuing on in the twilight, when we heard the tinkling of a cow-bell on the opposite side of the stream. Certain, from this sound, that there must be an encampment near, I halted and hallooed at the top of my voice. The halloo called forth a similar response, with an interrogation in English, "Who the devil are you—Spaniards or Americans?" "Americans." "Show yourself, then, damn you, and let us see the color of your hide," was the answer.

"Tell us where we can cross the stream and you shall soon see us," was our reply.

"Ride back and follow the sound of my voice, and be damned to you, and you can cross the stream with a deer's jump."

Accordingly, following the sound of the voice of this rough colloquist, who shouted repeatedly, we rode back in the dark several hundred yards, and plunging into the stream, the channel of which was deep, we gained the other side, where we found three men standing ready to receive us. We soon discovered them to be a party of professional hunters or trappers, at the head of which was Mr. Greenwood, a famed mountaineer, commonly known as "Old Greenwood." They invited us to their camp...about half a mile distant....

We found in the camp, much to our gratification after a long fast, an abundance of fat, grisly bear-meat, and the most delicious and tender deer-meat. The camp looked like a butcher's stall. The pot filled with bear-flesh was boiled again and again, and the choice pieces of the tender venison were roasting, and disappearing with singular rapidity for a long time. Bread there was none, of course. Such a delicacy is unknown to the mountain trappers, nor is it much desired by them.

The hunting party consisted of Mr. Greenwood, Mr. Turner, Mr. Adams, and three sons of Mr. Greenwood, one grown, and the other two boys 10 or 12 years of age, half-breed Indians, the mother being a Crow....Mr. Greenwood, or "Old Greenwood," as he is familiarly called, according to his own statement, is 83 years of age, and has been a mountain trapper between 40 and 50 years. He lived among the Crow Indians where he married his wife, between thirty and forty years. He is about six feet in height, raw-boned and spare in flesh, but muscular, and notwithstanding his old age, walks with all the erectness and elasticity of youth. His dress was of tanned buckskin, and from its appearance one would suppose its antiquity to be nearly equal to the age of its wearer. It had probably never been off his body since he first put it on. "I am," said he, "an old man—eighty-three years—it is a long time to live;—eighty-three years last—.[16] I have seen

---

[16.] Old Greenwood had been with the party who discovered South Pass, had trapped with Jedediah Smith, Jim Bridger, Thomas Fitzpatrick, and had lived with the Crow Indians when the famous Jim Beckwourth was their chief. He may have visited California in 1826, which would account for his seeing that country "twenty years ago." The Beer Springs he

all the Injun varmints of the Rocky Mountains,—have fout them—lived with them. I have many children—I don't know how many, they are scattered; but my wife was a Crow. The Crows are a brave nation,—the bravest of all the Injuns; they fight like the white man; they don't kill you in the dark like the Black-foot varmint, and then take your scalp and run, the cowardly reptiles. Eighty-three years last—; and yet old Greenwood could handle the rifle as well as the best of 'em, but for this infernal humor in my eyes, caught three years ago on bringing the emigrators over the *de*-sart" (A circle of scarlet surrounded his weeping eyeballs). "I can't see jist now as well as I did fifty years ago, but I can always bring the game, or the slinking and skulking Injun. I have jist come over the mountains...with the emigrators as pilot, living upon bacon, bread, milk, and sichlike mushy stuff. It don't agree with me; it never will agree with a man of my age, eighty-three last—; that is a long time to live. I thought I would take a small hunt to get a little exercise for my old bones, and some good fresh meat, The grisly bear, fat deer, and poultry, and fish—them are such things as a man should eat. I came up here where I knew there was plenty. I was here twenty years ago, before any white man see this lake and the rich land about it. It's filled with big fish. Thar's beer-springs here, better than them in the Rocky Mountains; thar's a mountain of solid brimstone, and thar's mines of gold and silver, all of which I know'd many years ago, and I can show them to you if you will go with me in the morning. These black-skinned Spaniards have rebel'd again. Wall, they can make a fuss, damn 'em, and have revolutions every year, but they can't fight. It's no use to go arter 'em, unless when you ketch 'em you kill 'em. They won't stand an' fight like men, an' when they can't fight longer, give up; but the skared varmints run away and then make another fuss, damn 'em."[17]

---

speaks of were at Soda Springs, Idaho. He had piloted the Stephens-Townsend-Murphy party in 1844, the first wagons to cross the Sierra.

[17.] Bryant, *What I Saw in California*, 353–56.

12. FURTHER ACTIVITIES OF HASTINGS

When Hastings arrived at Sutter's Fort, he found the American flag already flying, and Colonel Frémont recruiting volunteers for a campaign against the Mexicans. General Zachary Taylor had settled matters in the south, and the rule of Mexico in California was practically over. Hastings' long-cherished dream of being president of California was suddenly ended, and his frantic efforts to bring in settlers brought him no reward.

He was, however, apparently not one to grieve long over disappointment. Finding his plans frustrated, he did the next best thing under the circumstances, and volunteered to serve under Frémont, offering the services of the emigrants he had just brought over the mountains. For this offer he was elected captain of Company F, California Volunteers. These emigrants, together with Bryant and all the members of his party, served with distinction until the end of the campaign.[1]

The following entries in *Three Years in California*, the diary of Rev. Walter Colton, then acting as alcalde of Monterey, will throw some light on the activities of the emigrants during this campaign:

Oct. 31, 1846—Enlistments are going on actively among the emigrants recently arrived on the banks of the Sacramento. The women and children are placed in the missions; the men take the rifle and start for the battlefield: such is their welcome to California.

Nov. 12—Capt. Hastings is expected every day from San José with sixty men, well mounted, and twice that number of horses.

Jan. 5, 1847—Many of the emigrants who have recently arrived are now with Col. Fremont at the south....They are now receiving twenty-five dollars a month, and have few temptations for spending it; they will consequently find themselves in funds, small to be sure; but there is a period in almost every man's life when a penny takes the importance of a pound.

---

[1] Bancroft, *History of California*, V:359–60.

July 17—*That* unshrinking arm of the nation [the army] has done its work well and fast elsewhere, but only the vibrations of its blows have trembled across the confines of California. For matter of these the Mexican flag would still be flying over these hills and valleys. The seamen of the Pacific squadron, as reliable on land as faithful on the deck, and the emigrants, who have come here to find a home, have wrenched this land of wealth and promise from the grasp of Mexico, and unfurled the stars and stripes where they will wave evermore. Let the laurel light where it belongs.[2]

While at Sutter's Fort in February, 1846, Hastings laid out the town of Sutterville, now included in the city of Sacramento, being assisted in this by John Bidwell, who had crossed the desert in 1841 and had ever since been employed by Sutter. Hastings apparently expected a large emigration of Mormons overland in 1846 and was preparing to locate them as soon as they had crossed the mountains; Sutterville was intended for a Mormon settlement. When the Saints failed to arrive, Sam Brannan, who had some understanding with Hastings in this matter, had gone east early in the spring of 1847, to meet Brigham Young somewhere along the trail and guide him on to California. Brannan crossed the Sierra, passed the last survivor of the Donner party (Keseberg) being brought in to Sutter's Fort, and was the first aside from the relief parties, to view the horrors there revealed by the melting snow.

Brannan, full of enthusiasm for California, met the first company of Mormons not far from Hastings' old camp east of Fort Bridger, but was unable to persuade Brigham Young to continue on to the Pacific Coast; he returned to Sutter's Fort highly disgusted. Some sharp correspondence passed between these two Mormon leaders, and when Brigham later sent an emissary to California to bring to Zion the tithe of gold which Brannan had industriously collected from the members of his colony at Mormon Island, he refused to deliver the gold until, as he said, Brigham

---

[2] Walter Colton, *Three Years in California* (New York: A. S. Barnes & Co., 1850), 83, 92, 142, 201–02. Colton had been a chaplain in the navy. On account of trouble between Frémont, Kearny and Stockton as to which was the superior officer, the California Volunteers were never paid.

should give him a receipt signed by the Lord.[3] Brannan shortly after severed all connection with the church, started a store at Sutter's Fort, and in a year or two became the wealthiest man in California. While waiting for a receipt from Brigham, he invested the Lord's tithe in real estate.

Hastings, in promoting personally conducted tours to the West and in laying out the subdivision of Sutterville, claims a niche in the hall of fame as California's first realtor.

In spite of the defeat of his personal ambitions, Hastings seems to have been still interested in the welfare of the emigrants.[4] Josiah Royce, in his *California*, quotes the following from the *Californian* of March 13, 1847, written by Hastings under the nom-de-plume of "Paisano":

> "Those," he says "who have recently emigrated to this country came here with the well-founded [?] expectation that under the Mexican laws they would be enabled to secure a tract of land immediately upon their arrival; but they have been disappointed; and shall I state the cause of that disappointment?...It is simply this: The United States have acquired possession."...The remedy is, according to Paisano, "that the legislature be organized without delay, and that immediately upon their organization they proceed to the enactment of a law upon the subject. Let this law provide that every man shall be entitled to a certain quantity of government land; and let it further provide that, in order to acquire a legal right to the possession of the same, it shall be necessary for the claimant to have his lands surveyed and recorded. A law of this kind, I apprehend, would remove at once the chief cause of disappointment among the people."[5]

[3.] James A.B. Scherer, *The First Forty-Niner and the Story of the Golden Tea-Caddy* (New York: Minton, Balch & Company, 1925).

[4.] His interest, however, did not cause him to exert himself in behalf of the Donner party in their distress. He was in San Francisco when Reed arrived there on October 28, 1846 asking for assistance, but Bryant, who was with him, does not mention any effort on his part to relieve the people who were in distress through following his advice.

[5] Josiah Royce, *California* (New York: Houghton, Mifflin and Company, 1886. Reprinted Santa Barbara: Peregrine Publishers, Inc., 1970), 164.

Aside from the fact that there was no "well-founded expectation," his argument is sound, And it speaks well for him that, in spite of the great difficulties into which he led the emigrants, they sent him to the constitutional convention when it finally convened in 1849. This convention was presided over by Robert Semple, the giant who had accompanied Hastings over the Sierra on Christmas day, 1845, and the founder of California's first newspaper.

After various attempts to found new cities in California, Hastings was appointed judge for the northern district, a position for which his legal training fitted him. But the vocation of judge did not suit his restless temperament, and we later find him in various enterprises. At one time he recruited a company of volunteers to quell an imaginary uprising in the south. In the *Californian* of March 15, 1848, which contains the first announcement of the discovery of gold, we find an advertisement announcing the opening of Hastings' law office following communication from that gentleman himself concerns the "imaginary uprising":

In compliance with the orders of Governor Mason, the undersigned will visit all the principal towns and settlements in the Northern Department of California, for the purpose of conferring with the people in reference to the necessity of raising a Battalion of Volunteers in California, for the service in the south; and for the purpose of enlisting those of our patriotic citizens who feel a desire and determination to sustain the....[one line indistinct].

For the above purpose he will be, and remain at New Helvetia, from the 17th to the 22nd instant; at Suisan and Montezuma, from the 25th to the 28th; at Sonoma from the 3rd inst, to the 5th of April; at Benecia from the 6th to the 8th; at the Pueblo San Jose from the 10th to the 14th; and at San Francisco, from the 16th to the 20th of April.

While at the above places he will be prepared to give all those who desire to enlist all necessary information, relative to the terms of their enrolment, pay, &c. &c.

Persons at, or in the vicinity of San Francisco, wishing to enlist, will apply to G. H. Johnson, in San Francisco, for that purpose, at any time prior to the 20th of April, when all will be mustered into the service, as above stated.

L. W. HASTINGS.

In 1848 Lansford Warren Hastings was married to Charlotte C. Toler. In the late 1850s he moved to Yuma, Arizona, which was at that time headquarters for numerous filibustering expeditions into Mexico. He returned to California in 1862, his wife dying soon afterward. He then put his daughter in a convent at Benicia and returned to Mexico on some unknown business.

Hastings, although born in Ohio, became a sympathizer with the cause of the Confederacy. This may have been due to the influence of his father-in-law, who was a Virginian; but it is more probable that the underlying reason was his personal disappointment in not being able to make himself the leader of a great or spectacular movement, which seems to have been his burning ambition. Frustrated in this, he joined the Confederate cause, hoping to gain future prestige. For two or three years he served in the Confederate army, and his elaborate plans for the seizure of Arizona and New Mexico, revealed by his letters to Jefferson Davis, were only frustrated by the lack of money to execute them.

In 1867 Hastings spent six months in Brazil, seeking a suitable location for a colony of disappointed Confederates. He returned to Mobile, Alabama, and published his *Emigrant's Guide to Brazil*, hoping thereby to induce a large immigration to his new colony, as he had done previously in California. One shipload of colonists made the trip, and another followed the next year.[6] Only one copy of the *Emigrant's Guide to Brazil* is known to exist, owned by Albert Spence of Los Angeles, a grandson. Hastings died some time during the voyage with the second shipload of colonists, in the late 1870s.[7]

---

[6]. Biographical material from William J. Hunsaker, "Lansford Warren Hastings, Empire Dreamer and California Pioneer," *The Grizzly Bear* (May 1930). Hastings was an uncle of Mr. Hunsaker's mother.

[7]. For the final results of this colonization scheme see James E. Edwards, "'They've Gone—Back Home!' The Last of a Confederate Colony," *Saturday Evening Post* (January 4, 1941).

Bancroft says of him: "He was an intelligent, active man, never without some grand scheme on hand, not overburdened with conscientious scruples, but never getting caught at anything very disreputable."[8]

Of the Reverend McDonald who assisted in raising the money to publish Hastings' book, nothing further is known than that he preceded Hastings to California, probably in the summer of 1845, and tended bar in Voiget's saloon where Hastings later met him. If the money he collected for missionary purposes went into the "California Booster Fund," it might still be said that it was spent for missionary work, and the associated realtors of California will surely not hold it against him,

Hudspeth, who seems to have been the silent partner, had come to California with Hastings in 1843, having been a member of Dr. Elijah White's party to Oregon in 1842, He was a surveyor, and together with O'Farrell, laid out the town of Benicia for Dr. Robert Semple. He settled on a ranch near the head of navigation of the Sacramento. His housekeeper was an English girl who had escaped from Salt Lake City in an emigrant wagon. Hudspeth was a member of the California legislature in 1852.

---

8. Bancroft, *History of California*, III:779.

13. THE CUTOFF IN 1847

News of the Donner disaster reached the States too late in 1847 to have been responsible for the small California immigration of that year; unsettled conditions resulting from the war with Mexico probably kept the movement in check. Those who did go to California met eastbound travelers along the way who described the horrors at Donner Lake, and such reports may have had some part in persuading immigrants to keep to the older, well-known roads; there is no record of any wagon companies attempting the Salt Desert route in 1847.

There were, however, two eastbound parties of horsemen who this year traversed the Hastings Cutoff from its junction with the Humboldt River to Salt Lake Valley. Miles Goodyear, a trapper and trader who already had established a small post and farm on the site of Ogden, Utah, had taken a pack train load of dressed buckskins to California in 1846. Starting east from Sutter's Fort on June 2, 1847, with two Indian vaqueros to help manage his herd of California horses, he and his companions, John Craig, Truett and others as yet unidentified, decided to try the Hastings Cutoff, out of curiosity to see where the Donner party had met so much difficulty. They had been informed of the route by survivors of that expedition. Fortunately, a letter has just been discovered which describes this journey. While it is lacking a signature, internal evidence indicates it was written John Craig, from Ray County, Missouri, who had gone to California with a party of eight in 1846. The writer says:

> On my return home I suplyed myself with seven mules with packs and all things nessey and in company with seven others we started for home. On the 2th of June. On the fifth day we crosed the peak of the California mountains and had to travel about thirty five miles over snow varying from five to twenty foot deep and rode over numerous mountain streams on arches of Snow whilst we could hear the water roaring and dashing under our feet.

> My curiosity prompted me to return a Some what different road from that we went out For the war and death of Mr Standly [Larkin Stanley] prevented me going to Ore-

gon So I returned by the way of the great Salt lake running South of it and not far from the Utaw lake.

And with a few exceptions a more drery Sandy and barren country dose not (in my opinion) exist on Gods footstool. Excepting the great African desert. The intire country having a streaking and volcanic aprearence and abonding with hot and even boiling Springs. And if the different parts of our continents is cursed in proportion to the Sins of the inhabitants that formerly dwelt on them Then indeed must those ancient inhabitants have been awfully wicked for this is truly a land the Lord has cursed.

On one occasion we traveled over a vast Sandy and Salt plane a distenc of at least Seventy five miles without either grass or water and lost four head of horses that perished for want of water. We was 22 hours constantly traveling before we got to water And when we did come at a Spring the great Salt Lake lay off in full view having a number of high rocky barren Islands all through it.

But close arand the lake between the beach and high mountains that Serand it is considerable of rich land with abundanc of good spring water and ocasionaly Salt Springs But even here the county is nearly destitute of timber Onely here and thair a patch of willow and cotten wood on the Streams and a little ceeder and pine on the mountain arand. And the fourth and fifth of July I seen these mountains white in places with snow close arand the lake.[1]

This letter, which is reproduced in part through the courtesy of Mr. M. S. MacCarthy, of Glendale, California, omits to mention the writer's companions, particularly the mountaineer Miles Goodyear, [2] who was the real leader of this expedition; it also strangely fails to speak of the Donner wagons still standing on the desert and viewed by this party for the first time since their abandonment in 1846.

---

[1] Charles Kelly, "Gold Seekers on the Hastings Cutoff," *Utah Historical Quarterly* 20 (January 1952), 4–5.

[2] Charles Kelly and Maurice L. Howe, *Miles Goodyear* (Salt Lake City: Western Printing Company, 1937), 69–75.

Continuing east with his horse herd to trade with immigrant trains, Goodyear met the Mormon advance on the Bear River, July 10, 1847, reporting the desert route just traveled as unfit for wagons.

The second expedition was that of Captain James Brown who was returning from California with pay due the Sick Detachment of the Mormon Battalion. Tullidge records that:

...agreeable with directions which they had received from a surviving member of the Hastings company of emigrants...they left the old Fort Hall route, and took what was called "Hastings' cut-off." They had been informed that by taking this course they would reach Salt Lake with at least two hundred miles less travel. This course led them southward across what is known as the "Seventy-five-mile desert."

By the time they had reached the Humboldt their provisions had entirely given out, and their horses being considerably reduced in flesh they were unable to travel very fast, and the country had not proven as prolific in game as they had expected. They had yet to encounter their greatest foe. It was the desert of seventy-five miles in width. The weather was getting very cold, and light snow storms had not been infrequent from the time they had left the Humboldt region. They had supplied themselves with nothing in which to carry any quantity of water to speak of, and when they came to the desert they simply had to stem the hideous foe by launching out into this stretch of alkali bed with a determination to go through.

Three days were consumed in accomplishing the journey across the desert. They found water the third day about 2 o'clock. Some of the animals had given out, and had been left on the desert. For three days these five men had subsisted on three very lean geese which Jesse had killed the day before the company arrived at the desert; and during that length of time they had no water. One or two members of the party gave out, and were so weak that they had to be assisted on their horses by emaciated comrades. They arrived in Salt Lake City about the 1st of December, 1847, in an exceedingly broken up condition. This trip had reduced Captain Brown from 200 avoirdupois to 150, and the other members of the company were proportionately reduced.[3]

This party consisted of Captain James Brown, his son Jesse, Samuel Lewis, Lysander Woodworth, and Abner Blackburn. They left Sutter's Fort on September 5, 1847, and arrived in Salt Lake City November 16, notwithstanding the two different dates given by Tullidge. Fortunately we have a parallel account of their experiences by Abner Blackburn, an accurate observer, whose native humor, in spite of great adversities, is refreshing:

We shot more rabbits and hares. They went well with our boiled wheat. There was an awful goneness in our stomacks all the time....

Our boss[4] was a jolly chap. He would tell some outlandish story and put all in a good humor.

We next crost a salt plain.[5] The ground grass and the bushes were stiff with salt. One could smell it in the air. We were affraid to look behind for fear of being turned into a pillar of salt like Lots wife. I am sure we were no better than she was.

We expected to come to the Ninty Three Mile Desert anny time. Next morning [we] fill[ed] the canteens full of watter [and] cut some sage wood for the horses to eat.... Struck out and about noon began to be thirsty and drank spareingly and come to a large spring of good water.[6] We were not on it [yet].

Campt and prepared in earnest this time. Went on top of a high hill and could see far ahead on the dry bed of the old lake. The Salt Lake coverd a vast extent on the southern side of the lake at one time in the past and this is called the great dessert. Made preparation this time and no mistake.

---

3. Edward W. Tullidge, *Tullidge's Histories (Volume II), Northern Utah and Southern Idaho, Biographical Supplement* (Salt Lake City: Juvenile Instructor, 1889), 104–105.

4. Captain Brown.

5. Tecoma Valley.

6. Base of Pilot Peak.

Killed two crains. Layed in more wood [and] cooked an extra lot of wheat. Capt. Brown said he would cook it himself so as to have one good mess on the desert. He commenced to dance around and sing a dilly.

Pretty Betty Martin, tip toe fine.
She could not get a man to suit her mind.
Some were too coarse and some too fine.
She could not get a man to suit her kind.

At last word, he kicked out his foot and spilt all in the fire and cooked another.

In the morning the north wind was blowing cold. Started on the smooth bed of the ancient lake. Nothing but baked mud [with] no shells or sign of marine life. We supposed the watter had receded to the north. There appeard a mirage away to the north, but we could not tel[l] whether it was watter or not.

The [lake] bed we were traveling on appeard level and extend[ed] to the south as far as the eye could reach. It appeard like a few inches rise in the lake would send the watter over hundreds of miles of the old bed of the lake.

Not a bird, bug, hare, or coyote [was] to be seen on this wide desolate waist. Nothing but man and he was out of his lattitude or his natural seane. There was a mountain in the middle of this vast plain[7] and [it] appeard as though it had been surrounded by the lake at some past time. The wind blew cold and chilly as though it come off the watter towards us. This lake was in my old geography [named] Timpanagos and to the South to the Hela river was marked the unexplored regions.

[By] evening the ground was a little soft and the horses fag[g]ed out. Stopt at some abandoned waggons.[8] We

---

7. Newfoundland Mountains.

8. Except for Miles Goodyear and his party, no other white men had passed the Donner wagons since their abandonment, and this is the first written record by anyone who saw them. In 1929 I found at this spot the remains of five wagons, the number abandoned by the Donners, widely scattered. There was no large accumulation of tires and wagon irons, such as would have been seen if several wagons had been burned in one place. However, the remains found consisted mostly of wheels, which showed no

were cold [and] pulled the waggons togeather, set them on fire and had a good warm. Tied the horses [and] threw them the wood to eat. Rolled up in our blankets and the first night on the desert was gone.

The second day at noon, [we] left the bed of the lake and worried along until night whear there was som[e] little grass and some snow in drifts. The horses licked it up and so did we, for the watter was out.

Next day worried along and left one horse. [We] crost over a low mountain[9] and struck watter.[10] And now for rest. We had some brandy along and blew it in, which revived us excedingly. In the evening the horse we left behind come into camp. He thought it was a hard place to die and changed his notion. We forgot all about the desert and had a good supper of boiled hare, crane, and wheat.

In the morning [we] went down into a wider plain[11] and by the looks of the oposite mountain thought it was the Salt Lake Valley. The canion and other points looked familiar to us and [we] thought our journey ended. Our boss says, "Toot your horn Gabriel! We are most there."

The weather thickened up and began to snow. Expected to come to the Jordan River every hour. Come to riseing ground [and] then we knew we were mistaken in the country. Followed the mountain north to the Lake. Turned around the promi[n]tory on the beach of the lake[12] and camped under some shelving rocks, whitch shelterd us from the snow storm. Here we were on the shore of the great Timpanagos Lake, so named in the old geography. The sun rose clear the next morning [and] we could [see] in the distance about twenty miles. The smoke of the chimneys and all else looked right. One of the boys said he could hear the chickens crow....

---

signs of fire, and it may be that Brown's party gathered wagon boxes, rather than entire wagons, for burning.

9. Cedar Mountain.

10. Redlum Spring.

11. Tooele Valley.

12. Near Garfield townsite.

About three oclock we were on Jordans stormy banks and went up into the camp of the Saints, the New Jerusalem. Arived 16 November 1847....[13]

---

13. Will Bagley, ed., *Frontiersman: Abner Blackburn's Narrative* (Salt Lake City: University of Utah Press, 1992), 115–18.

14. THE STANSBURY EXPEDITION

On July 24, 1847, Brigham Young and the rear-guard of the Mormon Pioneer company reached Salt Lake Valley and founded Salt Lake City. This company had followed the trail of the Donner party, made the year before down Emigration Canyon, covering in a few days the distance which the Donners had spent three weeks in accomplishing. Salt Lake City was soon laid out at the foot of the mountains a little to the north of the Donner trail across the valley, and crops were planted that same year. Emigrants from the east during following years made it a point to pass through this new settlement, since it was the only town between Independence and Sutter's Fort. Having arrived at the Mormon village there were two routes by which they could reach California—one went north along the eastern shore of the lake until it intersected the Fort Hall Road; the other crossed the Salt Desert.

The fate of the Donner party, however, had been broadcast throughout the east, and for this reason no emigrant trains attempted the latter route during the years of 1847–48.

By 1849 the gold rush had begun; the Oregon Trail and the Fort Hall Road to California were crowded with excited gold-seekers. Transcontinental travel had assumed such proportions that the government interested itself in trying to locate shorter and better roads through the Great Basin. One of these surveying parties was under the command of Captain Howard Stansbury, who came west with instructions to survey a new road between Fort Hall and Salt Lake City, and also to survey and map Great Salt Lake.

Stansbury arrived in Salt Lake City on August 28, 1849. The Mormons had heard rumors that a company of troops were being sent to oust them from the lands which they had occupied, and they felt considerable anxiety. It was reported to Stansbury that the lives of himself and his men would not be safe in the Mormon colony. Stansbury, however, disregarded these warnings and upon his arrival went immediately to Brigham Young and stated the reason for his visit, convincing the prophet that his expedition was of a purely scientific nature.[1] Thereafter the surveying party was given every assistance in its work, and at the Pioneer Day celebration of the next year Captain Stansbury and Lieutenant Gunnison were honored guests.[2]

Except for the Stansbury party there was only one other party who took the Salt Desert route in 1849, as far as historical records available in 1969 show, and before recounting Stansbury's experience it might be well to list it.

J. Goldsborough Bruff mentions this party very briefly. It was captained by Dr. John McNulty and known as the Colony Guards. McNulty was a friend of Bruff, and the two companies passed and repassed each other several times on their journey across the plains. McNulty stopped in Salt Lake City to lay in supplies, where his party split, part going by way of the Southern Route (Old Spanish Trail) and part under McNulty taking the Hastings Cutoff. Bruff next met McNulty along the Humboldt River, where McNulty told Bruff about crossing the salt flats where, as Bruff briefly says "they suffered much."[3] We have no other information on this party and we do not know the exact date of their passing.

Being occupied first in locating a better road to Fort Hall, it was not until October 20 that Stansbury began his survey of the lake. He had been told that it would be utter folly to attempt a circuit of the lake so late in the season. But he did not wish to lie idle all winter and so decided to make the survey in spite of warnings. Following the eastern shore he finally reached the north end of the lake and struck out in the general direction taken by the Bartleson party in 1841. He had as guide a man who had crossed the desert with Frémont in 1845, probably Archambault, but whose name he unfortunately neglected to mention. The party, without any previous knowledge of the country, were often in difficulties, and when they reached Pilot Peak on October 29, had been sixty hours without water. But let Stansbury tell his own

---

[1] Howard Stansbury, *Exploration and Survey of the Valley of the Great Salt Lake of Utah.*

[2] *Deseret News*, August 10, 1850.

[3] Georgia Willis Read and Ruth Gaines, eds. *The Journals, Drawings and Other Papers of J. Goldsborough Bruff*, 2 volumes (New York: Columbia University Press, 1944), I:562.

story. After leaving the last waterhole on the journey toward Pilot Peak, he says:

Oct. 27—Resuming our journey, we took a course south by east, which led us past the ridge upon which we had halted two nights before....We then passed along the base of a range of low hills...After traveling ten miles, we came to a range of higher hills extending northwest and southeast...We then passed, in a southerly direction, through deep sand, along what at one time had been the beach of the lake....The country to-day has been similar to that passed over previously—dry, barren, and entirely destitute of water. We dug a well some five feet deep on the edge of the flat, which soon filled with water. The mules crowded around the hole, and seemed to watch the process of our labor, as if sensible of the object of our exertions, but upon tasting the water, refused to drink, although they had been travelling all day without a drop.

Oct, 28—Our little stock of water had become so reduced that we were compelled to forego our coffee this morning, and the most rigid economy in the use of the former was strictly enforced. We were on the road very early, and followed for several miles, down the edge of the sand at the foot of the range of hills on our right, when we ascended it...The ridge was about five miles wide....

Leaving the ridge, we entered upon a plain or sort of bay, partly covered with artemesia, and partly with mud and salt....The plain contained several island mountains, rising from it as from the water. To one of these, distant about twelve miles...we directed our course and reached it about an hour before sunset. Here we stopped for a short time to prepare our scanty supper....Not a drop of water had we met with the whole day; but at noon I had ordered a pint to be served out to each animal. Before arriving at this spot, one of the poor creatures "gave out," and we thought we would have to leave him to the wolves, but he afterward partially recovered, and another pint of water being given him, he went on....

It now became a matter of serious importance to find water for the mules, as they had been without for nearly forty hours, most of the time under the saddle, and al-

most without food. Nothing, therefore, remained but to
go on during the night, so as to reach the western ridge
bounding this basin as early the following day as practicable. We accordingly saddled up about dark and proceeded on the same course, directing our steps toward
another island in the plain, which appeared to be about
fifteen miles distant....Our course lay over a flat of damp
clay and salt mud, in many places soft and deep, which
made the travelling slow and laborious. All trace of vegetation had vanished, and even the unfailing artemesia had
disappeared. The animals were so tired and weak that the
whole party was on foot, driving our herd before us. The
mule which had given out in the afternoon was now unable to proceed, and had to be abandoned in the midst of
the plain, where it no doubt perished. Many others
showed symptoms of extreme exhaustion, so that their
packs had to be shifted and lightened repeatedly. I began
to entertain serious fears that I should not be able to
reach the mountain with them; nor was I certain that
when we did reach it we should be able to find water in
time to save their lives. The night was consequently
passed in a state of great anxiety. We continued on until
after midnight...when we reached a small isolated butte,
which was only a pile of barren rocks, with scarce a blade
of grass upon it. Wood or water there was none; so, although the night was quite cold, we laid ourselves down,
fireless and supperless, upon the sand, wearied to exhaustion by a continuous march of eighteen hours....

Oct. 29—On awaking early, we found the mules gathered
around us, looking very dejected and miserable. They had
searched in vain for food, and were now in nearly a starving condition. Before us, indeed, lay the mountain where
we hoped to find both food and water for them, but between lay a mud-plain fifteen or twenty miles in extent,
which must be crossed before we could reach it. I was
much afraid the animals were too weak to succeed in the
attempt, but it was our only hope. We set out, the whole
party on foot, pursuing the same general course....

The first part of the plain consisted simply of dried mud,
with small crystals of salt scattered thickly over the sur-

face. Crossing this, we came upon another portion of it, three miles in width, where the ground was entirely covered with a thin layer of salt...of so soft a consistence that the feet of our mules sank at every step into the mud beneath. But soon we came upon a portion of the plain where the salt lay in a solid state, in one unbroken sheet, extending apparently to its western border....Our mules walked upon it as upon a sheet of solid ice....

At two o'clock in the afternoon we reached the western edge of the plain, when to our infinite joy we beheld a small prairie or meadow, covered with a profusion of good green grass, through which meandered a small stream of pure fresh running water, among clumps of willows and wild roses, artemesia and rushes.[4] It was a most timely and welcome relief to our poor famished animals, who had now been deprived of almost all sustenance for more than sixty hours, during the greater part of which they had been in constant motion. It was, indeed, nearly as great a relief to me as to them, for I had been doubtful whether even the best mule we had could have gone more than half a dozen miles further. Several of them had given out in crossing the last plain, and we had to leave them and the baggage behind, and to return for it afterward. Another day without water and the whole train must have inevitably perished. Both man and beast being completely exhausted. I remained here three days for refreshment and rest. Moreover, we were now to prepare for crossing another desert of seventy miles, which, as my guide informed me, still lay between us and the southern end of the lake. He had passed over it in 1845, with Frémont, who had lost ten mules and several horses in effecting the passage, having afterward encamped on the same ground now occupied by our little party.[5]

Following the western edge of the plain at the foot of the range for three miles to the southern point of the mountain, Stansbury found a place where there had been an encampment of emigrants,

---

[4.] McHouston Springs.

[5.] Howard Stansbury, *Exploration and Survey of the Valley of the Great Salt Lake of Utah*, 107–11.

and where wagons and all kinds of valuable property had been abandoned.

That day, returning over the Donner trail, Stansbury traveled until past midnight. Some time during the night he passed five wagons and one cart which had become mired in the deep mud and had been left standing on the desert. There were also skeletons of oxen which had died under their yokes. Goods were scattered all about, among which were books, scientific instruments, medicine chests, tools and property of all description. The Indians had evidently looted the wagons for attractive trinkets. These were the wagons of Reed, Donner and Keseberg, together with the oxen of the last two, Reed's oxen having escaped.

At one o'clock that night Stansbury found the remains of a wagon with a broken ox yoke lying near. With this wood for fuel the party halted, made coffee, and camped for the balance of the night. In the morning, there being no more fuel, they resumed the journey without breakfast. During the morning they passed a place where emigrants had cached a wagon load of goods, but the cache had been robbed by Indians. Twelve ox yokes lay here in a heap.[6]

At noon of the second day, Stansbury was only about ten or twelve miles from Cedar Mountain, but so exhausted were the animals that it was dark before they reached its base, and here they were forced to camp without water. Two mules had to be abandoned during the afternoon. In the morning they succeeded in finding a little water, as it had snowed during the night, and here they rested for the whole day, recovering one of the mules abandoned the previous afternoon. The next day they crossed the ridge and found water at the little brackish spring on the opposite side.

Returning to Salt Lake City they completed the first circuit of the Great Salt Lake across or around the borders of the Salt Desert.

---

6. These yokes and extra wagon axles were still there in 1929, but were so weathered that it was impossible to salvage any of them.

15. THE GOLD RUSH

The story of the discovery of gold has often been told; but since some of those already mentioned in preceding chapters had an important part in that famous episode, it might be well to go into some of the details of the finding of gold, which precipitated the great gold rush.

James W. Marshall, credited with the first discover was a cabinet maker who had emigrated to Oregon in 1844[1] and later to California with James Clyman in 1845.[2] Being a good mechanic he was given employment by Captain Sutter. The heavy emigration of 1846 and 1847 had created a demand for lumber in the vicinity of the fort, and during the fall and winter of 1847 Marshall built a sawmill near some good timber on the south fork of the American River, at what is now Coloma. Sutter and Marshall were partners in this venture, Sutter furnishing the material and Marshall the labor. The contract between these two was drawn up by John Bidwell, who had crossed the desert in 1841 and who was still employed by Sutter, having charge of his property bought from the Russians at Bodega.[3]

Peter Wimmer, who had crossed the Salt Desert with Hastings, was also working for Captain Sutter at this time, and when Marshall began the construction of the mill, Wimmer was employed as a helper, and Mrs. Wimmer went along as cook. There were also employed on this construction several Mormons who had been discharged from the Mormon Battalion and who were on their way back to the settlement at Salt Lake. Sam Brannan, on his return to California after the unsatisfactory interview with Brigham Young, had met these men and told them that food was scarce in the new colony; that they should stay in California until the following year. They had heeded this advice and found employment with Sutter.

During the construction of the millrace tiny yellow flakes had frequently been noticed in the stream bed by Henry Bigler and

---

[1] George Frederick Parsons, *Life and Adventures of James W. Marshall, the Discoverer of Gold in California* (Sacramento: James W. Marshall and W. Burke, 1870), 7–8.

[2] Camp, ed., *James Clyman*, 170–71.

[3] Bancroft, *History of California*, II:719–20; IV: 186; and VI:29, 44.

some of the other Mormons working there. They presumed it to be flakes of mica and gave it no further attention. But one morning Marshall picked up a nugget below the millrace.[4] He still had no idea that it might be gold, but kept the nugget because in shape it somewhat resembled a bear.[5] Wimmer, having heard of placer gold from his wife, who had worked with her father and former husband in the Georgia diggings suspected its value and sent the nugget with one of his small sons to be examined by Mrs. Wimmer. At dinner that day she stated that she was certain the nugget was gold. Her husband and Marshall were still skeptical. To prove her theory she dropped it into a kettle of soap which she had on the fire, and boiled it all afternoon. At night it was still bright and shining, and she pronounced it to be gold without a doubt.

Some other small pieces were picked up from the bed of the stream and sent to Captain Sutter to be tested with acids. These proved to be genuine gold, and Sutter went to the millsite to investigate. By this time the Mormons had begun to pick up all they saw, and had collected a small quantity of it. When they heard Sutter's report they forgot all about the construction of the mill and began to dig in earnest. A bag of this was sent to San Francisco, where Sam Brannan saw it. He instantly saddled and rode to the site of the discovery. After examining the locality, seeing the quantity already dug, and digging some himself, he rode back to San Francisco and electrified the town by riding down the street at top speed shouting "Gold from the American River!"[6]

The town was deserted over night. Sam Brannan had started a store at Sutter's Fort in October, 1847, where, with the assistance

---

[4.] Marshall says January 19, 1848. Henry Bigler, in his diary, says January 24.

[5.] Marshall had previously been active in the "Bear Flag Revolution." See Parsons, *Life and Adventures of James W. Marshall*.

[6.] Scherer, *The First Forty-Niner*. The following, from the *Californian* of March 15, 1848, was the first printed announcement of the discovery: "Gold Mine Found—In the newly made raceway of the sawmill recently erected by Captain Sutter, on the American Fork, gold has been found in considerable quantities, One person brought thirty dollars worth to New Helvetia, gathered there in a short time. California, no doubt, is rich in mineral wealth, great chances here for scientific capitalists. Gold has been found in almost every part of the country."

of the tithing of gold dust collected from his Mormon followers, he laid the foundation of his fortune.

John Bidwell located Bidwell's bar, hired a number of Indians and took out $100,000 in a short time, being one of the few who used his money wisely. He later became known as California's first capitalist and foremost philanthropist.

James W. Marshall, John Sutter and Mrs. Peter Wimmer, the persons primarily responsible for the discovery, all died in poverty. Marshall's mill was torn down in the wild scramble for lumber, his claims were jumped, and bad luck followed him everywhere. Wherever he was seen gold-crazy miners rushed to the spot, never leaving him a moment in peace. He finally gave up in disgust and ceased digging entirely, whereupon an angry mob threatened to hang him if he did not reveal the secret of finding gold.[7] He finally died alone, in the direst poverty, in an abandoned shack.

Sutter's lands were overrun by gold diggers and his crops rotted in the fields. He was deprived of the lands granted him by the Mexican government, and died in Washington while trying to get redress from Congress. Mrs. Wimmer, who had been given the original nugget for a keepsake, was finally compelled through poverty to dispose of it to W. W. Allen, compiler of the *California Gold Book*.

News of the finding of gold soon reached the East; but it was not until 1849 that the richness of the gold began to be appreciated. In the spring of that year the vanguard of the gold rush started across the continent.

In the two years since its settlement Salt Lake City had become an active community and supplies could be purchased there. The first gold seekers, therefore, stopped in the new settlement to lay in supplies and to learn what they could of the country beyond. Here they found Captain Jefferson Hunt, of the Mormon Battalion, who said he could guide them to California over a route approximately the same as that now taken by the highway between Salt Lake City and Los Angeles. Being assured that it was much shorter and safer, these first gold-seekers decided to try it, although no wagons had ever been over the road. The train, consisting of several different parties, traveled south from Salt Lake City for several days, under the guidance of Hunt; but as they drew

---

[7.] Parsons, *Life and Adventures of James W. Marshall*.

nearer to the land of gold they became impatient and dissatisfied with the long detour to the south, which they began to think would not bring them out near the gold fields. One by one different parties left the train and struck out directly west over a country of which they knew absolutely nothing, and as they advanced and became involved in difficulties they split up into smaller groups until eventually it was every man for himself. Some of the wagons reached Death Valley where many died and the balance barely escaped with their lives. Their tragic story is told by William Lewis Manly, one of the survivors, in *Death Valley in '49*.[8] Those who remained with Captain Hunt arrived safely.[9]

When spring of 1850 had rolled around the whole country was gold crazy, and everyone who possibly could sold out and started for the gold fields. The story of the gold rush has already been told many times, but the journals of those travelers usually begin after they reached the diggings, and few have left any account of the overland journey. One such, however, written by John Wood, describes his crossing of the Salt Desert with the gold-seekers, and it appears from his record that there was a constant stream of traffic over the Hastings Cutoff that summer. Having heard that two or three hundred miles could be saved, many were anxious to take it at all hazards, to reach the land of gold before all the precious metal should have been dug. Cholera had taken a heavy toll of the emigrants that year and the people were desperate, willing to take any chance which would sooner get them out of the mountains and across the deserts into fertile country.

Following the shore of the lake the Ogle–Robinson party, of which John Wood was a member, reached Skull Valley, where they laid in a supply of water and grass for their cattle. Crossing the valley to Cedar Mountain they camped at the brackish spring at the foot of the pass, fighting for an opportunity to water their cattle at the little seep which scarcely furnished enough moisture for one team. It was noon of August 5 before they left the spring and the rest of the day was spent in getting over the ridge. Stopping a short

---

8. William Lewis Manly, *Death Valley in '49* (San Jose: The Pacific Tree & Vine Co., 1894).

9. James S. Brown, *Life of a Pioneer; Being the Autobiography of James S. Brown* (Salt Lake City: George Q. Cannon & Sons, Publishers, 1900).

time for refreshment, they continued their journey throughout the night. Toward midnight Robinson, who was captain of the train, passed a wagon in which a sick man seemed about to perish of thirst, and carried him in his own wagon until he was revived. By morning they found that some of their cattle were nearly done, and many of the emigrants were not much better off.

On the morning of the sixth they rested about an hour, gave each of the cattle a quart of water and some hay, and then resumed the march. Cattle now began to drop from exhaustion and the party began to wonder if they would ever reach the mountains on the other side. Continuing until dark they came to what is now called Silver Island, a rocky promontory projecting into the desert. All now thought that they had reached Pilot Peak and would soon find water, but were dismayed to learn that water was still twenty-five miles ahead. During this last stretch of twenty-five miles calamity began to howl closely on their heels. Cattle dropped dead, the dryness and heat of the desert caused the wheels to shrink and the iron tires to drop off and stragglers were left on the desert to make their way in as best they could. They passed an old woman carrying a coffee pot full of water to her husband who had become exhausted and lay down to die twenty-five miles out on the salt. Another woman, Mrs. Hall, was left with a wagon while her husband drove the oxen to water.

All along this last drive the trail was lined with dead and dying cattle and abandoned wagons. John Wood says:

Aug. 6. ...Several of our cattle about dark are giving way and cannot go much further; they look awful bad, and I know they feel worse than they look. I judge them by myself. Soon after dark another steer gave way in our team and he was left, and some others in the company have gone the way of all flesh, but we are going to see how many can get through, roll on is the cry now with everyone; we are going through or die. We have not an ox in the company now but what will take hard cracking with the whip and never flinch, but they certainly can endure more fatigue than I ever expected.

About 10 o'clock two more steers gave out, which left us but two yoke to take our wagons through; some other teams gave way entirely and stopped for the night. When we got within 10 miles of the water our cattle seemed to know, by some instinct, that water was not far ahead, and became animated with new life, and the two small yoke we had attached to our big wagon, walked as fast as I could, and sometimes would trot, and when we got within a mile of the water, I had to walk before them to keep them from running. Who could not sympathize with flesh and blood, suffering in this way?

It was one o'clock at night when we got through. This was the severest trial I have had by far, the desert proving to be 93 miles instead of 75, as we had understood, and having to walk all the way almost without stopping, with but little to eat and drink, and no sleep, was soul-trying in the extreme. We dropped our bodies under the wagons and in less than five minutes were in a state of unconsciousness....

Aug. 7. ...This morning our case is deplorable, notwithstanding it is heart-cheering to see water and grass; our team is broken and we must leave McLean's last wagon; the only resort we have now is to make pack saddles and pack our provisions on our remaining cattle, as many others have had to do.

Emigrants are arriving here all the time from the desert, almost famished for water; they say men, women and children are dying with thirst and fatigue. All start in ignorance of the distance across, and many take but little water and they must perish. Mr. Hall, who left his wife on the desert yesterday, is preparing to go back after his wife and wagon.

Our company rigged out a wagon loaded with water and have gone back on the desert to relieve the suffering, without money and without price. They found many at the point of death, and saved them, many suffering extremely. Mr. Ogle, who carried water back in the desert on his back, 20 or 30 miles, tells of one man that could not speak, whom he relieved, and many others in almost similar condition.[10]

[10.] Charles Kelly, "Gold Seekers on the Hastings Cutoff," *Utah Historical Quarterly* 20 (January 1952), 23–24.

*

The *Deseret News* began publication in Salt Lake City on June 15, 1850, at which time the gold rush was on in earnest. Registration at Fort Laramie showed that 11,443 men, 119 women and 99 children had passed there up to June 3. Many of these went to Fort Hall and thence to the headwaters of the Humboldt, but hundreds who found themselves short of provisions stopped in Salt Lake City. The Mormons had raised three crops and were able to supply some grain and vegetables to the emigrants. Brigham Young issued orders that no one in distress should be turned away if it were possible to aid him. To add to its limited revenue, the new publication offered to publish the names of emigrants passing through, at twenty-five cents each, copies of the paper to be mailed to relatives and friends in the east. Each issue during that season contained long lists of such names. Among those registered were E. S. Hall and wife, of Cincinnati, who arrived July 13 and departed July 30, the day on which the Ogle–Robinson party left the city. This is the Mr. and Mrs. Hall mentioned by Wood, who were in difficulties on the desert.

This letter from the *Deseret News* of August 10, 1850 proves the Hastings Cutoff had been traveled previously that season:

—CUT OFF—

Pilot Peak, July 29, 1850.

Capt. Hooper—

Sir, I am across the great Desert after a hard drive, this *Desert is over 80 miles* without any doubt. Should any Emigrants call on you for information, you can say to them with confidence, that they *cannot* get through with their animals without at *least 2 gallons of water* to each *animal* and one gallon for each person; without they can carry this quantity of water with a supply of grass; no man should ever attempt to cross. There was a great deal of suffering among those who came over at the same time I did, but no lives lost, but no doubt a great many would not have got through, had it not been for the active part of those that got across early and hauled water back, for those behind.

The road is very fine especially across the desert, and plenty of grass and water on this route with the exception of the desert; I hope no one will endeavor to come this road without they are well prepared.

Yours in haste,
JNO. B. McGEE.

Capt. Hooper vouches for Mr. McGee's veracity. [11]

The Ogle–Robinson party reached Pilot Peak on Aug. 7, one week later than the date of this letter. John Wood mentions meeting with some Mormon guides returning from piloting emigrants over the desert, and these guides must have been with the McGee party. No explanation of any kind accompanies this letter, but it is probable that Captain Hooper had made arrangements with McGee in Salt Lake City to inform him about the condition of the cutoff.

Another account of travel in 1850 is given by John Udell, on his second journey across the plains as emigrant guide. In his book *Incidents of Travel to California* he says:

[July] 19th [1850]. We put our goods on our horses... and threw away part of our clothing. We then resumed our journey [from Salt Lake City] taking an entirely new route. Passing west of the city one mile; crossed the Jordan and journeyed west to the Bluffs. Camped near a small lake and springs of brackish water. Plenty of grass, but no wood.

20th. Traveled to the clear cold springs—five miles. Mountains close to the left. Bluffs and Big Salt Lake to the right. The waters of this lake are so *dense* that a person cannot sink, and dry salt may be shoveled up on its beach. Seven miles and fifty yards of rocky road to a lone craggy rock on the left. This is a blind road, and we steer westwardly to the mountains on the opposite side of the valley. Large springs in a deep ravine, quarter of a mile from the town off the road on the right. All the water, so far, is brackish, but can be used. Good grass, but no wood; hard, rough gravelly road. Fifteen miles to Willow Creek, for eight miles of the way no wood except some brush; the rest of the way good willow brush for wood, and fine camping ground. Thirty-three and a half miles' travel; camped on Willow Creek.

[11.] John B. McGee died of cholera in Sacramento, October 13, 1850. From Vital Statistics, California State Library.

21st Sunday. Thirty-five miles' travel to the next fresh water....the road turns to the right, leaving the mountains and a marsh on the left, until you come down to the Sweet Water springs. We passed several brackish springs; their water is often used, however.

22nd. From the fresh water springs you travel a little to the north west across the low ground to the mountains on the opposite side. The road keeps on into the bluffs. On the left we found sulphur springs in a deep ravine, and some other springs, mostly of brackish water. This water has a very unpleasant taste, but can be used by those on the plains.

23rd. We left the brackish springs and crossed the Great Desert. We could only obtain vessels enough to carry two gallons of water. This was insufficient for four persons forced to travel thirty miles under a burning sun. We were but one day going through. Before night several had become speechless from extreme thirst, and would have perished, had not others been able to go forward and bring water to the suffering. After passing around several high mountains, we came to a vast plain which presented a most singular appearance. There was no vegetation on it, and the whole expanse was covered to the depth of five or six inches with a white substance resembling gypsum, that reflects the heat of the sun's rays, making a bright glaring atmosphere, which together with the dust, causes extreme faintness and thirst.

24th. This day we concluded to rest from the fatigues of traveling.[12]

Udell's description of his route from Salt Lake City to and across the salt flats is very incomplete and confusing. He speaks of springs where there are no springs, fails to mention the miles of sand dunes just east of the salt flats, gives the distance across the salt flats at thirty miles instead of seventy, and does not mention Pilot Peak. It is difficult to explain his record. But he definitely describes Silver Zone Pass and Flowery Lake beyond so he must have been traveling in the tracks of the Donner party and others.

---

[12]. John Udell, *Incidents of Travel to California* (Jefferson, Ohio: Printed for the Author, at the Sentinel Office, 1856), 25–26.

He also fails to mention the Donner wagons, still standing in the mud. From his description it might be inferred that he wrote his record some time after his actual passage and failed to remember definite details.

Another account of the crossing of the Hastings Cutoff during the gold rush is given by William P. Bennett, a young emigrant from Canada. He was apparently a member of some company other than those already mentioned, but gives us little information about his companions. In his book *The Sky-Sifter*, principally devoted to other matters, he says:

> Traveling through the "Valley of the Shadow of Death"— graves to the right and graves to the left of us as we toiled on our way—we reached Salt Lake City, July 14th [1850]. There we were told of a much shorter route than that taken by wagons, through which we might "swiftly glide" on horseback, with pack animals. We believed in this "cut-off," therefore sold oxen and wagons, and bought horses and pack animals. For the oxen we got about what we paid, but all else went for a song—a song that was sung by Mormons with voices tuned to the sharp notes of Mammon, "god of the Syrian."

> ...We left Salt Lake [July 22] to take the much-lauded cut-off, under the guidance of a Frenchman [Auguste Archambault] who said he had traveled that way two or three times with Fremont and others. We took with us provisions for only fifteen days, as our guide said that in that time he would land us in California, instead of which we came out at the end of the period of time named, upon the main wagon road at the head of the Humboldt River. We had constantly traveled through a succession of waterless deserts, one of which was ninety miles across. In all of these deserts we were obliged to carry water and grass, and to travel much of nights.

> We were more dead than alive when we reached the Humboldt, and our animals were barely able to crawl after us when led. At the Humboldt we learned, to our rage, that in taking the "cut-off" we had traveled one hundred miles farther than would have been required had we followed the main wagon road. It was a trick of the Mor-

mons to send emigrants packing through the so-called cutoff of the deserts in order that wagons, supplies, and all except what could be carried on horses and mules, might be "dumped down" at Salt Lake and almost given away. How well they did at this may be imagined when I say that in our one party there were no fewer than three hundred men. Party after party were deluded into taking this cut-off, and the Mormons always had in readiness one of "Fremont's old guides" to steer them through at a salary of about twenty dollars a day.

We were landed on the head of the Humboldt River almost destitute of provisions, and the stock of the wagon trains which had preceded us had devoured nearly all the grass. The carcasses of hundreds on hundreds of dead animals of all kinds tainted the air. We were thirteen days on the Humboldt and were often obliged to swim or ford the river in order to get a few handfuls of grass for our starving animals. As for ourselves, we were glad to make a meal of such frogs as we could catch, or at times to pick the bones of cattle slaughtered by parties ahead of us, then to crush the bones and make soup of them.[13]

Bennett's company of three hundred men on horses, according to the dates given, may have been led by McGee, whose letter has been quoted. If McGee was traveling with wagons, Bennett must have passed him in Skull Valley.

The mention of "Frémont's guides" is interesting, but unfortunately no names are mentioned. It is not unlikely, however, that some of Frémont's French-Canadians did actually act as guides during the gold rush. The Frenchman mentioned was Auguste Archambault, who first crossed the desert with Kit Carson in 1845.

*

Another fragmentary record of the gold rush is contained in *Recollections of a California Pioneer* by Carlisle S. Abbott. The author did not cross the Salt Desert, but gives the experiences of some of his friends who took that route. The incident is not without its humorous side. He says:

[13.] William P. Bennett, *The Sky-Sifter; the Great Chieftainess and "Medicine Woman" of the Mohawk* (N.P., 1892), 278–79, 287–88.

From Salt Lake City there were two routes westward, the main road around the north end of the lake and the other, called the "Southern Route," [Hastings Cutoff] around the south end of the lake,—the southern being one hundred miles shorter than the main road, but necessitating the crossing of a ninety-mile desert. Both routes again merged at the Carson River. Two or three of the companies went by the shorter route, while our company determined to take the main traveled way.

One of the companies that took the shorter route was composed of a man by the name of Marsh, another by the name of Allen, and four other men whom Allen and Marsh had taken into their company upon the payment of a stipulated sum of money. Marsh was a short, thick-set man, and as tough as a pine nut, while Allen was over six feet tall, rather slim, and was, moreover, the most profane man who ever honored me with his acquaintance.

Happening to meet Marsh in Sacramento two years later, I asked him how he got along on the ninety-mile desert. He replied:

"Bad."

He then told me that they had started out early in the morning expecting to get across the desert by the following morning, but, as teams do not travel as fast by night as they seem to, their expectations were disappointed, and by eleven o'clock of the following morning all their horses lay dead in their tracks, and the canteens were empty; that they had taken a small quantity of food from their wagons and started for the shore (as the edge of the desert was called), intending to refresh themselves at the big spring and then return to their outfit, removing and taking away with them all the food they could carry; that while the road was good and hard, being composed of mixed sand and salt, it gleamed and glistened in the sun, and the heat was vicious as it was bewildering, and finally Allen and one of the other men dropped to the ground exhausted, when, to the amusement of the others, Allen began to pray:

"O Lord Almighty, send us just one drop of rain!"

Immediately from a few fleecy clouds scattering rain drops began to fall, and as Allen and his companion had a rubber blanket, they quickly spread it out. But not a sufficient quantity of water fell to admit of its running together.

"The damphool," said Marsh; "might just as well have prayed for a barrel of water as for a drop, for he got ten times as much as he asked for."

Marsh and the other three men reached the spring, and after resting a few minutes, filled their canteens and started back. When the cool of the evening set in Allen and his companion were revived and had started on, and a little after dark they were met by Marsh and the others, were given water, and then all returned to the wagon, only to find that some thieving emigrant had stolen everything that was edible. Taking their rifles, they returned to the water, filled their canteens, and now, without an ounce of food, took up the trail for "the land of gold,"—the distance to the junction of the roads, where it would be possible to procure food, being nearly three hundred miles. On the way they shot a sage hen, a prairie dog, and two pigeons, all of which were quickly devoured, and thus they poked along, with a cane in each hand, until they reached the junction where they obtained food from the traders located there.[14]

Another very brief account of crossing the salt flats is by James Mathers, reproduced in *Overland in 1846* by Dale L. Morgan:

13th Went up the valley 5 m and encamped by fresh water and grass—.[15]

14   Remained in camp

15th Went to springs in the mountain[16]   12 m.

16th Started on the long drive and after traveling until near the middle of the next day without resting but a little we were obliged to leave two waggons and go on with

---

14. Carlisle S. Abbott, *Recollections of a California Pioneer* (New York: The Neale Publishing Company, 1907), 53–56.

15. The spring at Iopesa.

16. Redlum Spring.

the third so as to get the cattle to water the sooner, the distance still being more than 20 m. I remained with the waggons on the salt plain until the evening of the 20th when Carolan came back with the oxen and the next day about 11 o'clock we reached the camp at the foot of the mountains, the whole distance without water about 65 m. On the 18th there was a violent wind and the salt drifted over the plain like snow.   65

22nd Removed our camp about 4 m.—Course on the long drive W.N.W.   4

23rd Drove 30 m. and reached water and grass about 2 o'clock A.M. on the 24th The road for 18 m. was bad except 3 m. from the top of the mountain it was better course south & west   30

August 25th Traveled south parallel with the mountain 14 m.—hard travelling—plenty of grass & water—days hot & nights cold—froze ice in a basin more than 1/4 of an inch thick.[17]

One of the best accounts of crossing the Salt Desert is by Madison Berryman Moorman, as edited by Irene D. Paden.

—Dr. T.[homas] was trying to converse with an Indian who it seems was well acquainted with the Desert and the Dr. wanted him to guide us. He promised to do so and was to be back early the next morning. We gave him and his two companions their dinner, soon after which they started and said they would kill us an antelope. They were fine looking fellows and had no little shrewdness; were of the Utah tribe and were dressed tolerably well.

July 29th.—Our Indian guide "came up missing," as we a little suspected, which put us to no inconvenience whatever.—We soon made the distance to the next spring where we found Mr. K.[ingston] with his wagon all the rest of the boys had left about midnight for the next and last spring before entering upon the Desert. We had provided us a supply of water [in Skull Valley], before starting, for drinking purposes as we understood it was the last good water we would have before crossing the dreaded

---

17. Morgan, *Overland in 1846*, I:231.

waste.—A short time was consumed here in watering our animals and seventeen miles more brought us to the last watering place—a number of small wells dug in a ravine that were ever kept stirred up and muddy [Redlum Spring]. The water would have been bad enough had this not been the case, it being very brackish, but now intolerable.—We found the van of our train encamped near by and their mules about half a mile off in the hills upon good bunch grass where we soon had all the balance. We had no time to lose;—our grass, to last us across a desert of seventy five miles, was to [be] cut and arranged—cooking for the same had to be done, and many other little things of importance were to be attended to.

July 30th & 31st.—A double guard or rather twice the usual number of men were put upon duty last night, so that no one should stand more than two hours. I was on the first watch and the entire guard were to take their blankets and spend the night in the mountains with the mules. The first relief, from some cause or other did not relieve, which kept me on duty till 12 o'clock, and when I did lie down the relief kept so much noise in herding the mules—which were very much disposed to run about, that I did not sleep more than an hour.

At 3 o'clock P.M. we started on our dreaded tour and after travelling six or eight miles over a very rough and mountainous road [over Cedar Mountain], we struck the immense barren plain covered with a white saline incrustation. The road here was very dusty and the train already strung along for a mile or two. The sun was nearly down, shining directly in our faces and the dust rose straight up in dense clouds that nearly choked us—there being no breeze to fan it away. Each couple had to provide for their mules, which left but one saddle mule to two men—the other packed with grass. We travelled on in this way and about 8 o'clock we were on the summit of a low mountain twenty miles out [Grayback]. We made a stay of near an hour awaiting the coming up of several of the men who had got behind. All came up but Messrs. W. M. M.[athews] and J. W. W.[ilson], who we supposed had got with the wagon and would travel with it—their pack

mule being a little sick the last time they were seen.—
About 11 o'clock the moon rose and showed us that our
road was much better—which, with the fine light of the
moon and the reflection of the white plain, cheered us no
little on our way.—The night was pleasantly cool and
about the dawn we stopped to feed our animals and give
them a short rest. I was nearly dead for sleep and fell
down upon the ground, with the *laryette* [*sic*] in my
hand, and was soon asleep. The hour seemed to be but a
few minutes.—About 8 o'clock we stopped again, in sight
of the point of a mountain, at which we had expected to
find water & grass. We gave our mules the residue of the
water and grass & ate a little ourselves. Several wagons
were here being guarded by several men, while the rest of
their parties were gone on with their stock in search of
grass & water, which, they told us, were *twenty five miles
off*. This unfavorable inteligence [*sic*] gave us a good deal
of uneasiness. There we were without grass and not more
than a quart of water. The sun was already oppressively
hot and one or two of our mules began to show signs of
"*caving in*." We tarried but a short time and when we had
travelled five or six miles—which brought us to the point
of the mountain above mentioned [Silver Island], one of
the mules refused to go any further. We gave it the last
drop of water we had, which was but a few swallows and
the train moved on leaving Dr. [illegible] with his mule.
After travelling a short distance we met a wagon loaded
with water which had been sent out by subscription to relieve the distressed. The teamster gave us as much as *we*
could drink but would not let us have any for our mules.
We told him of Dr. T.[homas]'s situation and pushed on—
seeing numbers of poor animals dead & dying and about 3
o'clock P.M. we reached the long looked for fountain,
gushing out of the earth in a large bold stream while all
around were emigrants and their stock grazing upon the
immense meadow. In the lapse of an hour or two Dr.
T.[homas] came in leading his mule, almost exhausted.
We soon had a good supper prepared, which seemed to be
more appreciated than any we had partaken of in our
lives. We felt grateful that we had been so fortunate in

crossing what was called a *"Seventy-five mile Desert,"* but is, in reality, according to several *Viameters, Ninety miles!* The hastily prepared supper was hastily eaten we were soon scattered around on our respective pallets in deepest slumber.

Aug. lst.—They still continued to pour in from the Desert, many of whom were almost exhausted. Great suffering of man & beast reported. About 11 o'clock last night Messrs. K.[ingston], J. W W.[ilson], & W. M. M.[athews] got through but did not find our camp till this morning. The latter two, as before stated were left behind, & they had the misfortune to lose one of their mules soon after entering the desert—which caused them to have a hard time of it—having to walk nearly the entire distance with a very scant supply of water.—The wagon had been left twenty miles out in charge of Dr. P.[atterson] & Bl'k Walker. We had all the tanks filled with water and a considerable quantity of grass cut and packed upon mules and sent back to relieve them and bring in the wagon. The company contributed to the relief of the suffering still out, some of whom were reached just in time to save life.—I felt much better to-day than it would be supposed—having slept but one night in three and in this interrupted to stand guard for an hour.

Aug. 2nd.—Very early all were up and looking after the mules which were very much scattered and in great danger of being stolen—there being a great deal of thieving rascality carried on at this juncture.—Soon after breakfast Walker came in, having left Dr. P.[atterson] alone before the relief arrived.—Messrs. S. L. S.[haw], J. W. W.[ilson], A. M.[ills], Bl'k Jno. & myself started on a tramp to Pilot's peak—the base of which, appeared to be not more than two miles off. We travelled seven or eight miles before we could discover that we were ascending much & after going two or three farther we came to a bold stream of icy cold water, which refreshed us no little.—This stream lost itself in the arid valley long before reaching the fertile meadow that skirted along the desert about half a mile wide, abounding with springs—the outbreaks, no doubt, of these mountain streams, but in quality of water, very far inferior—yet pretty good.—We pursued our winding course up the steep and rugged mountain side and at 2 o'clock we were about twelve miles up the mountain (this is from camp) where it was covered with cedars—large forest pines—innumerable flowers, many of which of exquisite beauty—and an abundance of raspberries of rich & delicious flavor. The surface of the mountain, from the plain below, looked to be regular and smooth—covered with luxuriant grass. The *even surface* we found to be the most rugged—sometimes almost bidding defiance to another step upwards. The *luxuriant grass* we found to be large forest pines & cedars. The immense mass of rock that lay in one confused pile—covering the greater part of the mountain is a kind of sand stone, of a very fine and sharp grit—resembling very nearly that used for *oil stones*, and for which purpose would answer admirably. Here, J. W. W.[ilson] & A. M.[ills] turned back and the three remaining ones of us went on. When we had clambered about two miles further Jno. & myself felt willing to stop—though S. L. S.[haw] remonstrated. We told him we would wait till he went to the summit & return if he would accomplish it in a given time as we did not care about night overtaking us in that wild looking place—with nothing to eat or cover with. He hurried on and was gone but little over his time. We then commenced descending by leaping from stone to stone at a precipitous and rapid rate, after l[eaping] over deep chasms, into which the least blunder would have consigned us. It was very tiresome—much more so than going up, and long before I reached the base, did I wish myself safe in camp.— We reached camp just before dark and found that all the train had come in, wagon and all—though several of the mules were very much worsted.—After supper we entered into a confab—which increased to be a debate. The topic was—"Whether we were then in the U. S. or not." S. S. P.[hillips], D. S. W.[oodward], A. M.[ills] & myself in the negative against the rest of the camp, save one or two who occupied *neutral ground*. The subject was discussed with increased ardour until 11 o'clock—when, by mutual consent, it was *lain on the table*.

Aug. 3rd.—The day was employed in making preparations to start on the following day. I did my first washing which blistered by knuckles severely.—Several of us in the after noon took our guns and went out after hares, which are very abundant through the sage region, and are three times as large as the common hare and much wilder. Several were killed and cooked for supper which gave us a delicious meal. The question of the evening before was taken up again and after an animated discussion of more than an hour—the affirmative party acknowledged that *being in the U. S.* and being *in the U. S. Territory,* was not the same, which they contended for in the premises. So our argument was ended.

Aug. 4th.—Another Sunday found us in an oasis of the desert. Till 5 o'clock P.M. was spent in cooking, eating and sleeping, when we once more took up the line of march.—For six or eight miles from the point we struck at the Desert are plenty of grass and water; after which we entered an arid sandy region—destitute of water and producing nothing in the way of vegetation but hardy clusters of dwarfish sage.—We travelled on, with no light but that of the stars to show us our road, which was very difficult to keep in this sandy region, for about fifteen miles which took us till near 11 o'clock. We stopped—unpacked our mules—tied them as securely as we could to the sage, and made our beds down upon the sand—which afforded us an agreeable resting place. For the last two or three miles travelled our speed was very much retarded on account of a weak mule, which was left about a mile back to remain until morning.[18]

*

Under date of September 7, 1850, Elijah Ward advertised in the *Deseret News* that he will guide emigrants over the Southern Route (now followed by the highway to Los Angeles) for ten dollars per wagon; and under date of October 5, Joseph Cain advertises maps of the Southern Route for sale to emigrants. It therefore seems that emigration was directed over the Southern Route, be-

---

[18.] Irene D. Paden, ed., *The Journal of Madison Berryman Moorman, 1850-1851* (San Francisco: California Historical Society, 1948), 55–59.

ginning late in the season of 1850, and that thereafter the Hastings Cutoff was abandoned. There is no further mention of it in any of the pioneer records.

In the fall of 1849 Joseph Cain, Major Jefferson Hunt and several others left Salt Lake City with instructions from Brigham Young to "dig gold in California and then go on a mission to the Sandwich Islands." Evidently the latter part of their instruction was not carried out, since under date of October 2, 1850, the *Deseret News* prints a letter from Joseph Cain, who had just returned with his party from California. He says:

> We met a number of persons who had come "Hasting's Cut-Off," who have all declared it is a much longer road, and a much more dangerous one, on account of the Desert of 91 miles, and also the Indians; many of the Emigrants having to travel on foot, packing their provisions on their backs, the Indians having driven off all their animals.

This would bring the last crossing of the desert down to about September 15 of that year, and since emigration was about over for the season early in October, it is probable that those were the last parties to cross.

16. THE BECKWITH SURVEY

The famous Hastings Cutoff was apparently never again used after 1850. For the next few years emigration followed either the Fort Hall Road, with various new short cuts, or took the Southern Route. But the latter also had its disadvantages; during the hot months of summer it was dangerous or impossible to attempt certain portions of the road due to long stretches of deep sand and the great distance between waterholes. It could only be safely traveled in the cool months of the year. The Fort Hall Road was best in summer and the Southern Route best in winter.

Emigrants were still complaining about the long detour to the north over the Fort Hall Road; and if they took the Southern Route that brought them out at Los Angeles, they still had to travel up the coast to San Francisco to reach the gold fields.

The unprecedented emigration since the discovery of gold had started agitation for a transcontinental railroad; and in 1854 Lieutenant E. G. Beckwith was sent to Utah to make a survey for a practicable railroad route to the Pacific.[1]

Beckwith followed the well known trail from Salt Lake City south of the lake, arriving in Skull Valley where he saw Frémont's trail of 1845 crossing Cedar Mountain. Instead of following this trail, however, which would have taken him over the very route where the Western Pacific later built its line, he went farther south in Skull Valley and crossed the ridge between two of its highest points, now known as Beckwith Pass. From there the survey led to Granite Mountain, a large rocky island half way across the desert, but many miles south of the Hastings route. This pile of granite is the pinnacle of what was once probably the highest mountain in the Great Basin—a mountain which was almost submerged by the cataclysmal subsidence which caused the formation of the lake. Here at Granite Mountain, Captain Beckwith found a fine spring of good water. Continuing across the salt, he reached the opposite side without mishap, and then turned northwest through various

---

1. E.G. Beckwith, *Reports of Explorations and Surveys, to Ascertain the Most Practicable and Economical Route for a Railroad from the Mississippi River to the Pacific Ocean*, Volume 2 (Washington, D.C.: Government Printing Office, 1855).

valleys until he finally struck the Hastings road beyond Pilot Peak, on its way to the Humboldt.

A new route across the Salt Desert was thus laid out which had the great advantage of being much safer, since water could be had in the middle of the desert, and the total distance across the salt flats was only forty miles. This is the route which Hastings should logically have chosen if he had studied the country more carefully, and one which would have been followed by the gold-seekers if it had been known. It would have saved untold suffering and prevented the loss of many cattle and much valuable property. If Hastings had taken this route, he might possibly have arrived in California at the psychological moment and have made California, for a time, at least, an independent republic.

Beckwith's new route was used several years by freighters to Nevada mines, whose heavy wagons were drawn by many teams of mules. Its only disadvantage was the extreme steepness of the trail over the pass, ten to twenty teams being required to draw one loaded wagon. Even as late as 1875 an ox team crossed Beckwith Pass, bearing in the wagon box the body of a certain "bad man" who had been killed by a timid little Scot in self defense. So steep was the grade that the body of the erstwhile gun-fighter fell out of the back of the wagon and never stopped rolling until it reached the foot of the mountain.[2]

[2.] Information from Mr. Dan Orr, Grantsville, Utah.

17. The Simpson Survey

One more road was yet to be surveyed across the Salt Desert before the railroad came. This was laid out by Captain Simpson, a government surveyor, who was instructed to find a better wagon road from Salt Lake City to Carson Sink.[1] To avoid the steep grade of Beckwith Pass, and to eliminate long drives without water, Captain J. H. Simpson, in 1859, laid his route through Tooele and Rush valleys and over Johnston's Pass, where there was plenty of feed and several good springs, crossing the extreme southern tip of the desert at Fish Springs. His route for the most part was level, and there were no great distances to be traversed without water. It was a logical route, and a safe one—except for Indians. Over this road came the Pony Express,[2] established by Colonel William Hepburn Russell.[3] Along this road the transcontinental stages were later run, and the first telegraph line built. At Fish Springs and at Callao could still be seen, as late as 1932, the old stone relay stations where fresh horses were kept in constant readiness. Stumps of the old telegraph poles are still preserved in the mud there.

---

[1] J. H. Simpson, *Report of Explorations Across the Great Basin of the Territory of Utah for a Direct Wagon-Route from Camp Floyd, to Genoa, in Carson Valley, in 1859* (Washington, D.C.: Government Printing Office, 1876).

[2] Howard E. Egan, *Pioneering the West, 1846–1878* (Salt Lake City: Skelton Publishing Co., 1917).

[3] The William H. Russell who founded the Pony Express is not the same person who traveled with the Bryant-Russell party in 1846.

18. A Bicycle Crosses the Desert

On May 10, 1869, the two ends of the first transcontinental railroad which had been built from the east and the west, were joined at Promontory, Utah, on the east side of Great Salt Lake. Until this time the Oregon and California trails, with their various cutoffs and detours, had been kept open for wagon traffic. But as soon as the transcontinental railroad had become a reality the old freighting wagons were seen no more on the desert—the prairie schooner of the homeseeker became a novelty. It was not long until the old trails were neglected and forgotten by all except those who had traveled them in early days. Wagon roads now radiated north and south from the railroad, tapping fertile sections close to the transcontinental line, but there was no through east and west traffic.

Then came the bicycle. As this forerunner of the automobile gained in popularity there was a great public clamor for better roads. Bicycle clubs were organized all over the country and young men of those days began to explore the highways and byways. Endurance runs became weekly events; in some of the clubs it was requisite for the applicant for membership to be able to ride a hundred miles continuously in one day. Such speed had never before been obtained on dirt roads, and the bicycle was taken up by the signal corps of the U.S. Army and various commercial enterprises.

In 1896, at the height of its popularity, William Randolph Hearst conceived the idea of a transcontinental relay bicycle dispatch. He had just started a newspaper in New York, and he thought it would be a great publicity stunt to send a message by bicycle from his San Francisco *Examiner* to his New York *Journal*. To conceive was to do—and scouts were sent out to locate a route across the continent.

No difficulty was encountered until the scouts reached the great plains and deserts of the West. Wagons no longer attempted to cross the great open spaces; there were no roads of any kind and even the location of the old pioneer trails had been forgotten.

It fell to the lot of William D. Rishel, a young man who was then president of a bicycle club in Cheyenne, Wyoming, to locate a practicable route from that place to Truckee, California.[1] Having no maps of the trails, this young man started out across the deserts in the general direction of San Francisco, on a bicycle. Many times he crossed old trails; but since pioneers and gold-seekers had been forced to make their way from waterhole to waterhole, their route was considerably longer than necessary for the swift-moving bicycle.

On his westward scouting trip young Rishel took the northern route around Great Salt Lake—the old Fort Hall Road. But, like those who had gone before him, this route seemed too much of a detour to the north. Returning from Truckee, he followed the general route of the railroad along the Humboldt River, but decided to save time and mileage by riding across the Salt Desert instead of around it. In this he was following the ideas of Hastings in 1846 and, like Hastings, the route seemed feasible to him as he stood on the northwestern edge of the great level expanse and looked across its smooth surface.

Those of whom he inquired told the intrepid young scout that such a journey meant sure death. But like the earlier pioneers he disregarded their warnings and decided to make the attempt. From an old "desert rat" he obtained a rough map, on which was marked the location of only one place where water might possibly be obtained. His route lay somewhat to the north of the old Hastings Cutoff and passed to the east of the Lakeside Mountains, a range of hills on the eastern edge of the salt flats, near the lake. In these hills Cook's Spring had been indicated by the "desert rat."

Starting from Terrace, a station on the railroad which had by then been built around the north end of the lake, Bill Rishel, with one companion, began the first and only crossing of the Salt Desert on bicycles. They carried two army canteens each, and some sandwiches. It seemed to the young riders that this would be the easiest part of their journey, as the desert appeared perfectly level and the surface was covered with a hard crust of salt. Leaving Terrace at two o'clock in the morning to take advantage of the cool hours of night, they began their ride, the desert being brilliantly lighted by a full moon. The first few miles were marvelous—the salt made the finest possible traveling surface and they had no difficulty in making twenty miles an hour. But they soon discovered

---

[1.] Information from Mr. William E. Rishel, Salt Lake City (1929).

that all is not salt that glitters in the moonlight. The hard salt beds were quickly passed and they then struck mud flats where even in July the mud never dries. After a few rods of this their wheels were so clogged with mud they were compelled to dismount and carry their bicycles for many miles at a stretch—they could not even lead their machines through the sticky mass. The sun rose then, and they discovered that a day in June on the Great Salt Desert was very far from being perfect. They tried to conserve their water supply, but all four canteens were empty by early afternoon, and they were still only half way across.

Striking toward the lake they found sandy stretches where it was possible to ride for short distances. The going was still terrible, but much better than the mud.

Rishel and his companion, Charlie Emise, now fixed their hope on being able to find the spring marked on the crude map. In such a desolate waste it was extremely difficult to identify landmarks which the old prospector had described. But eventually they neared the highest point of the Lakeside Mountains, and finding what seemed to be a very dim trail, followed it into the hills for several miles. Here they found the spring. Instead of the gushing water which they had expected, they found a depression about the size of a derby hat, which was kept half filled by a tiny drip from the ledge above. Drinking sparingly of the water in the spring, they set their canteens under the drip. Two hours they waited and still there was no more than a swallow in the canteens.

While they rested at the spring evening came, and from their elevation they could see directly across the lake the lights of Saltair Pavilion, a resort which had been built on the shore nearest Salt Lake City. In the clear evening air it seemed only a short distance, yet to reach those lights they would have had to travel more than a hundred miles. Refreshed by their rest and the cooler air of the evening, the two bicycle scouts again resumed their journey, riding along the shore of the lake for many miles and then across the marshy ground at the entrance of Skull Valley, which the emigrants had been forced to avoid on account of the weight of their wagons. This was the most exhausting part of the whole trip, and the marsh seemed endless, besides being filled with clouds of mosquitoes. But every journey must have an end, and at twelve o'clock that night two young men rode into the town of Grantsville, having been the first—and also the last—to cross the Salt Desert on bicycles. They had been in continuous motion for twenty-two hours and had covered more than one hundred miles.

The transcontinental relay bicycle race was run shortly after, using six hundred riders, and the message was carried from San Francisco to New York in thirteen days of continuous riding day and night. The route selected, however, went north of the lake and not across the salt. Rishel declared that a million dollars would not tempt him to again cross that desert on a bicycle.

19. THE RAILROAD AND MODERN HIGHWAY

By 1906 the Hastings Cutoff had been entirely forgotten, Beckwith's route had been deserted, and the Overland Stage road abandoned. No road of any kind crossed the Salt Desert.

In 1907 the Western Pacific Railroad was built, and in seeking the shortest route laid its rails directly west across the Salt Desert from the station of Delle on the east to Wendover on the western edge, south of Pilot Peak. Thirteen miles west of Delle the railroad crossed the trail of the pioneers of 1846 just at the foot of the pass over Cedar Mountain, where the old trail is still visible.

The automobile was now becoming popular, and a transcontinental highway was being talked of. There were still no continuous roads from east to west, but as the popularity of the automobile increased it became evident that a practicable route would sooner or later have to be found across the great barren wastes of Utah and Nevada. Again the old question arose, "Can we cross the Salt Desert, or must we take the longer road north of the lake?" When this question began to be agitated who should appear on the scene but William D. Rishel, now located in Salt Lake City as a sort of unofficial automobile pathfinder for the whole of the Great Basin country. Breaking new trails had become an obsession with him— he had already opened the first automobile road into Yellowstone Park and the Grand Canyon.

In the same year that the Western Pacific was built, this modern counterpart of the Hastings of 1846 drove the first automobile to the edge of the Salt Desert for the purpose of ascertaining if it were possible to cross. The day was hot and clear, and when he arrived at the edge of the salt flats he found they were almost completely covered with water—or so he thought. So perfect was the mirage that even this automobile pioneer was deceived. He returned to the city and reported that the route was impossible.

In the meantime automobiles had begun to follow the old pioneer roads—the Fort Hall Road and the Southern Route. But the tourists, like the forty-niners, all complained that the road was much longer than necessary. Rishel, having discovered his mistake of 1907, was frantically trying to find some way of crossing the mud flats of the desert by automobile. Some money was eventually secured, and a dirt embankment was graded for forty miles along the railroad right-of-way, over which the first automobile was driven in 1916. But the desert mud did not lend itself readily to road building purposes, and during the next winter most of the embankment was washed back into the desert. Even at best it was only wide enough for one car and was consequently a one-way road.

Agitation for a road across the Salt Desert now began in earnest, and in 1918 a road was constructed across the southern end of the desert, near Beckwith's route, where the mud flats were only eighteen miles wide. Since there were then no Federal funds for the purpose, the road was financed by Eastern tire and automobile manufacturers, as a stimulant to transcontinental traffic, and $196,000 was sunk in those eighteen miles of mud, which was then made a part of the Lincoln Highway. In dry weather this stretch could be crossed, after a fashion, but when wet it was worth one's life to attempt it. Moisture drawn up from below kept the roadbed soft and it was still next to impossible for two cars to pass.

After Rishel had organized the Utah State Automobile Association he began a real campaign for a safe road across the desert, which he thought should follow the line of the Western Pacific, since that was the most direct route. But the mud flats at that point were forty miles across, and with the earlier experiences of the Goodyear Cutoff farther south, it seemed the expense would be prohibitive.

The fight of different factions over this short stretch of transcontinental highway was long and bitter. Government engineers were finally sent out, who carefully surveyed all the different projected routes and reported that the Wendover Cutoff, while expensive, was the logical route. The Federal Aid Bill was passed by Congress that same year, and in consequence the road was eventually built by government engineers.

Profiting by previous attempts, and conducting numerous experiments, the engineers in charge evolved a unique method which had never been employed elsewhere. They found that if the roadbed was built directly on the salt, it would sink, due to the percolation of water through the salt bed underneath, which is porous. The road embankment, being absolutely level for forty miles, constitutes a dam across the salt flats. If water collected during the winter on the surface to a greater depth on one side than on the other, the pressure on the higher side would force the water through the porous bed of salt beneath, dissolving it away and allowing the roadbed to sink.

To overcome this, a novel method was adopted. A trench three feet wide was dug down through the salt to the mud beneath. Other trenches were dug at some distance from the first to a depth of fifteen feet. The salt from these trenches, which in some places was four feet deep, was discarded but the mud from below the salt was used to build the grade, directly on top of the first trench. Thus the mud in the first trench, connecting with the embankment above and the mud beneath, formed a dike which was impervious to percolating waters and prevented the salt from being dissolved away. The grade was then topped with eight inches of gravel, and the road was complete.

The Wendover Cutoff, following in general the route of the old Hastings Cutoff, was finished in 1924, and was one of the finest pieces of road engineering on the Victory Highway. For forty miles it lies absolutely level and straight. Thousands of automobiles now cross the Salt Desert annually over this road at fifty and sixty miles an hour.

Here, within sight of the old trail where ox teams passed in 1846, one may now ride in comfort, passing the slower moving trains in a high-powered car, and in turn being passed by jet planes which glide overhead, all following the trail first blazed by Kit Carson under Frémont in 1845; later followed by James Clyman, Bryant, Young and Harlan, the Donner party in 1846; Captain Howard Stansbury in 1849; and the gold rush of 1849.

How many tourists, who cover the entire desert in the brief course of an hour, ever stop to think of the dangers and sufferings endured by those brave old pioneers who first crossed with ox teams? Few even know that such crossings have ever been made. The Great Salt Desert, terror of the emigrant, has been conquered at last, and the easterner who still hears echoes of the cry "Gold in California!" can now travel the same trail between Independence Missouri, and San Francisco, in six days by automobile, which his grandfather traveled by ox team in six months.

20. TRAILING THE PIONEERS

Eighty-three years after the passing of Hastings and the Donner party in 1846, I followed their old trail from Salt Lake City across the Salt Desert to the foot of the Pequop Mountains in Nevada.

In Utah and Nevada, fortunately, the old trail is still comparatively well preserved, due to slight rainfall and the fact that it has not been traveled for the greater part of its length since 1850. With the exception of a few miles now under cultivation on each side of the Jordan River in Salt Lake Valley, the old desert trail lies just as it was left by the pioneers. Parts of it, to be sure, have seen the passing of a few sheep wagons during the winter months but the most interesting part, that which crosses the Salt Desert itself, lies unchanged, preserving in the desert mud the footprints of horses, oxen, men, women and children who toiled across its salt-encrusted surface so many years ago. Probably no where else in the world are found the same peculiar combination of conditions which are responsible for the preservation of the individual footprints of pioneers who have long since passed on.

The little town of Grantsville, Utah, located at the "Twenty Wells" spoken of by the Donner party was settled in 1852, and is the nearest settlement east of the Great Salt Desert. Its pioneer inhabitants were naturally interested in the earliest stories of the difficulties of the Donner party brought to Utah by returning members of the Mormon Battalion, and many of these are still remembered there. All such stories contain some truth and a considerable amount of misinformation.

The first news of the fate of the Donner party was brought to Utah in the summer of 1847 by Sam Brannan, leader of the Mormon colony in California. After locating his flock there, Elder Brannan hurried back across the mountains to meet Brigham Young, who was then enroute, and guide him on to the land of promise. But Elder Brannan also brought the information that California had been taken by the Americans and was no longer Mexican territory, which information may have decided Brigham to stop in Utah. From this decision, confirmed by a vote of the people themselves, Brigham could not be moved, and Elder Brannan returned to California in disgust.

On his way east over the Sierra, Brannan had passed the camp where the Donner party had spent such a disastrous winter. Except for members of relief parties, he was first to see the remains of bodies lying about, which had been used for food by their starving companions. The Mormons, having been forcibly expelled from Missouri, always bore the greatest hatred toward anyone from that state, and when it was learned that some of the Donner party were from Missouri, they considered that the Lord had dealt out a fitting punishment to their enemies, after first using them to build a difficult road through the wilderness. I quote from the Sunday School Lesson of the Church of Jesus Christ of Latter-day Saints, for September 15, 1929:

> After establishing his colonists near San Francisco, he [Sam Brannan], with two companions, had braved the wilderness to come and meet President Young, requesting that he go on to California and not stop in the Great Basin. As he came east he had found the camping grounds where a company bound for California [the Donner party] had been snowed in for the winter, and about forty or fifty had perished and had been eaten up by their fellow sufferers. "Their skulls, bones and carcasses lay strewed in every direction." He also met "the hindermost of one of these unfortunate creatures [Keseberg] making his way into the settlements. He had lived upon human flesh for several weeks." Part of the Donner Company was among the persecutors of the Saints in Missouri. They helped make the road in 1846, which the Pioneers were now following.[1]

It was generally believed in Grantsville, until a few years ago, that all of the Donner party had perished in the Salt Desert except six who crawled twenty miles on their hands and knees to water. Just where this story originated is unknown.

The first persons to see the wagons left in the desert were those engaged with Captain Stansbury in surveying the lake in 1849.

[1.] Church of Jesus Christ of Latter-day Saints, *Church History Sunday School Lessons*, "This is the Place," Vol. 2, No. 9 (September 15, 1929). By his own account, Brannan set out with three companions. Levinah W. Murphy was the only member of the Donner party who had once been a Mormon. There is no proof of the claim that members of the Donner party were persecutors of the Saints in Missouri.

Five or six of Stansbury's men were hired in Salt Lake City, one of whom was Albert Carrington, a surveyor, after whom Stansbury named one of the islands in the lake. These men from the Mormon settlement so recently established determined to return when the weather should be more agreeable, and salvage some of the valuable property and wagons. Iron in particular was very expensive so far from the source of supply, and some of the wagons contained valuable goods intended for trade in California. The Donners had passed only three years before, and the wagons were still standing with their contents fairly well preserved.

Some time during the latter part of 1849 or the early spring of 1850 this stuff was brought in to Salt Lake City.[2] Apparently the expedition was kept a secret, lest the sudden acquisition of so much wealth might excite the cupidity of certain individuals. So far as I am able to ascertain there is only one man living today (1930) who has any knowledge of this transaction. Certain it is, from reasons which will appear, that the goods abandoned on the desert were brought in. Albert Carrington kept a detailed diary during his lifetime, and it doubtless contained the facts regarding this matter, but the diary was burned at his express order, in his old age, and whatever record he may have made is lost to us.[3]

The experiences of this salvaging party, if known, would be almost as interesting as the story of the Donner party. In winter the desert is covered with a sheet of salt water a few inches in depth, which does not entirely disappear until hot weather, when, on account of the great distance between watering places, it is almost impossible to cross with oxen. The only possible way in which these men could have brought in the goods or wagons, would have been to cross the entire desert to Pilot Peak, rest their animals a few days and then return, picking up the goods on the return trip.

Not all the wagons found there were brought in at that time, and it is thought that no other attempt was ever made, since several wagons have remained there to the present.

The next persons to see the remaining wagons were Dan Hunt, Quince Knowlton and Steven S. Worthington. These men were

---

[2] Mr. Don Maguire, Ogden, Utah. According to Tullidge the stuff was brought in by Cyrus Call and Samuel Mecham from Tooele in 1849.

[3] Information from Mr. Calvin Carrington, Salt Lake City.

driving cattle from Deep Creek to Grantsville, probably about 1875. The cattle were taken from Deep Creek, southwest of the desert, to Pilot Peak, and from there eastward to the south point of Newfoundland, a rocky desert island north of the old trail, on which there were found "tanks" of water in the rocks; and from Newfoundland over Low Pass in Cedar Mountain to Grantsville.

Traveling eastward from Pilot Peak and Silver Island, these men saw the remains of the wagons deserted in the "deep mud." Some of them had fallen down and had begun to collect mounds of sand. Fragments of the heavy canvas covers still clung to the old wagon bows, and many of the wheels were fairly well preserved. Either at this time or shortly afterward, an old leather boot, containing about seven dollars in small coins, was found by Lard Naylor.

The location was apparently never visited again until 1897. That year was the fiftieth anniversary of the settlement of Salt Lake City, and the Mormons were planning a Jubilee celebration for Pioneer Day, July 24. In looking about for old emigrant wagons to drive in the parade on that day, it was discovered that none were to be found—they had all been worn out and discarded. But the fiftieth annual Pioneer Day would not be complete without some of those old relics of the past to revive memories of the great emigration of 1847. In their dilemma Steven S. Worthington remembered the old wagons he had seen in the desert on the Donner trail and was commissioned to bring some of them in to Salt Lake City if possible. For this he was to receive $175, if successful.

Accompanied by his son, Hamp, Mr. Worthington drove a team and wagon back over his cattle trail of 1875, to Pilot Peak. But the years had raised havoc with the wagons left there, and not even one complete pair of wheels could be brought back, so badly were they deteriorated by the action of salt water and the weathering of sixty-one years.

Several articles, however, were recovered and turned over to the committee in charge of the celebration. Among these was a medicine chest, still containing three bottles in which were rosin, turpentine and camphor; an ox yoke and some ox shoes; dishes, old shoes, tinware, the barrel of an old rifle which had been driven into the mud and a log chain which had rusted together in a heap.

About fifteen years later Silas Gillette, Ed and Alvin Orem made a trip into the desert, for the purpose of burying the bones of the emigrants who were supposed to have died there. Just why they should have decided to bury these bones, after so many years, I am not able to ascertain. Silas Gillette says they did find and bury a box full of bones, but he is not sure that they were human bones, as no skulls were found. As a matter of fact there is no historic record of anyone having died in the Salt Desert, and the bones they found were undoubtedly those of oxen or horses. They left no marker, and the exact spot is unknown.[4]

Since 1897 no one, so far as I am able to ascertain, visited the vicinity of the old trail until 1927, when Captain Charles E. Davis came from California and obtained parts of some of the old wagons for the Sutter's Fort Historical Museum at Sacramento. Mr. C. F. Hartmeyer, a grandson of the last member of the Donner party to be rescued, is custodian of this museum. Captain Davis believes he found parts of James F. Reed's big wagon. Through his activities I first heard of the existence of the Salt Desert Trail, and determined to follow it from Salt Lake City entirely across the desert, noting every landmark mentioned by the pioneers.

The different excursions made in tracing this old trail mile by mile, over the mountains, through the valleys and across the Salt Desert, have proven interesting far beyond the fondest expectations, and it is with the idea of preserving the information discovered during these trips that I have undertaken this story. Thirty years ago first-hand information might have been obtained; now we must be content with second-hand facts. In another thirty years there will be nothing but vague legends. I consider myself fortunate to have been able to uncover a number of facts, considering the length of time which has elapsed.

The old Donner trail, later followed by the Mormons, comes down Emigration Canyon into Salt Lake Valley. The last mile or two was still visible there until 1960. Passing the site of Salt Lake City it crossed the Jordan River and led toward the south end of the lake, eighteen miles west, where it passed between the lake and the point of the mountain near Black Rock. Part of this section is now under cultivation, and the old trail at the point of the mountain is now occupied by a concrete highway, which, in passing the point, must of necessity occupy the old trail.

[4.] Dr. A. L. Inglesby, then of Bingham Canyon, Utah, was also a member of this party, and says he saw no human bones.

Passing this point we enter Tooele Valley. Just at the edge of the lake, after entering the valley, is a spring. Here the Donner party rested after their first day's journey from the Jordan, and it was here that Reed broke an axle on his wagon and spent all night repairing it. It was also while camped at this spot that one of the Donner wagons came up bearing the body of Luke Halloran.

About two miles west of this spring stands a peculiar group of rocks, like a monument rising from the floor of the valley, and toward this the trail goes in a curve following the solid ground above the shoreline of the lake. It then circles the large spring at "E. T. City" (present Lake Point), an early settlement now [in 1930] almost abandoned, and from this spring goes directly toward Grantsville, following the curve of the shoreline, and using a natural grade which runs for several miles, marking one of the lower shorelines of old Lake Bonneville.

At Grantsville the emigrants found the "Twenty Wells." Most of these have been filled up, but some still remain, just as described by the Donner party in 1846 and John Wood in 1850.

From Grantsville the trail leads around the foot of the mountains to avoid the sloughs at the edge of the lake. It was a long day's travel from the wells at Grantsville to the springs in Skull Valley where they rested their stock before attempting the desert. On this part of the trail they passed many salt springs, the largest of which is found just after entering Skull Valley. This Big Salt Spring is mentioned by nearly all early travelers, but today runs a stream considerably larger than in 1854, when it was carefully described by Lieutenant Beckwith.

Several miles south in Skull Valley the emigrants found fresh springs, and at the southernmost of these, now called Burnt Spring, near Iosepa, they camped. The modern highway closely follows the old trail as far as the Big Salt Spring; but from these fresh springs on to Pilot Peak the old trail has been traveled in few places since the pioneers passed, and then only by the wagons of occasional sheepherders in winter.

From these springs the trail makes a straight line west to the foot of Cedar Mountain, which separates Skull Valley from the Salt Desert. The detour to the south from the entrance of Skull Valley was necessary for two reasons: first, it was impossible to go directly west along the shore of the lake to Low Pass on account of the marsh which filled the north end of the valley; second, it was necessary to rest the animals and lay in a supply of water and grass.

Arriving at the foot of the pass over Cedar Mountain, the trail crosses the ravine and follows up the left or south bank. In the bottom of this ravine, just at the point of crossing we found the damp sand which Bryant scooped out to obtain the bitter water which he carried with him across the desert. The Donner party evidently did not discover water here, and it is not to be wondered at. Only an experienced mountain man would have been able to find it at that season of the year.

Samuel C. Young crossed this mountain during the night. After leaving the springs in Skull Valley all the different emigrant trains kept moving day and night until they reached Pilot Peak. But this pass offers considerable difficulty, even in daylight, and if Young and Harlan made this first passage with wagons during the night, they certainly deserve the highest credit for persistence under difficulties. The pass is still called after Hastings, although Kit Carson discovered it, when with Frémont in 1845.

From the summit of Hastings Pass, one thousand feet above the valley, the emigrants had their first view of the Great Salt Desert which they were about to cross. Immediately below lay several miles of sage-covered plain. A few miles to the west ran a ridge of volcanic hills. Beyond the hills the white and barren salt flats stretched away westward as far as the eye could see, with here and there a mountain rising like an island from a lake of salt. On the far horizon, seventy-five miles away, loomed Pilot Peak, their objective, at the foot of which flowed the springs which were to furnish them with their next water. There was no turning back from this dreary prospect; it was either do or die. After passing the springs in Skull Valley there could be no stopping until Pilot Peak was reached.

A direct line from Hastings Pass to Pilot Peak runs a little north of west, and the emigrants chose a direct line as being the shortest route between two given points. They might have saved much labor by circling Grayback Mountain, the last hill before striking the salt flats, but instead they traveled in a straight line, crossing the ridge at a point about five miles north of the present Victory Highway.

Between the western side of the pass and Grayback, I found the old trail is almost obliterated. Greasewood and sagebrush dwindle in size as the trail approaches the desert, and the flats are gradually being covered with fine silt and windblown sand. The only evidence of the trail over this stretch is a slight discoloration of the vegetation, which can be seen in the distance, but disappears upon a closer view. It was only through the guidance of Mr. Frank Durfee of Grantsville, that this part of the trail was located. He remembered seeing it quite plainly marked when he was a boy, and except for this fact it would have been entirely lost.

Upon reaching Grayback we were unable to find where the trail crossed; evidences of it were apparently obliterated by erosion. But upon following the crest of the ridge, we began to pick up articles which had been lost or discarded, and shortly found the exact spot where wagons had been brought over the hill. It was an exceedingly steep climb, and some digging had been done on the east slope to prevent the wagons from overturning. Here were found a few pieces of wagon boxes made of chestnut and oak. We also picked up the horn of an ox, probably broken off during the struggle to reach the top. Since it is impossible for cattle to live in this dry desert, this weathered old horn could have been left there in no other way.

Reaching the top of the hill we discovered fragments of two broken jugs. Upon reaching this place the emigrants had been without water for about twenty-four hours, and from here on the trail is littered with discarded jugs, bottles, kegs and barrels. When a vessel was emptied it was discarded to lighten the load.

On the very pinnacle of this hill was found a cedar club which had been used to urge the oxen up the steep slope. The driver could see no more hills in the distance, and presumed he would have no further use for it. A cobbler's hammer was also found here.

West of Grayback the trail for many miles has not been traveled since 1850, and we were fortunate enough to find it just as the pioneers left it.

Resting their oxen after the strenuous climb, the emigrants searched for the easiest way to get down the opposite slope. The western side of this hill slopes more gradually, but is covered with volcanic boulders of all sizes. To prevent breaking the wheels of their wagons—a very serious accident at this stage of the journey— they rolled aside the largest of these boulders and made a reasonably safe road. But at best it was an extremely rough passage for the next mile; for this reason we found the hillside literally strewn with articles which had been jolted out of the wagons. Here was a coffeepot, there a tin pail, mashed by the wheels of the wagons. Broken bottles and jugs were scattered all down the hill. Lids of pots and pans were numerous, and along here we found fragments of the first old-fashioned whiskey flask, and the remains of a bottle of bitters, a good substitute for whiskey in those days. The emigrants, realizing that the great struggle was immediately before them, thus fortified themselves for the ordeal.

The most important find on the whole trail was made just at the foot of this hill. There in the sandy soil among the rocks lay an old Kentucky rifle, the barrel forty-four inches long, and the stock decorated with carefully shaped brass fittings. The wood of the stock was almost gone, the lock was rusted away, but the heavy octagon barrel was still in good condition. It had been bent in two places, probably to destroy its usefulness if found by Indians. With this rifle was also found the stock of another and cheaper gun.

From the top of Grayback we could plainly see the streak of darker green which indicated the trail below, leading away to the west across a perfectly level and increasingly barren sage flat.[5] At the foot of Grayback we had found a stave from an old wooden bucket; at intervals for the next five miles we picked up nearly all the other staves of this bucket, which had apparently dried out and started to fall apart.

At the end of five miles we came to the first of a long series of sand dunes. These dunes indicate the last shore line of the old lake, and a water level can still be traced along their sides. They are composed of very fine grayish-yellow sand, held in place by a thin salty crust, the interior being soft and spongy like new ashes. The dunes average probably thirty feet in height, and between the lines of dunes are lagoon-like basins covered with salt, foretaste of the great salt flats beyond.

Across these lagoons the wheelmarks of the old wagons can still be seen as plainly as though made last week. In places the individual footprints of the oxen and loose stock can be seen.

On the edge of the first lagoon we found a spot marked with broken jugs and bits of wood, where still remained the distinct footprints of a man, a woman and a child, together with the tracks

---

[5.] Here Bryant saw the illusion of breaking waves. It is still to be seen, although the flat is now partly covered with stunted greasewood.

of oxen. The animals, from all appearances, had given some trouble at that place.

The trail through the dunes has been obliterated by wind-blown sand, but Mr. Durfee, who accompanied my brother and me over this part of the trail, is an expert tracker, and by walking ahead of the car was able to pick up enough bits of broken wood and old square iron nails to indicate the trail.

When we struck the dunes it appeared we could go no farther in the car. But after several attempts we found the crust would hold sufficient for one passage of the wheels—if we were compelled to back down, we could not again follow the same tracks, but were forced to make new ones. After a few trials we were able to make slow headway over what at first appeared absolutely impossible.

On the opposite side of the second line of dunes, we found a spot where the emigrants had stopped for refreshments. Here were bits of charcoal, and scattered about were more fragments of the old whiskey flasks, turned blue by the sun, together with small pieces of badly rusted iron, a few old nails, a broken jug, three jug stoppers and the bung of a large barrel. Here we found the bottom and the hoops of the wooden bucket which had been scattered all along the trail. Near here also was found a walnut tent stake and a piece of chestnut board with the initials "H. P." carved in it.

After passing the second line of dunes there is a stretch of perhaps two miles of level going over the soft surface of the desert, dotted here and there with clumps of salt sage which have gathered about their roots small dunes of sand. After this comes another series of dunes and lagoons, and it would appear from the remains scattered along the trail that the emigrants were beginning to suffer severely at this point. In such terrific going as they encountered with their heavy narrow-tired wagons in this loose ashy sand, the oxen must have begun to show signs of great distress.

At the foot of the dunes on the west side of the next lagoon, we found an old army canteen of the period of 1845, still in a fair state of preservation considering its age. This may have belonged either to some of Frémont's men or to some member of Stansbury's party. I prefer to believe the latter since by the time Stansbury reached this place going east, he was entirely out of water.

Another dune was crossed and still another. Then, on the opposite side of the next lagoon we found the remains of several ox yokes and heavy wagon timbers, some improvised from mountain cedars, and some made of oak brought all the way from Missouri or perhaps even Illinois. Here were tent stakes standing in the ground and the remains of a fire, and here the wagons had spread to the right and left of the trail, apparently to rest and feed the oxen and to make coffee. This stop was probably made about morning of the second day. Stansbury, passing this place in 1849, found signs of a cache of goods which had been robbed, and a pile of twelve ox yokes. Just who made this cache, who robbed it, and why the ox yokes were left at this particular spot is unknown.

Climbing the dune beyond this resting place, Frank Durfee found that the dunes continued for at least three miles farther without a break, and at first glance it looked absolutely impossible to get a car through such treacherous ground. But since we had come so far without mishap it was voted to make an attempt. Here the trail was invisible and we were guided solely by Durfee's sense of direction. Toward the western edge of these bad lands I turned somewhat south, feeling sure the trail lay in that direction; but when we finally surmounted the last obstacle and struck the level desert again, we were obliged to turn north to locate the wagon tracks, which we found just at the spot indicated by Durfee.

There, we found ourselves on the very edge of the REAL Salt Desert. Before us lay an absolutely level expanse of salt-encrusted mud as far as the eye could see, with nothing between us and the hazy outlines of Pilot Peak on the distant horizon. No vegetation of any kind dotted this limitless expanse, and here we became aware of the full beauty—and terror—of the desert mirage.

The old trail lay before us glittering in the sun. Here were no ruts, to be sure—the surface was perfectly smooth and level—yet the trail stretched away to the west as plainly as though the pioneers had passed only last year. The surface of the desert here consists of several layers of fine silt, some light gray, some dark gray, and some nearly white. At a depth of about twelve inches lies a layer of white crystals of sodium sulfate, several inches in thickness. Beneath this again is more gray silt, the whole saturated with salt. The narrow tires of the emigrant wagons cut through these various layers of silt, bringing to the surface sometimes darker and sometimes lighter material. Then, when melting snows of winter or occasional summer showers cause this level surface to be covered with a shallow film of water for a short time, the salt and lighter sediments gradually settle and fill these old ruts, leaving the surface perfectly smooth, but making a distinct discoloration which remains permanently. Thus it happens that each individual wagon track, unless merged with another, is still plainly visible on the surface of the desert, and the main trail, where wagon followed wagon, lies like a white ribbon streaming toward the west.

Setting their course directly for Pilot Peak, the emigrants started across the vast level salt plain, probably with many misgivings; for let it be recorded here that even we, with a mechanically perfect car, plenty of water, with shovels for digging out, and with the modern highway only ten miles to the south, felt a peculiar sinking sensation as we set out from the last of the dunes on our journey across this terrifying desert. Ahead of us, shimmering in the sun, lay what appeared to be beautiful lakes of clear water, and as we advanced the lake closed in behind us, so that we were apparently surrounded with water. The sensation was like being on a floating island in the ocean.

The wheels of the car made a deep impression in the soft desert mud, but still we made good progress in high gear over the smooth surface, from which there was no vibration whatever. The large size of our tires, together with the crust which had begun to form, prevented our breaking through to the soft slime underneath. We had been told that as we advanced we would find the surface softer, until finally we would be compelled to retreat. However, we were determined to see for ourselves, and since the car still traveled easily, we kept moving forward. Nearly ten miles we traveled in a straight line, finding nothing of unusual interest. Then, in the distance, a grove of trees began to take form. In the midst of the grove were towers rising far above the trees, which seemed to float on the surface of the lake. Another mile and we came to a small sand bar, on which grew a few stunted sagebrush, and as we drew nearer the trees disappeared; but the towers remained.

Stopping here to investigate, we walked toward one of these towers, which disappeared as we approached, then reappeared near at hand; what we found was almost as strange as anything we could have imagined. Here was the nest of some kind of large bird, probably an osprey, which had been built up a little each year from pieces of sagebrush and greasewood, the wind filling the interstices with sand until the whole structure had grown to be more than ten feet high. A few stray feathers in the deserted nest on the top of this pinnacle showed that it had recently been occupied. To the right and left were three or four similar structures, with some smaller ones which were not as old. Here, year after year, comes some bird to build her nest, finding both solitude and safety in this dreary waste. How she rears her young in such an environment, thirty-five miles from the nearest water, and nearly that far from any kind of food, is a riddle which must be solved by the ornithologist.

On this slight sandy elevation the emigrants had stopped to rest and make coffee. Here we found the remains of a fire, much charcoal still remaining, and near the fire a broken blue china saucer, and part of a white china plate.

Scattered about were many pieces of wood, parts of wagon boxes and running gears, some heavy pieces badly decomposed which may have been ox yokes or extra axles, and pieces of old iron, very brittle, staining the salty mud for a considerable distance. There were pieces of boot soles, with the wooden pegs still preserved; knots of hemp rope in surprisingly good condition, and the remains of a tar bucket which had hung underneath one of the wagons.

When the emigrants reached this place their oxen were still moving, but must have begun to suffer terribly from thirst. They refused the hay which had been brought in the wagons; their tongues were so dry they could not eat it. Some had probably given out already, but so far no wagons had been deserted.

Leaving this resting spot we began to go forward again toward the west. Pilot Peak now loomed up somewhat larger, although many miles away. Between us and Pilot Peak, however, began to loom another smaller ridge of mountains called Silver Island. Apparently insignificant foothills from the eastern edge of the desert, they now assumed the form of real mountains, and as we advanced, began to shut off our view of Pilot Peak altogether, since they stand twelve miles nearer. Finally the distant mountain was entirely lost from view; here the trail swerves slightly to the north, toward a low pass between two of the peaks of Silver Island. This "island" extends into the desert for forty miles, north of Wendover, being a chain of volcanic mountains with low passes between.

When the Donner party passed here, it was a moonlit night; as they neared this ridge they lost sight of Pilot Peak entirely. In their state of exhaustion and mental depression they thought this "island" was the mountain they were seeking, at the foot of which they would find water. So they swerved toward the right to pass what appeared to be the north point of the mountain, but which turned out to be a low pass between two of the mountains of this small chain.

Soon we noticed that our wheels were skidding slightly, and the engine began to labor. The tires made a deep and ragged impression in the mud. The surface took on a sickly gray color in spots, and when we struck these spots the wheels went down several inches into the muck. Still, since we had come so far in safety, we decided to go as far as we possibly could, hoping that the surface would be slightly drier farther on and enable us to make the entire crossing of the desert, something which had never been accomplished in a car.

Half a mile or so from the last stopping place we began to find the remains of discarded wagons. First we found four large iron tires, lying close together. No wooden parts were found with these, and we surmised that the hubs and spokes had been burned by some of the parties which passed in 1850. A little farther on lay the iron axle and two tires of an old-fashioned buggy—probably made into a cart. Stansbury mentions seeing the remains of a cart. Still farther along we found six wagon tires lying near each other, with the same appearance of having been burned. They were so brittle we could not lift them out of the salt.

In the distance, at the foot of Silver Island, now began to loom up the outlines of Floating Island, a volcanic upthrust which apparently made its appearance in the bottom of old Lake Bonneville. Around the "shores" of this island considerable sand has been deposited by the wind, and on this grows bright green greasewood, which from a distance appears like beautiful green grass. When the emigrants sighted this island, which is the first "land" after crossing the desert, they probably thought that water might be found at its base, and consequently the trail makes a bend to the left toward it.

So level is this desert that any small object projecting above its surface a few inches, can be seen for a mile or more, and on account of the mirage is magnified many times. As we changed our course toward Floating Island, we saw in the distance what appeared to be a large mound. Arriving at this mound we found it to be an old wagon box lying on the surface, which the wind had completely covered with sand of the consistency of brown sugar. Protruding out of this sand was the axle and part of the running gears of a light wagon. Although exposed to the elements, this axle, on account of its raised position, was protected from the action of salt water, and consequently was almost as sound as the day it was left there. The wagon box, likewise, had been protected from the action of the air by being buried in damp sand, and was still sound and all complete. Wood, when buried in the salt mud or sand, is perfectly preserved. But when exposed to both salt water and air, it becomes as pulpy and light as cotton. The iron parts of this wagon, likewise, where exposed to the atmosphere but not to the salt, were well preserved.

Here we made a stop to examine our find. The wagon box was empty, and there were no wheels near it, nor any other parts of the gear. After photographing this relic, we climbed back into the car preparatory to resuming our journey, which now seemed assured of success. In the distance we could discern other similar mounds and our hopes were high. But when I stepped on the gas the wheels began to spin in the soapy slime; before I could take my foot off the throttle both rear wheels were mired to the axle.

Evidently we had not been misinformed about the condition of the desert. Our journey was at an end for the present; but with the aid of shovels we anticipated we would be on our way again in a few minutes. Digging a trench in front of the wheels I again applied the power. But so soapy was the mud after the thin crust had been broken that there was no result except to sink the car deeper into the mud. Now the rear axle was embedded and the exhaust pipe plugged with mud. Water began to seep into the bottom of the ruts.

Here we were in the middle of the Great Salt Desert, mired to the axle, with no grass, sagebrush or rocks to lend traction to the wheels, no fence posts to lay in the ruts, and nothing on which to set a pry or jack, even if we could have gotten the jack under the axle. To make matters worse, the afternoon was rapidly passing, and in the distance, coming toward us, was a thunder shower, hanging like a curtain across the sky. If the rain should strike us and dampen that slimy surface, we knew there would be no more traveling until it dried out again. We were now thirteen miles north of the highway. Exhausted by our efforts to move the car, we sat down to decide what must be done.

Although the prospect seemed hopeless, yet there must be some way out, if we could only discover it. Suddenly it dawned on us that the old wagon box might yet be the solution of our difficulty, and it was the work of only a few minutes to dig out the two old end-gates. Much as we regretted having to disturb this old relic of pioneer days it was our only salvation. We supposed that the boards would be too rotten to hold the weight of the wheels; but in this we were pleasantly surprised—they were almost as strong as when new. Using the old light wooden axle as a lever, our jack as a fulcrum, and one of the end-gates as a base to prevent the jack from sinking in the mud, we gradually raised one of the wheels and inserted the other end-gate under it. Then, procuring one of the old sideboards, we placed it likewise under the other wheel. Applying the power, the wheels still spun on the soapy boards, and we were no better off than before. Finally, in desperation, we carried hatfuls of the sugar-like sand which had accumulated in the old wagon box, packed this around the wheels to give them traction, and with a last final attempt, pulled out of the hole. Keeping the car in motion we circled around on to the accumulated sand near the wagon box, loaded on our life-savers, the old axle and boards, and eventually made our way south to the highway, avoiding the difficult sand dunes behind us.

Since it was found impossible to cross from the east, our next attempt was made from the west. Following along the foot of Silver Island we struck the old trail just north of Floating Island. Here the tracks of the pioneer wagons are widely scattered; many had driven miles out of their way trying to locate water or feed somewhere on the island, only to be disappointed. There is an overhanging bluff on this island, and at the foot of this bluff the sand is slightly damp, supporting a few bunches of grass. Here we found the skull of an old horse which had been abandoned on the desert and had come here to pick what grass there might be and paw at the damp sand in hopes of finding a drop or two of moisture. At this damp spot it had remained until it died of thirst, and the coyotes had carried away everything but the skull.

Although many wagons had explored the vicinity of Floating Island, the main trail, half a mile north, was well marked. On this trail, nearly opposite the island, we first found another heavy piece of wood, part of a wagon, and several smaller fragments of cedar. A short distance farther on was a shapeless heap of fibrous wood which had collected a small mound of sand. Carefully removing the sand we discovered that the fragments of wood to be barrel staves, badly decomposed where exposed to the air, but perfectly sound where buried in the damp sand. Clearing these away we found the head of the old barrel intact and just as sound as when left there by the emigrants in 1846. This barrel had evidently been abandoned when empty; on one side of the head are still preserved the fine lines made by a knife when it had been used as a table upon which to slice bacon. Part of the old hickory staves were also preserved under the sand.

We were now traveling eastward, toward the place where we had been forced to turn back on our westward journey, and it should be kept in mind that in the deep mud which had forced our retreat previously lay the wagons deserted by the emigrants, and that this part of the trail had been traveled by the occupants of those wagons on foot.

A little farther east from the spot where we found the barrel I saw what I took to be a small stake, protruding two or three inches above the surface. Stopping to examine this, it was found to be the breech end of an old rifle barrel, which had been driven into the mud. A half hour's work in the sticky mud with a shovel brought to light the balance of the gun barrel, which was encrusted with two or three inches of iron-impregnated mud. The end which had protruded above the surface was in good shape, showing the tube of the old flintlock, and the threads of the breech-block; but the balance of the barrel was very brittle and in places eaten through to the bore. Even so it is a priceless relic. It had evidently been discarded along here either because it had become broken and useless, or because its owner, now many hours without water had become too exhausted to carry it farther. Just why it should have been driven into the mud is a mystery.

Walking in circles around this point, looking for a possible cache, I found, lying on the surface, the two halves of a small folding brass comb. In spite of the fact that it had lain there in the salt crust for more than eighty years, it was still in excellent condition, the fine teeth being apparently as strong as ever. The slight oxidation was easily removed, and the metal underneath found not to be injured in any way by its long exposure to the elements.

Leaving Floating Island behind we now began following the trail toward the east. For several miles we traveled, finding nothing. The going became again difficult, the wheels skidding on the slippery surface, the dangerous gray spots began to appear, and so we decided in the interest of safety to leave the car and cover the remaining distance across this mud on foot. Just how far it might be back to where we had abandoned the search on the eastern side of the deep mud we did not know, since there were no guiding landmarks of any kind.

Walking became rapidly more difficult as we entered this imperceptible depression which constitutes the "deep mud." Our boots picked up enormous quantities of it, which was shaken off with difficulty, and it can easily be imagined what must have happened here to the wheels of the emigrant wagons. In attempting to remove this mud with a shovel, the shovel becomes burdened with the sticky mass, which clings to everything it touches. In their already thirsty, sleepless, exhausted and irritable state, the emigrants must have suffered the torments of hell when they found themselves mired in this bottomless glue.

After proceeding two or three miles on foot we noted in the distance some dark objects beginning to loom up on the horizon. These, we knew, could be nothing else but the remains of the old wagons, around which the wind had collected considerable sand. Hastening our steps we finally reached the first of these low mounds and looked upon what must have been the remains of the big wagon belonging to James F. Reed, which was left standing in the desert in 1846.

Here were the four wheels, lying close together, the hubs only showing above the sand. These hubs, from their enormous size together with the heavy oak wheels which we soon exposed to view, indicated a wagon of unusual proportions, being larger and heavier than any others we found there. One of the hubs still retained the broken end of an axle.

These old wagons were of the linch-pin variety, in which an iron pin is inserted through the end of the wooden axle to prevent the wheel from coming off. The axle could be replaced, and frequently was, but the wheel and hub could not be repaired by any but an expert wheelwright. The ends of the wooden axles were reinforced with strips of iron on the under and upper sides, and the weight of the load rested upon the two points of contact between these strips and the iron boxing in each end of the hub. Through a loop of iron in the end of the axle was inserted the linch-pin.

Our shovels had been left behind in the car, but clearing away the sand with our hands we uncovered two of the wheels, one of which was nearly intact. The spokes still sat solidly in the hubs, all the iron hoops and friction rings were in place, although badly eaten by the salt, and the tires were still strong enough to be handled without breaking. Even the old linch-pins were in place.

Digging in the sand we uncovered what had been an enormous log chain, all rusted together in one big red lump. With a little scraping, however, the links could be distinguished. Here were fragments of boards, parts of axles, and many odd pieces of iron, so badly decomposed that we could not identify them. Much more still lies to be uncovered at some later time.

At one end of this long heap of sand-covered remains we found the skeletons of two oxen. Here, then, was the whole tragedy lying before us in the mud—the deserted wagon, left standing on the desert, with the exhausted oxen still in their places.

Continuing eastward, we shortly encountered the remains of another wagon, not as large, but in the same condition as the first. Much iron was lying about, a few boards still remained, and here again was the skeleton of an ox. A short distance farther was found two other heaps representing wagons, and in between were the bones of another ox. Still another wagon lay just off the trail in the near vicinity.

Here, within sight of each other, and approximately in a group, lay the remains of five wagons. These probably were the three left by Reed and one each by Keseberg and Donner.

On the horizon to the east we could see still other heaps of sand, each marking the site of some disaster. Sometimes it would be part of a box; in other places only wheels. Often there was nothing left but the iron tires, or perhaps a group of hub rings. In the whole desert we did not find a complete wagon in any one spot. This, I believe, is due to the fact that the best parts of these wagons were salvaged in 1849, and that much of the remaining lumber was probably burned for fuel by the gold seekers of 1850.

Eventually we reached the spot where we had been forced to turn back on our westward trip, near the old wagon box, which had served us so well, having covered the entire trail as far west as Floating Island. Retracing our steps toward the car, which was now a mere speck on the distant horizon, we endeavored to read the story which the pioneers had left written in the desert mud.

Up to the point where the deep mud begins, the wagons had kept together, most of them using the same track. Here and there one would stop to rest his oxen and the man behind, becoming impatient, would circle around him. Here and there we could plainly see where an ox had given out and been taken out of the team. Occasionally a wagon would pull out to the side of the trail to let others pass.

But as the trail became softer, each one apparently made his own trail, rather than follow in the deep ruts of the wagon ahead. Here, in the worst going, the tracks of the individual wagons are spread out over a width of a long city block. These sometimes cross and weave about, but for the most part are parallel.

Here, with calamity upon them, and with their oxen giving out one by one, the women and children were compelled to walk beside the wagons to lighten the loads; and here, in the desert mud, covering nearly every square foot of this part of the trail to the width of a city block, are the faintly visible footprints of those pioneers who walked to lighten their wagons—or because their wagons had already been left behind.

According to the record of survivors of the Donner party, the contents of two wagons were buried "in the desert." It has always been thought that this cache was made in the salt mud near where the wagons were abandoned. But no indications of a cache have ever been found in that locality, and the nature of the country would discourage any such procedure, since an excavation more than eight inches deep immediately fills up with salt water.

Of the large amount of valuable goods, books and scientific instruments seen by Stansbury in 1849, nothing whatever was found. It may be that Indians carried off everything that was left by Carrington and his friends. Indians did occasionally frequent this waterless and barren section of the desert, as is proven by their camp sites on Silver Island. During the winter it would be possible for them to obtain water by melting the snow. In winter also, antelope and mountain sheep were found on Silver Island.

Whatever may have become of all the small articles such as dishes, bottles and tools, remains a mystery. Nothing now remains except heavy pieces of iron, old log chains and scattered fragments of wood.

Nothing of particular interest was discovered on our return along this part of the trail, with the exception of a heavy oak bolster from one of the wagons some distance off the trail, with the kingpin still in place; one spot the size of a wagon box covered with what appears to have been blacksmith tools; and the spout of an old-fashioned teakettle.

Returning to the car, loaded with relics, we rested a half hour and then drove back past Floating Island and began following the trail on westward. Within a mile or two we struck the base of the mountainous Silver Island, and followed northward along this for several miles.

Along this part of the trail on a subsequent trip, Mr. Dan Orr, of Grantsville, found a number of interesting relics. Lying on the rocks just above the trail was a heavy log chain, in perfect condition, except that one hook was broken. Near this lay a short end-gate chain, with "finger-hooks," also in perfect condition. Near the same spot he found a yoke ring and staple partly buried in the soil. Excavation showed that the wooden parts of at least one wagon had been burned there, and the soil was full of rusted iron bolts and braces. On a mound below the trail lay a broken earthen jar and near the mound a large pile of log chains rusted together in a heap. A dim trail was found running from this rocky point directly toward the deserted wagons, which in all probability is the trail of those who returned to salvage the supplies of food left in the abandoned wagons; they saved a mile or two by taking a more direct route. Farther along the foot of Silver Island was found a broken cast iron frying pan; still farther north and a considerable distance from the trail was found a complete hub and linch-pin, together with an iron tire and hub rings.

Reaching the pass over Silver Island, the trail climbs the steep face of a bluff and strikes directly west. Once over the bluff the pass slopes gently to the east and west and is probably four or five miles in width. At the summit the emigrants had their first near view of Pilot Peak, and far in the distance, at its base, they could discern clumps of willows which represented the vicinity of water—the first signs of water they had seen since leaving the springs in Skull Valley, sixty hours before, during all of which time they had been in constant motion. Their feelings can better be imagined than expressed. Only one who has seen this trail can have any adequate idea of its depressing desolation. But, even though signs of water were now in sight, there were still twelve miles of salt mud to be crossed. After leaving the opposite side of Silver Island the going was almost as bad as the deep mud on the eastern side, but as they progressed it gradually became more firm, and the oxen, smelling water while still many miles away, took a new lease on life, and hurried forward. The trail across these twelve miles can be plainly seen from the pass, and strikes directly west for the nearest clump of green.

Just before reaching the salt plains west of the pass we found the remains of a wheel. It was one of a pair which were seen still standing about ten years ago by Charles McKellar. Its mate had been carried to a sheep camp farther north where we later found the tire and hub rings. A badly decomposed ox yoke of unusual size was also found on the edge of the salt.

In our car we crossed these salt flats to the springs in half an hour. But to the emigrants who had by then been from two to four days and nights without water, constantly on the move without sleep and with very little food, this last stretch of the trail, with the springs in sight, must have been the most trying of the whole journey. Oxen dropped in their tracks and the wagons became mired here within plain sight of water. Even to those who were able to keep moving the distance must have seemed interminable. With the peculiar conditions existing here on account of the absolutely level plain, the mirage, and the great mountain behind, one seems to travel endlessly, the objective seeming to be no nearer, until almost upon it.

The spring which the emigrants first found breaks out of the ground just a few rods from the very edge of the salt mud. It is easily located by the dense growth of reeds, and the peculiar jointed canegrass which grows there, mentioned by Edwin Bryant. The stream flowing from the spring never reaches the salt flats, but sinks in the sand and gravel within a short distance. When the emigrants stopped here in 1846 the desert for some distance around the spring was covered with a dense growth of willows; but since these were the only available fuel for the pioneers who stopped to recruit their strength they soon disappeared, although the dead stumps remained for many years after.

There is now a ranch at this emigrant spring, at the end of the long, dry trail. The spring waters a small garden and some fruit trees and alfalfa, assisted by a limited underground flow. It is primarily a cattle ranch, a watering place for stock roaming the long slope of Pilot Peak. The owners, the Cummings Brothers, gave us much valuable information.

After exploring the vicinity for traces of pioneer equipment we turned south and traveled two miles to another spring of the same kind, at which is located the McKellar ranch. Here we found Mr. Eugene Munsee, eighty years old, who had originally homesteaded the land fifty years before.

It was just getting dark when we arrived, and we had traveled all day without stopping for lunch. But after stating our object in crossing the desert and asking a few questions I soon discovered that Mr. Munsee was the one man I wanted to talk to about the Salt Desert trail. Forgetting we had not eaten all day, I spent the hours until midnight questioning him about what he had seen around those springs when he first camped there fifty years before.

"Were there any wagons or goods found here when you first came to these springs?" I asked.

"Well I should say there was!" he replied. "The whole desert for half a mile out and all around the springs was covered with parts of old wagons, tools, goods, log chains, ox yokes, and everything you could think of. I first saw this place about thirty years after the Donner party had passed, and of course by that time there were no whole wagons standing. All of them had begun to fall down, and most had been taken apart, to use the strongest parts of each. Whenever an emigrant came by here, he stopped to repair his wagons while his cattle were resting, and helped himself to anything he found. A box would be missing from one wagon, a wheel or two from another, a tongue from another, and so on. Many of the wooden parts of the wagons had been burned for fuel, after the willows gave out, and the ground all around here was covered with the remains of old fires. There were tons of old iron scattered around—wagon tires, hub rings, iron braces, farming implements, blacksmith tools, and dozens of heavy log chains."

"What ever became of all that stuff?" I asked.

"Well, you know, in the early days iron was expensive and scarce in these parts. By the time you had hauled iron across the plains, it cost money. So when the country began to be settled up over in Nevada, the settlers used to come here and haul away wagon loads of old iron to be worked over into tools and repairs for their own wagons. I remember even as late as when the railroad was built around the north end of the lake, a Chinaman from Tecoma, Nevada, came over here with a team and hauled away a big load of old iron which he sold for junk. Of course, people who heard of the Donner party have carried away a lot of things for souvenirs and we have used some of the stuff around the place here, until there is hardly anything left anymore. We used to pick up old guns, broken dishes, bone buttons, old whiskey flasks, ox shoes and the like. They were scattered all over the flats out there."

"Have you ever been out to the place where the wagons were left standing in the desert?" I inquired.

"No, I never have. I have been all over Silver Island, not far from there, and I know about where they are located, but I have never seen them. I never had any occasion to go there, and you know that is a dangerous country to travel on a horse; it's too far from water. So I usually stick around pretty close to the springs. I used to run sheep on Silver Island in winter when there was snow on the ground, and I have found stuff scattered all over them mountains. Yes sir! Saddles, parts of wagons and buggies, pieces of harness, and log chains. You see that peak out there, that highest one? Well sir, a good many years ago I climbed that mountain, and right at the top I found a broken ox yoke. I could never figure how it got there, but there it was. It's there yet, I guess, if somebody hasn't packed it off, and I don't think they have."

"Were there any wagons left on the trail between Silver Island and this place when you first came here?"

"No, I don't remember seeing any. They were all hauled in to the springs from this side of the island. But I remember many years ago when I was riding along the foot of those hills there, two or three miles south of where the trail crosses, I found the remains of a buggy, with the skeletons of two horses, with the harness still on them. They had given out along there, and the owner had probably walked to the springs and left them standing on the desert. A horse, you know, is different from an ox. An ox, left like that, will start to hunt water; but a horse will stand right where you leave him until he dies of thirst, unless you unhitch him. No, I couldn't take you to that place now—I looked for it last summer, but couldn't find a trace of the buggy or the bones. Must have been covered up with sand I guess."

"How do you account," I asked, "for the fact that there are so few skeletons of oxen along this trail? The old accounts all state that scores of oxen were left exhausted on the desert. Why did we not find their bones?"

"Well now, that's a fact, I never saw many bones along there; but if you have ever driven oxen, you can understand that. You see, driving those oxen so long without water, they got tuckered out, and just quit; couldn't go any farther. But an ox is different from a horse. When a horse quits, he is done for; he gives you all he's got, and when he stops he drops dead. But an ox, if you let him rest awhile, let him get cooled off, he probably will get up and go on again. But these emigrants were scared, and they wouldn't wait. They were thirsty, of course, and anxious to get out of there as quick as they could. When an ox laid down they left him and went on. They figured he was a dead ox. But those oxen, after they laid there awhile, and it cooled off at night, and they got rested up some, most of them started to hunt water. They could travel a long ways yet, without a load, and that's just what they did. Most of them got on their feet after awhile and wandered off into the desert toward the bills looking for water. Some of them found water, too—a lot of them. You'd be surprised."

"How do you know that, Mr. Munsee?"

"Well, I'll tell you how I know. You see, there used to be Indians living near the springs along this mountain when the emigrants came through. Some of them lived around here for a long time after I came. I knew one of these young Indians quite well, and one day I asked him if he knew anything about the Donner party. He sure did. He told me all about how they crossed the desert and left a lot of wagons here at the springs; he said that his grandfather and others who lived around here in those days had gathered in most of the cattle left by the Donners, and eaten them. The cattle would be found wandering in the foothills, and the Indians would drive them to camp and kill them. They sure lived high that winter. If the Donner party had had a little more patience, they could have saved most of their cattle and wagons."

"Is there any water on Silver Island, Mr. Munsee?"

"Yes, there are two springs over there—not very big springs— there wouldn't be enough water there for all that stock to drink at one time, but there was plenty for the people to drink, if they had known it. One spring is in a cave on the side of the mountain, only a little ways from the trail. But they never found it. A mountain man would have found it, but those people didn't know how to look for water in this kind of country. And I guess they were in too big a hurry."

I then asked if he had ever found any human bones on the desert or near the springs.

"No," he said, "I never did. Lots of the old-timers believed that the Donner party died on the desert, all but six, who crawled to the springs on their hands and knees. But I never found any proof of that. There were no graves here that I ever saw, and no human skeletons. I think they all got across."

We spent the balance of the night with Mr. Munsee, had breakfast with him in the morning, and then started to follow the trail westward into Nevada. The state line runs between the ranch house and the mountain.

Directly west stands Pilot Peak like a huge pyramid, blocking the trail in that direction. It therefore turns south along the foot of the slope, passing in the next two miles the last of the springs. From this point to the next water is forty miles, which distance the emigrants covered in about twenty-two hours of constant travel. Considering the condition of their cattle and the short period of rest they had been allowed at Pilot Peak, it is remarkable they could have made the next forty-mile stage without serious mishap.

Turning southwest the trail passes over a range of low hills. Beyond these it can still plainly be seen stretching away across the next valley, probably fifteen miles wide, toward Silver Zone Pass, the only possible crossing of the next range of mountains. The trail here has never been used except by an occasional sheep wagon, and we were compelled to fill many gullies and washes before we could get the car across.

We reached the opposite side of the valley, however, without mishap, and entered Silver Zone Pass. Here the modern Victory Highway follows in the exact footsteps of the pioneers of 1846— there is no other way—and the railroad closely parallels it.

Emerging from the pass we found ourselves in Steptoe Valley. Here the trail turns southwest, crossing the valley in a slightly angling direction direct for the springs known as Flowery Lake, ten or twelve miles below the station of Shafter, Nevada.

Flowery Lake deserves special mention here, on account of its many peculiarities. In the center of a shallow depression covering perhaps ten acres, are several low mounds, each of which covers considerable ground, and out of the top of which flow many springs of slightly saline water. Some of these are cool, others lukewarm. The mounds are completely covered with "endless grass" in which one sinks almost to the knees. The water from the springs oozes down through this deep grass and collects at the lowest point of the shallow basin, where it sinks again. The marsh so formed is at certain times of the year covered with a peculiar variety of blue flower, from which the place takes its name. The water is clear, and good enough, if one is thirsty. Walking on top of one of these mounds shakes the whole structure. The sensation is like walking across an enormous glass of jelly.

The records of the Donner party state that at this place were buried the contents of several more wagons which the oxen were too weak to pull any farther. We were unable to find any traces of a cache here, but it would be practically impossible to do so at this late date, since two old deserted cabins show that the springs have been the watering place for hundreds of cattle within the past few years.

From Flowery Lake the trail strikes west, crossing the mountains at Flowery Lake Pass, and the next water is found on the opposite side, eighteen miles distant, at some mound springs very similar to those just described.

As the trail bends south to round the southern point of the Ruby Mountains, many springs were found, the emigrants calling this the "Valley of Fifty Springs."

No particular difficulties were encountered by the emigrants from this point to the sink of the Humboldt, and from that point onward their hardships have been adequately described by McGlashan, Mrs. Houghton, Thornton and other writers. Their trail, after striking the Humboldt, has been traveled by thousands, many of whom left their bones by the wayside. The modern highway and the railroad follow the old pioneer trail, so that it is not possible to locate it exactly, except in places.

The Great Salt Desert, however, preserving as it does down to the present generation, the actual tracks of the emigrant wagons, and the footprints of the emigrants themselves, is strikingly unique. Nowhere else in the world are the peculiar conditions duplicated which have preserved for us to this day such a wealth of pioneer relics. In no other spot can one say with assurance, "These are the wagons of certain known pioneers, and in this exact spot certain difficulties overtook them." No other stretch of pioneer trail in the West has been visited so seldom and about no other part of the entire trail has there been less reliable information.

The emigrants who crossed the Salt Desert trail may have been foolish, but they cannot be accused of cowardice; they may have been misled, but they had no thought of turning back. They may have been no better nor worse than we of a less romantic age, but they persisted in the face of almost insurmountable difficulties— they conquered the Great Salt Desert. To those brave old pioneers who knew not defeat, who braved the most treacherous desert in America, I dedicate this book.

INDEX

Composed in 10 pt. Adobe Caslon 224 Book text and
12 & 14 pt. Caslon 224 Bold headings by

Will Bagley
of
The Prairie Dog Press

Printed at Publishers Press
Salt Lake City, Utah